HIGHER EDUCATION
IN SOUTHEAST ASIA

INTERNATIONAL PERSPECTIVES ON EDUCATION AND SOCIETY

Series Editor: Alexander W. Wiseman

Recent Volumes:

Series Editor from Volume 11: Alexander W. Wiseman

Volume 21:	The Development of Higher Education in Africa: Prospects and Challenges
Volume 22:	Out of the Shadows: The Global Intensification of Supplementary Education
Volume 23:	International Education Innovation and Public Sector Entrepreneurship
Volume 24:	Education for a Knowledge Society in Arabian Gulf Countries
Volume 25:	Annual Review of Comparative and International Education 2014
Volume 26:	Comparative Sciences: Interdisciplinary Approaches
Volume 27:	Promoting and Sustaining a Quality Teacher Workforce Worldwide
Volume 28:	Annual Review of Comparative and International Education 2015
Volume 29:	Post-Education-For-All and Sustainable Development Paradigm: Structural Changes with Diversifying Actors and Norms
Volume 30:	Annual Review of Comparative and International Education 2016
Volume 31:	The Impact of the OECD on Education Worldwide
Volume 32:	Work-integrated Learning in the 21st Century: Global Perspectives on the Future
Volume 33:	The Century of Science: The Global Triumph of the Research University
Volume 34:	Annual Review of Comparative and International Education 2017
Volume 35:	Cross-nationally Comparative, Evidence-based Educational Policymaking and Reform 2018
Volume 36:	Comparative and International Education: Survey of an Infinite Field 2019
Volume 37:	Annual Review of Comparative and International Education 2018
Volume 38:	The Educational Intelligent Economy: Big Data, Artificial Intelligence, Machine Learning and the Internet of Things in Education
Volume 39:	Annual Review of Comparative and International Education 2019
Volume 40:	Annual Review of Comparative and International Education 2020
Volume 41:	Building Teacher Quality in India: Examining Policy Frameworks and Implementation Outcomes
Volume 42A:	Annual Review of Comparative and International Education 2021
Volume 42B:	Annual Review of Comparative and International Education 2021
Volume 43A:	World Education Patterns in the Global North: The Ebb of Global Forces and the Flow of Contextual Imperatives
Volume 43B:	World Education Patterns in the Global South: The Ebb of Global Forces and the Flow of Contextual Imperatives
Volume 44:	Internationalization and Imprints of the Pandemic on Higher Education Worldwide
Volume 45:	Education for Refugees and Forced (Im)Migrants Across Time and Context
Volume 46A:	Annual Review of Comparative and International Education 2022
Volume 46B:	Annual Review of Comparative and International Education 2022
Volume 47:	How Universities Transform Occupations and Work in the 21st Century: The Academization of German and American Economies
Volume 48:	Annual Review of Comparative and International Education 2023

INTERNATIONAL PERSPECTIVES ON EDUCATION
AND SOCIETY   VOLUME 49

HIGHER EDUCATION IN SOUTHEAST ASIA

EDITED BY

LORRAINE PE SYMACO
Zhejiang University, China

United Kingdom – North America – Japan
India – Malaysia – China

Emerald Publishing Limited
Emerald Publishing, Floor 5, Northspring, 21-23 Wellington Street, Leeds LS1 4DL.

First edition 2025

Editorial Matter and Selection © 2025 Lorraine Pe Symaco.
Individual chapters © 2025 The authors.
Published under exclusive licence by Emerald Publishing Limited.

Reprints and permissions service
Contact: www.copyright.com

No part of this book may be reproduced, stored in a retrieval system, transmitted in any form or by any means electronic, mechanical, photocopying, recording or otherwise without either the prior written permission of the publisher or a licence permitting restricted copying issued in the UK by The Copyright Licensing Agency and in the USA by The Copyright Clearance Center. Any opinions expressed in the chapters are those of the authors. Whilst Emerald makes every effort to ensure the quality and accuracy of its content, Emerald makes no representation implied or otherwise, as to the chapters' suitability and application and disclaims any warranties, express or implied, to their use.

British Library Cataloguing in Publication Data
A catalogue record for this book is available from the British Library

ISBN: 978-1-80262-514-1 (Print)
ISBN: 978-1-80262-513-4 (Online)
ISBN: 978-1-80262-515-8 (Epub)

ISSN: 1479-3679 (Series)

Printed and bound by CPI Group (UK) Ltd, Croydon, CR0 4YY

INVESTOR IN PEOPLE

CONTENTS

About the Editor	*vii*
About the Contributors	*ix*

**Chapter 1   Higher Education in Southeast Asia:
Issues and Challenges**
Lorraine Pe Symaco   *1*

Chapter 2   Higher Education in Cambodia
Say Sok and Rinna Bunry   *5*

**Chapter 3   Indonesian Higher Education: Issues in
Institutional and Individual Capacities**
Nurdiana Gaus   *19*

**Chapter 4   Higher Education in the Lao People's
Democratic Republic**
Nanludet Moxom and Richard Noonan   *35*

Chapter 5   Higher Education in Malaysia
Cheong Kee Cheok   *49*

**Chapter 6   Higher Education in Myanmar: Coup,
Conflict, and Educational Crisis**
Mark Brown   *67*

**Chapter 7   Higher Education in the Philippines:
Issues and Challenges**
Maria Alicia Bustos-Orosa and Lorraine Pe Symaco   *91*

**Chapter 8   Higher Education in Singapore:
Challenges for Institutions of Continuous Learning**
Shien Chue   *103*

Chapter 9   Higher Education in Thailand
Oliver S. Crocco and Sukanya Chaemchoy   *119*

**Chapter 10   Developing Higher Education in Timor-Leste:
A Work in Progress**
Margie Beck   *139*

**Chapter 11   Achieving Vietnam's Sustainable Development
Goals in the Higher Education Sector**
Le-Nguyen Duc Chinh and Martin Hayden   *151*

Index   *169*

ABOUT THE EDITOR

Lorraine Pe Symaco is Professor at Zhejiang University, China. She was UNESCO Chair in international and comparative educational research with special reference to Southeast Asia and founding Director of the Centre for Research in International and Comparative Education (CRICE) at the University of Malaya, Malaysia.

ABOUT THE CONTRIBUTORS

Margie Beck has lived and worked in Timor-Leste for more than 20 years. After a career as a Teacher before moving into the tertiary education sector, she came to Timor to work with the Marist Brothers to set up a teachers' college. She has had extensive experience in all aspects of education in Timor-Leste.

Mark Brown is an Independent Analyst. His work focuses on rural and higher education in Myanmar. He co-founded a school for rural youth in Northern Shan State, taught international and community development in Yangon, and worked with local community-based organisations to provide research skills training to persons with disabilities.

Rinna Bunry is Chief of the Policy and Curriculum Office, Department of Higher Education. She is also Head of the Governance and Higher Education (HE) Institution Management Reform team, which initiates and implements HE governance and management reform in Cambodia.

Maria Alicia Bustos-Orosa is a Professorial Lecturer of the Department of Counseling and Educational Psychology at De La University Manila and is also a University Administrator at Baliuag University in Bulacan, Philippines. Her research focuses on literacy studies, assessment and learning.

Sukanya Chaemchoy is an Associate Professor of Educational System Management Leadership at Chulalongkorn University, Thailand. Her research focuses on educational policy, management and leadership.

Cheong Kee Cheok was Senior Research Fellow at the Faculty of Economics and Administration, University of Malaya. He was Senior Economist at the World Bank's Economic Development Institute and coordinated training programmes in China, Vietnam, Cambodia, Mongolia, Lao PDR and Moldova.

Shien Chue is a Senior Research Scientist at the Centre for Research and Development in Learning (CRADLE) at Nanyang Technological University Singapore. Her research interests include transitions, workplace learning and curriculum implementation. She has published in areas of workplace learning and is currently examining work-study programmes for fostering career resilience.

Oliver S. Crocco is an Associate Professor of Leadership and Human Resource Development (HRD) at Louisiana State University, United States. He also serves as a Special Lecturer in the Faculty of Education at Chulalongkorn University, Thailand. His research focuses on leadership, higher education and HRD in Southeast Asia.

Le-Nguyen Duc Chinh is a Researcher at the School of Medicine, Vietnam National University HCMC, Vietnam. He was awarded a PhD in Education by Southern Cross University, Australia, in 2016. His research focuses on disciplinary culture, research university development and flagship universities.

Nurdiana Gaus is a Professor of Higher Education Policy and Leadership at Graduate School, Universitas Gadjah Mada, Yogyakarta, Indonesia. She has published on issues relating to the impacts of globalisation, neoliberalism and internationalisation in Indonesian universities.

Martin Hayden is an Emeritus Professor of Higher Education at Southern Cross University, Australia. He was awarded a PhD by the University of Melbourne in 1988 and has published extensively on higher education. He has been actively engaged as a Higher Education Consultant in Vietnam, working on projects for the ADB, the World Bank and various national governments.

Nanludet Moxom is Lecturer and Quality Assurance Manager at the National University of Laos, where he has been working for over two decades. His research focuses on higher education governance, leadership, communication, curriculum development and research methodologies.

Richard Noonan studied Comparative Education and Economics of Education at Columbia University (EdD.) and Stockholm University (PhD). As an Education Economist, he has served as Consultant to UNESCO, the World Bank, the Asian Development Bank, the International Labor Organization and many other multilateral and bilateral international development agencies.

Say Sok is Technical Adviser on governance, policy and planning, and project management for the higher education improvement project. He holds a PhD degree from Deakin University, Australia. He is a Board Member at the Cambodia Development Center and an Advisor and Adjunct Lecturer at the Department of Media and Communication, Royal University of Phnom Penh.

CHAPTER 1

HIGHER EDUCATION IN SOUTHEAST ASIA: ISSUES AND CHALLENGES

Lorraine Pe Symaco

Zhejiang University, China

Higher education in Southeast Asia has developed considerably over the past decades. Marked with economic and socio-political differences across countries, the role of higher education in development is common. As one of the most compact and culturally diverse regions of the world with a population of over 692 million (Worldometer, n.d.), a more regional push for the higher education sector and markets is seen through initiatives such as the ASEAN Mutual Recognition Agreements (MRAs) which advocates for a free movement of professionals across the region. The Association of Southeast Asian Nations (ASEAN) was established in 1967 as a political and economic alliance and now consists of 10 country members, with observer status for Timor-Leste. Despite the diversity found across countries in the region, common themes relating to higher education issues are prevalent. Issues of quality, access and equity, governance, financing and employment, among others remain at the forefront of higher education development in Southeast Asia.

This book brings together country experts in higher education, with each chapter focussing on the relevant issues facing individual countries. Shared goals for quality and access relate to linked SDG ambitions for the sector as highlighted in each chapter. This book covers nine country members of the ASEAN and Timor-Leste, making for the most comprehensive reference work on higher education in Southeast Asia to date.

The following section will outline the distinctive themes discussed in each chapter.

Higher Education in Southeast Asia
International Perspectives on Education and Society, Volume 49, 1–4
Copyright © 2025 by Lorraine Pe Symaco
Published under exclusive licence by Emerald Publishing Limited
ISSN: 1479-3679/doi:10.1108/S1479-367920240000049001

HIGHER EDUCATION IN SOUTHEAST ASIA

Quality in higher education is a shared issue in all country cases. In Cambodia, this links to concerns of governance, strategic finance and human resources management which often point to an inefficient system characterised by bureaucracy. Rising from the Khmer Rouge and the Cambodian–Vietnamese War, the country's higher education has expanded since. Say Sok and Rinna Bunry however report on the need for a more goal-oriented strategy in higher education, accompanied by transformative leadership, noting how the highly centralised civil service system limits attracting the best talents for higher education governance. And while access in the sector has increased in absolute terms, concerns in terms of access for the marginalised remain a challenge.

In discussing higher education in Lao PDR, Nanludet Moxom and Richard Noonan likewise point out the issue of quality as it relates to financing and governance. The low budget given to higher education institutions (HEIs) undermines research performance, among others. Concerns of late budget delivery also often mean unspent monies which end up being sent back to funding sources. The highly centralised system also results in less autonomy while meritocracy in leadership appointments is often lacking. Gaps in terms of access to basic education also bear consequences in terms of higher education enrolments, with the country showing rates well below most ASEAN countries. Nonetheless, education support for the disadvantaged and female students is forwarded by the government to help with access concerns.

Higher education in Vietnam exhibited rapid growth in the early 2000s with a gross enrolment rate rising from 9% in 2000 to 29% in 2019. Le-Nguyen Duc Chinh and Martin Hayden report gender equality in the education system as supported by mandated laws in the country, though some gaps are evident in postgraduate studies and STEM enrolment (both favouring males). Also, despite the expansion of higher education in Vietnam, access to the sector is behind other ASEAN nations, with enrolments falling behind Indonesia, the Philippines, Malaysia and Singapore. Student loans are available to those seeking tertiary education but are said to be insufficient and repayment is difficult to achieve upon graduation. Management and autonomy are also concerned in the sector where public HEIs are managed by varying ministries and autonomy may mean focussing priorities on finance generation over other concerns.

Higher education in a fragile and post-conflict context is investigated by Mark Brown for Myanmar and Margie Beck for Timor-Leste. The military coup of 2021 and the COVID-19 pandemic held consequences for the higher education sector of Myanmar, hampering possible medium-term progress made from 2011 when a nominally civilian government was put in place. Universities as an avenue for public discussion and resistance in the country continued well after the coup but serious challenges remain in terms of achieving related SDGs such as quality and access to higher education. The cost of higher education for rural students and the inability of persons with disability (PWD), among others, to access the sector remains a significant problem. The damage to the higher education sector due to the ongoing civil war is also yet to be fully realised.

Timor-Leste has the youngest higher education system in Southeast Asia, with the first university opening in 1986 during Indonesian rule. Since its independence in 2002, the sector has grown substantially, now with over 20 accredited institutions. Quality and access are concerns in the country. The push for quality has resulted in an initial licencing and accreditation of HEIs in 2008, also, access to tertiary education beyond the larger cities of Dili or Baucau has set in motion the provision of this in other municipalities. Nonetheless, issues relating to quality such as graduate-job market mismatch and the need for qualified academic faculty staff persist. Also allotted country observer status at the ASEAN, the country aims for full membership wherein initiatives in the higher education sector (e.g. ASEAN's MRA) may help it.

With more than 3,000 HEIs, Indonesia has the largest higher education system in the region. Apart from the challenge of ensuring quality in such a large system, access relating to quality concerns is prominent given the concentration of HEIs granted autonomy in Java Island. Nurdiana Gaus notes the need to further quality in the sector through increased internationalisation, autonomy and effective leadership. The political manifestation in terms of choosing the best person to lead universities is seen through the 35% vote of the education ministry for Rectors, bearing consequences in choosing the most eligible to lead. The race to world rankings of the country's HEIs also displays the increasing neoliberal approach of the system, yet questions in terms of its contribution to quality continue given among other things, the lack of funds allotted to research and development, and rising predatory publication in the country.

Next to Indonesia, the Philippines has the second largest higher education system in the region with over 2,000 HEIs and 3.4 million students. The country's young median age of 25 also exhibits the importance of higher education. Despite this, a gross enrolment ratio in tertiary education of 34.89% shows the country trailing behind its ASEAN neighbours. Alicia Orosa and Lorraine Pe Symaco note the concentration of HEIs in Metropolitan Manila and its surrounding provinces relating to access concerns, and the significant concentration of enrolments in public institutions despite a more pronounced private system (1,729 HEIs). The latter may carry significant effects on funding mechanisms, especially with the newly enacted law which institutionalises free tuition (and other fees) in public institutions. The move to quality linked with internationalisation is also manifest in the push for transnational education, although the ability to implement remains a challenge.

Higher education in Malaysia has exhibited increased access and supply through the Private Higher Education Act of 1996. Cheong Kee Cheok also notes the criticisms of affirmative action through the New Economic Policy introduced in the 1970s which continue, pointing to the differential and segregated university intake in public HEIs. The shortage of STEM graduates is also detrimental to the country's push for developed status, in addition to the lack of autonomy, thus stifling academic freedom and the political hold inherent especially in public HEIs. The mismatch of skills of graduates to that demanded by the industry is also a concern alongside the low female participation in the labour force, both issues bearing economic implications for the country.

As the most highly ranked university system in Southeast Asia, Singapore places importance on its higher education system being attuned to the needs of the future. One such focus is on digital transformation as discussed by Shien Chue, through curriculum and pedagogy, and educating the workforce through professional learning modules on digital transformation. Revamp in the curriculum also reflects the emphasis on producing job-ready graduates via greater links with industries. The introduction of more weighted aptitude-based university admission in 2020 also highlights the efforts by the government to push for greater flexibility in education pathways. Nonetheless, balancing the expectations of formal certification of graduates and the ability to realise learning and applied focus in training is needed.

Thailand is the only country in Southeast Asia that was not officially colonised yet still has a degree of Western influence and international orientation in early universities. Oliver S. Crocco and Sukanya Chaemchoy discuss the challenges in the sector which include bureaucracy and administrative fragmentation, in particular where various ministries offer higher education services making central coordination difficult. Quality is also an issue when gauged with international rankings, showing below-average performance of local universities. Issues of skills mismatch among graduates are also present, alongside language proficiency in English. Government initiatives to address such concerns are provided to help rise to these challenges.

CLOSING REMARKS

Despite the varying higher education systems in the region, the move towards a more sustainable sector is envisioned in all countries through improved quality, access, equity, governance, autonomy and better market orientation. Rising to the needs of modern times, a more adaptable and flexible curriculum and a more student-centred and critical-based assessment are favoured. Alongside the contemporary demands of higher education, ensuring an equipped system able to respond to emergencies such as the COVID-19 pandemic is at the forefront of Southeast Asian government policies with the push for a more innovative and accessible higher education for all. Even with the different levels of achievements in the tertiary sector as manifest in the chapters in this book, the common goal of guaranteeing the role of higher education for human capital formation and broader development of countries is underscored. It is hoped that towards this goal, a more integrated and robust Southeast Asian higher education will emerge.

REFERENCE

Worldometer. (n.d.). *Southeast Asia population*. Retrieved June 18, 2024, from https://www.worldometers.info/world-population/south-eastern-asia-population/#:~:text=South%2DEastern%20Asia%20Population%20(LIVE)&text=The%20current%20population%20of%20South,of%20the%20total%20world%20population

CHAPTER 2

HIGHER EDUCATION IN CAMBODIA

Say Sok[a] and Rinna Bunry[b]

[a]*Royal University of Phnom Penh, Cambodia*
[b]*Ministry of Education, Youth and Sport, Phnom Penh, Cambodia*

ABSTRACT

This chapter examines five systemic issues that are at the core of the development of Cambodia's higher education sector. These are goal-oriented sector and university development strategy, transformative institutional leadership, strategic human resource management, strategic financial management, and achieving Goal 4.3 of the Sustainable Development Goals. A goal-oriented strategy is fundamental, with its implementation carefully monitored to ensure a focus on quality. Transformative institutional leadership is, therefore, necessary, as is the need for strategic human resource and financial management practices that support the strategy.

Keywords: University development strategy; transformative leadership; strategic human resource management; strategic financial management; systemic university transformation; Cambodian higher education

INTRODUCTION

Higher education in Cambodia dates back to the Angkor period when two important learning centres were established at the Preah Khan and Ta Prohm Temples (in modern-day Siem Reap) to support Hindu religious scholarship (Tao & Kao,

---

Higher Education in Southeast Asia
International Perspectives on Education and Society, Volume 49, 5–18
Copyright © 2025 by Say Sok and Rinna Bunry
Published under exclusive licence by Emerald Publishing Limited
ISSN: 1479-3679/doi:10.1108/S1479-367920240000049002

2023, p. 8). These institutions fell into disarray when Buddhism became the preferred belief system of the nobility. Buddhist pagodas sprinkled across the country became the new centres of basic and religious education. Under French colonial control, from 1964 to 1953, the need for higher education provision was overlooked. It was not until the period of the People's Socialist Community (*Sangkum Reastr Niyum*) between 1954 and 1970 that a need finally began to be identified, and higher education development started. However, from 1970 to 1975, with the Lon Nol regime progressively losing control of the country, the higher education sector suffered neglect. Then, from 1975 to 1979, under the Khmer Rouge regime, all higher education institutions (HEIs) were closed or destroyed, with many scholars killed or fleeing Cambodia to save their lives (Ayres, 2000). Some sector recovery occurred between 1979 and 1991, mainly with support from the Soviet Union and Vietnam. However, it was not until the early 1990s that significant foreign aid enabled the process of recovery to become more sustained. Noteworthy developments in 1997 included the establishment of the first private university and the granting of more autonomy to a selected number of public HEIs by giving them the status of public administrative institutions (PAIs). Since the early 2000s, public HEIs have received significant financial assistance, initially primarily from bilateral sources and recently through funding obtained from the World Bank (Sok & Bunry, 2021b). Investment in private HEIs from the owners and students has been substantial.

The higher education sector has changed significantly since the 1990s. There are now many more HEIs in Cambodia than at that time. In 1996, there were only eight public HEIs. By 2024, there were 169 HEIs, 91 of which (accounting for about 60% of all enrolments) were privately owned. Public HEIs are supervised by as many as 17 ministries or ministerial agencies, though most are under supervision by the Ministry of Education, Youth and Sport (MoEYS) (17 public and 73 private HEIs) or the Ministry of Labour and Vocational Training (MoLVT) (36 public and 18 private HEIs) (MoEYS, 2024). Most HEIs in Cambodia are located in Phnom Penh, the national capital, though now there are HEIs in all provinces.

The higher education student population increased from 13,465 (including 2,140 females) in 1996 to 284,599 (including 148,757 females) in 2023. Most (83.3%) students in 2023 were enrolled in bachelor's degree programs. A further 11.6% of all students were enrolled in two/three-year associate degree programs, 4.6% were enrolled in master's degree programs, and 0.5% were enrolled in PhDs.

Around 70% of all bachelor's degree enrolments in 2023 were in social sciences and humanities majors, and 31% were in STEM-related majors, amongst which enrolment in natural sciences and mathematics accounted for 12%, computer sciences 32%, engineering 29%, agriculture 10%, and health sciences 18% (MoEYS, 2024). According to UNESCO statistics, there were 7,401 students studying abroad in 2021, with the most popular destination countries being Australia, the United States, France, Vietnam, and Thailand. The number of international students enrolled in study programs in Cambodia is small but increasing (Sok & Bunry, 2021a).

The number of academic and general staff members has also been increasing. In 1996, there were 1,247 employees in the higher education sector. By 2023, the

Higher Education in Cambodia

number had risen to 21,329 (including 5,117 females). As many as 4,817 of these employees had a bachelor's degree, 10,335 had a master's degree, and 1,968 had a doctorate (MoEYS, 2024).

There are four foreign branch campuses: the Limkokwing University of Creative Technology, the Raffles International College (Tek & Leng, 2017), the East Asia Management University, and the De Montfort University. Nagoya University has also established a satellite campus at a few public HEIs. No official records of joint degree programs offered with foreign providers or programs taught in foreign languages exist. However, in a survey of 15 HEIs conducted in 2017, 3 had twinning arrangements with foreign institutions, and 14 had international joint degree programs. The number has increased substantially in recent years. There are some programs that use English as the medium of instruction (Sok & Bunry, 2021a), and this is increasing.

The higher education sector remains at an early development stage and faces many challenges. The government's national university development strategy is not taken seriously, and strategic management at the institutional level is weak. University leadership is typically characterised by command and control rather than a transformative model for long-term institutional and social development. The sector is preoccupied with administrative and regulatory compliance regarding academic, personnel, and financial management matters, with little attention paid to long-term vision, strategic goals, strategic university management, and transformative university leadership.

This chapter examines five strategic issues relating to the development of Cambodia's higher education sector. These concern the need for a goal-oriented sector and university development strategy, transformative institutional leadership, strategic human resource management, strategic financial management, and achieving Goal 4.3 of the Sustainable Development Goals (SDGs). In addressing these topics, the authors draw on published and unpublished materials, together with their knowledge of and experience within the sector over several decades.

A GOAL-ORIENTED UNIVERSITY STRATEGY

Traditionally, there has been an absence of strategising in Cambodia's higher education sector. Public HEIs have tended simply to reproduce the aspirations expressed in the strategic plans of their relevant supervising government ministries. Sok and Bunry (2021a) have reported how these aspirations are too ambitiously written, excessively lofty, and poorly connected with realistic strategies or measures for their implementation. Where expressed, implementation measures are often vague and imprecise, with no accountabilities assigned or timelines specified for their attainment. In addition, institutional plans tend to lack any reference to the investment funds required for their implementation. In this regard, public HEIs function like branches of government administration (Mak et al., 2019a). The articulation of aspirations of private HEIs is often similarly lofty and ambitious, without clear performance targets, and adequate investment. The need for a goal-oriented development strategy for the sector is urgent.

The kind of goal-oriented strategy required is one that expresses specific targets to be achieved across the sector within a declared timeframe (Yates, 2004). Individual HEIs would then set the targets specific to their role and strengths, with the attainment of these targets carefully monitored. This process would require adequate institutional investment and ongoing mentoring for the change agents within HEIs who are responsible for its success. Without such mentoring, HEIs will develop slowly, with inadequate care for quality and relevance to national development (Sok & Bunry, 2021b). Being strategic also involves mandating inter/multidisciplinary academic collaboration among supporting units and across academic and research programs.

The Directorate General of Higher Education (DGHE) within MoEYS has been experimenting with developing this kind of long-term strategising. Working with six public HEIs, it has created a *Development Strategy for 2021–2030* and a similar long-term strategy for the participating HEIs. The strategy, which aims to improve the quality of teaching, research and institutional governance, focuses on producing programs that meet national and international standards and research programs that can promote development and innovation. Achieving international standards requires development of quality academic programs and the promotion of research for development and innovation.

The *Development Strategy for 2021–2030* provides an explicit blueprint for developing the institutions selected for inclusion. It focuses strongly on identifying a shared vision, mission, and set of goals and articulating relevant strategic implementation measures. It takes account of a 4Es leadership framework (i.e. envision, enable, empower, and energise) (Yates, 2004) and the World Bank's monitoring and evaluation (M&E) system. Goals are measurable, and responsibility for their attainment is assigned to the institutional governing board and senior executive managers. Regarding the 4Es, envisioning involves having a clear goal for the future. Enabling entails having appropriate organisational structures, functions, tasks, tactics, and standards. Empowering includes having a 10-year results framework, an M&E system, human resource development, and strategic budget planning. Energising involves developing individuals' annual result agreements, performance evaluations, career pathways, and system sustainability. In addition to measures implemented under the *Development Strategy*, various interlocking operation systems including internal quality assurance and results-based public investment programs, are being developed and piloted.

While this endeavour looks promising, its success cannot yet be assessed. Its success will inevitably depend on university senior leaders' and managers' collective commitment and capability to steer the implementation and sustain proactive support from politicians and senior technocrats. The latter will play essential roles in close monitoring and providing sustained investment, mentorship, and support for this critical reform agenda.

Poor execution of strategic plans by public HEIs has been enabled by weak monitoring and evaluation and internal quality assurance processes. The execution of strategic plans has not been regularly monitored, and timely corrective actions have not always been taken. Mechanisms to monitor and evaluate achievements have been absent, and the tools for monitoring and evaluation have

Higher Education in Cambodia 9

been inadequate. The values associated with internal quality assurance have yet to be acculturated and institutionalised. Poor performance in this regard is linked to a lack of capable executives with a firm commitment and relevant expertise. Furthermore, relevant national agencies do not yet sufficiently support the implementation of internal quality assurance.

Currently, expectations of 'large-scale' success are small, and mobilising large-scale collective goodwill to implement the *Development Strategy for 2021–2030* may be challenging (Sok & Bunry, 2021b). First, senior politicians can have short-term political agendas. There have been inadequate proactive and frank dialogues between them, senior technocrats, and university executives. Individual politicians can have different political patrons and agendas, and their promotion of a collective plan for higher education development can be insufficient (Sok et al., 2019). Second, there are too few examples of senior technocrats and university leaders being genuinely committed to and skilful in implementing strategic reform and providing a role model for social change. This is partly because strategic, transformative leadership is a new phenomenon in the higher education sector in Cambodia. University leaders and executives are more accustomed to a traditional leadership style (Sok & Bunry, 2021b), and are often not professionals in their areas of responsibilities. Third, the *Development Strategy for 2021–2030* requires public investment for its implementation, but an outcomes-based approach to public investment is new in the context of national investment expenditure in the higher education sector (Mak et al., 2019b).

STRATEGIC, TRANSFORMATIVE UNIVERSITY LEADERSHIP

Leadership is about making the right decisions to achieve a development strategy; and management is about doing whatever is necessary to implement a strategic plan. However, the current regulations and practices for promotion and performance management cannot ensure the recruitment of a team of the best and brightest leaders to perform the management role and hold them to their duties and performance commitment. Shortcomings in appointing governing board members of universities in Cambodia are discussed elsewhere (Mak et al., 2019a). Rather than focusing on strategic decisions and mobilising funds, governing boards in public HEIs focus mainly on routine management oversight and reporting (Un & Sok, 2018). For public HEIs with PAI status, all board members must be Cambodian. This requirement limits their opportunities to learn from foreign experience and restricts their ability to pursue international engagement. Additionally, governing boards of public HEIs have relatively few members, are government-centric, and have limited internal and no external non-government representation (Mak et al., 2019b).

The appointment and promotion system for senior executives requires dramatic reform to enable the recruitment of the best and brightest professionals as leaders. These individuals must be committed to university development and achieving transformation. As mentioned, public HEIs are restricted to recruiting civil servants as senior executives. Private HEIs have more freedom in this regard and may appoint expatriates. In public HEIs, the appointment process is centrally managed and not adequately participatory. In private HEIs, appointment decisions are made by the governing board itself, which the shareholders dominate. For public HEIs, the minister retains authority in the nomination process, and only one candidate is proposed for appointment. In principle, selecting appointees for deanships and other positions should involve all lecturers. In practice, the power to choose appointees to these positions rests with a few top executives and the preferences of external authorities.

There is no written regulation on recruiting chief executives for public HEIs, and regulations on internal promotion are patchy. Politicisation and favouritism in nominations and appointments happen, and seniority and other non-academic considerations dominate as the primary considerations ahead of professional competence, relevant experience and academic attainments (Ahrens & McNamara, 2013; Chet, 2009).

Without a robust post-audit performance management system for executive appointees and appointment practices, a spirit of teamwork among university executives at public HEIs is weak (Mak et al., 2019a). The government's centralised system of promotion and appointment works against the development of effective succession plans and gets in the way of smooth leadership transition and mentorship processes. Public HEIs have no term limit for all executive positions, with everyone appointed for life (Chet, 2009). In private HEIs, regulations approved by shareholders determine contract terms and the duration of leadership and management appointments.

Across the sector, a result-based performance management ethos is absent. For public and private HEIs, executives generally focus on routine daily paperwork instead of addressing strategic matters, collective institutional goals, and university-wide collaboration. Besides, in public HEIs, the chief executive makes final decisions in almost every matter relating to expenditure and new appointments because of legal requirements and established practices (Mak et al., 2019b). This centralisation of decision-making locks the chief executives into unnecessary duties, creates indecision at lower levels, and perpetuates a lack of transparency, accountability, and participatory decision-making. There is an inadequate linkage between performance and rewards, and for public HEIs, rewards, especially for the chief executives and governing board members, are managed tightly and at their discretion (Mak et al., 2019a).

Appointing and promoting only civil servants to all executive positions in public HEIs discourage recruiting the most competent individuals from the private sector and abroad. Furthermore, the absence of rigorous performance management and credential-based promotion systems creates conditions not conducive to attaining managerial competency. Another concern is that, for public HEIs, the authority to decide the reward system (i.e. payment and other monetary incentives) is concentrated in the Ministry of Economy and Finance, meaning it is highly centralised and bureaucratic. In general, the decision-making process is slow and stifles institutional efficiency and the creation of a vibrant university work culture (Ford, 2006; Sok & Bunry, 2021b).

Moving towards reform requires formalising inclusive internal systems and mechanisms for recruitment and selection, making the promotion and appointment system and mechanisms more participatory, accountable, and decentralised. For public HEIs, the reform process requires decentralising appointment and promotion authority to institutions, with opportunities made available to appoint chief executives and senior managers from outside the public service, including non-Cambodians. As practised in Thailand (Mak et al., 2019b), the appointment of new chief executives should coincide with the termination of previous holders of these positions, and chief executives should be able to nominate deputies for appointment by the institution's governing board. Appointment terms should be specified and decentralised to the governing board. The selection and promotion of the best executives should encompass the adoption and enculturation of a strong results-based performance management culture linked to attractive pay, sanctions, and continuous professional development (Trost, 2020).

Moving in this direction will be a challenge, especially in an entrenched system and mindset of centralisation, favouring the government's tight control of public HEIs and private HEIs by their owners. For public HEIs, such reform is only possible with a strong political commitment to move the appointment and promotion process towards one based on professionalism, academic credentials, and the decentralisation of appointment and promotion authority. Before public HEIs have more authority and to ensure that the power is not misused and abused, there is a need to institutionalise regulations on the leadership and management and for such appointments and promotions to be conducted with the highest degree of transparency and professionalism.

Public HEIs should be allowed to appoint board members and include more representatives from industries, students and staff, and overseas university partners (Mak et al., 2019b). For private HEIs, balancing the power of the shareholders in dominating the boards can be done by having more independent members duly selected. The selection process of these members should strictly adhere to legal requirements instead of continuing to be a process for recruiting allies of the owners as members of governing boards (Un & Sok, 2018).

STRATEGIC HUMAN RESOURCE MANAGEMENT

Strategic human resource management involves managing human resources to enable employees to achieve institutional strategic goals. It consists in making decisions that embody best practices regarding recruitment and appointments, performance management and appraisal, adopting appropriate and incentivising remuneration systems, and so on (Trost, 2020). In public HEIs, there has been some steady progress in personnel reforms, for example, by providing HEIs with authority to vet candidates taking civil service exams (DGHE, 2021b) and allowing them to fill positions at all levels from deputy deanships downwards to contract officers. However, significant challenges remain. Civil service management requires that national rules and regulations are followed; there is no scope for institutional statutes to govern all employees. The government manages the selection of civil servants, and there is little flexibility in the recruitment and selection tools and procedures employed (DGHE, 2021b).

A current deficiency in human resource management is that there are few professors appointed and none appointed for HEIs under MoEYS's supervision until 2023. There are no results-based career paths for academic and support staff members. It was in 2023 that 328 lecturers from 9 HEIs under MoEYS's supervision were appointed professors, following an attempt by MoEYS to improve the relevant appointment criteria and mechanisms. Unlike practices in some other ASEAN countries, which decentralise the selection and appointment of professors in HEIs (DGHE, 2021b), Cambodia's government requires it to make the final nomination, with appointments then approved by the King. Results-based performance management, including strong staff profile management, is absent in Cambodia's higher education sector.

The government also manages salary payments for civil servants. The pay is low, supplemented by the income HEIs independently generate, and is often paid as hourly wages for teaching civil servants and contracted instructors and as monthly salary top-ups/salary for executives and support staff. Moonlighting and free-riding such as personal consultancy businesses, and working in multiple institutions are common. Non-civil servants in public HEIs and teaching staff in private HEIs are short-term service contractors. The labour law is not applied in contract management; hence, they have no employment scheme, career track, or path. The pay can be as low as US$5-6 per hour for lecturers holding bachelor's degrees. Service contractors are considered non-staff, making employment security and opportunities for promotion impossible (Mak et al., 2019b).

Recent attempts have been made to move towards performance-based human resource management practices, but legal requirements and entrenched practices have presented many obstacles. The fragmented nature of the human resource system makes for ineffective, inefficient human resource management. The random, non-systematic nature of contract employee selection and management in public and private HEIs tends to prevent recruiting and retaining high-quality employees for jobs (DGHE, 2021b). The dual recruitment and hiring system involving civil servants and contracted employees in public HEIs cannot guarantee the best talent recruitment, making human resource management a complex issue.

The workload of academics in public and private HEIs is strongly skewed towards teaching. Large-scale use of short-term, casual employment fails to create and maintain a talent pool. Sometimes, teaching is used as a stepping-stone for further education and/or lucrative second jobs (Mak et al., 2019b). In public and private HEIs alike, annual performance appraisal and continuing professional development are routinely neglected. There are generally no internal systems and mechanisms and institutional budgets for continuing professional development. Likewise, there is a weak effort to create a robust staff appraisal system; the absence of a staff appraisal system prevents HEIs from establishing reasonable payment and promotion systems that reward good performance and sanction poor performance (DGHE, 2021b).

Public HEIs have an insufficient regulatory framework for incentive payments. Some HEIs adopt their own practices, with or without endorsement from the Ministry of Economy and Finance, creating a fragmented payment system.

There are no systematic internal institutional systems and mechanisms for managing salary top-ups for civil servants and monthly salary schemes for contract employees. An hourly payment for contract teaching services and other non-systematic seasonal and annual payments is not the most efficient payment and employment system. The practice has created a high rate of staff turnover. Besides, for public HEIs, the two-track monthly salary top-up payment system for executives and administrators and hourly pay for teaching staff has disadvantaged the latter. Furthermore, though senior executives and board members at some large public and private universities receive good pay, income levels for faculty and staff generally fall below the market rate for employees with similar responsibilities (Mak et al., 2019b).

Support staff in public and private HEIs, including those of the Personnel Office, often have lower qualifications, limited professional experience, and little exposure to innovative expertise and practices. This situation has hindered their contribution to strategic university management (DGHE, 2021b). Additionally, the centralised nature of civil service appointments and terminations makes terminations for ineffective performance very difficult. These circumstances discourage the proper execution of national regulations (Mak et al., 2019b).

Given all these conditions, if the status quo persists, there is little hope for creating an excellent talent pool of academics, executives, and professionals in higher education in the country. The dual employment system in public HEIs has entrenched the privileges of civil servants (especially senior leaders and executives), and put contract employees into a second tier, with negative implications for their sense of belonging and collegiality (Sok et al., 2019). In the medium term, public HEIs should move towards strategic human resource management, managing their staff to achieve strategic goals, strategic alignment of human resource management, and ensuring the best staff members are employed to manage resources (Hum et al., 2024; Trost, 2020).

Human resource needs should also be carefully devised to achieve institutional goals. Annual performance appraisals should be professionally conducted and linked to an efficient rewards system. Furthermore, appraisal results should form a basis for continuing professional development and the application of rewards and sanctions. In the longer term, public HEIs should be fully empowered to manage their own human resources, improve succession planning, abolish the civil servant system, and move towards a unitary time-based university employment scheme (Hum et al., 2024; Sok, 2016; Trost, 2020).

Reforming the human resource management system in public and private HEIs is a challenging, complex agenda. Thus, strong, genuine political commitment from the top political leadership and from the owners of private HEIs' owners is needed (Sok & Bunry, 2021b). Sustained dialogue between concerned state institutions at the political and senior technocratic levels is required.

STRATEGIC FINANCIAL MANAGEMENT

Strategic financial management is the second most crucial element in helping to mobilise revenue for strategy implementation. In Cambodia, the government funds public HEIs and uses the historical funding modality (i.e. how much the government-funded HEIs in previous years). Public HEIs usually have meagre financial resources given by the government. The funding scheme for these institutions is also typically outdated, with line-item budgeting based on the government's chart of accounts and line-by-line negotiations. This funding mechanism provides little flexibility, with heavy control on expenditure by the Ministry of Economy and Finance. Additionally, itemised budgeting creates complexities in making results-based planning and execution effective, especially in proposing activities with required budgets from multiple lines. Movement of credit across budget chapters needs authorisation from the Ministry of Economy and Finance, requiring manual processing of substantial paperwork, which is time-consuming and may be susceptible to irregularities (Mak et al., 2019a).

Private HEIs, on the other hand, have tuition fees as their primary source of income and are usually focused on achieving a profit. Budget planning and execution are often done *ad hoc*, generally with the approval of the top executive and the governing board.

Unlike more decentralised financial management systems in Thailand, Malaysia, and Singapore, where significant decision-making authority is delegated to boards, in Cambodian public HEIs, every dollar spent needs approval from the Ministry of Economy and Finance or its representative. Given the heavy focus on compliance, HEI management focuses inadequately on revenue mobilisation and incentivising revenue generation (e.g. matching funds and result-based contracts for priority programs). This funding modality does not encourage HEIs to venture into more creative revenue generation activities, as they rely mainly on budget support and accessible monies (mainly from tuition fees) (Sok et al., 2019). Strategic financial management remains a challenge to public HEIs. For instance, the governing boards are usually stand-alone with no permanent committees. They have less oversight authority, act more like a review body for the relevant supervising ministry, and play a negligible role in internal audits, external linkages and fund mobilisation (Mak et al., 2019a). Restricting members of these boards to Khmers also results in restricted access to non-government sources of income.

Cambodia does not legally acknowledge the delegation of authority from the rectors/directors in public HEIs to cost centres within these institutions. Therefore, budget decisions are ultimately controlled by a few individuals, with every decision needing approval from the head of the institution and endorsement by a national treasury accountant and financial controller or Minister of the Ministry of Economy and Finance. This level of centralisation and often poor work culture have hindered the development of strategic financial management planning and execution. Additionally, chief finance officers and others responsible for financial matters usually have limited professional experience and knowledge of strategic financial management (DGHE, 2021a; Mak et al., 2019a). In private HEIs, the owners' relatives or close allies often hold these positions.

The government makes all appointments to financial management positions in public HEIs, and all key positions are allocated to civil servants who hold the positions indefinitely. Appointing individuals with under-par qualifications and experience is typical. Furthermore, finance and accounting offices are usually understaffed, and junior employees frequently have inadequate knowledge and experience in strategic financial planning (DGHE, 2021a; Mak et al., 2019a). Continuing professional development is minimal, while results-based performance is absent. Performance is not adequately linked to promotion and pay raises. The salary for junior officers can be as low as US$200 per month. This situation has created a narrow pool of qualified applicants, resulting in rigidity in staff appointments and the lack of optimal management in finance positions.

There is also no legal basis or mention of how units must be involved in public HEIs' financial management. Public HEIs have little reallocation freedom after the government approves the adjusted budget. The practice of centralised budget management and random expenditure requests has created an entrenched culture of budget centralisation and opaque budget execution.

Existing regulations do not provide ultimate authority to the public HEIs to produce internal financial management regulations, with such authority commonly vested to the institutional governing board in more advanced systems in the ASEAN. When issued, these should conform to Cambodian national regulations or be approved by the Ministry of Economy and Finance and the technical supervising ministry. The approval process is usually bureaucratic; hence, many resort to 'informal practices', such as having the matters endorsed by the board (Mak et al., 2019a). The lack of formal internal regulations poses significant challenges to accountability and transparency.

It should be noted that there is little strategic linkage between the university's financial and annual operation plans (DGHE, 2021a; Mak et al., 2019a). The manual process for petty cash advance disbursement for the government's budget support and disbursement in public HEIs also consumes significant human resources and time. The request for disbursement may take a few months and can invite irregularity. Another issue is that public HEIs are responsible for asset management but are limited. For instance, HEIs cannot enter into contracts for long-term leases of their assets or get into a joint venture to capitalise on such assets. This practice restricts the possible resource generation that HEIs need (Sok, 2016)

It is likewise vital to connect HEIs with the private sector and expose them to advanced university governance in the region. Annual performance contracts should ideally also include the capacity to generate revenues for the HEI. To ensure that qualified professionals are recruited for public HEIs, legal reform is needed to enable the employment of non-civil servants, with terms of appointment set and decentralised to the HEIs (DGHE, 2021a; Mak et al., 2019b). Additionally, an external audit by an independent agency is ideal, where reports are sent to the board and relevant government agencies.

ACHIEVING SDG GOAL 4.3

Given the challenges discussed in the previous sections, the government's intent to improve the higher education sector is evident in policies, for instance, through the MoEYS's development of *Cambodia's Education Roadmap 2030: Sustainable*

Development – Goal 4, i.e. 'to ensure equal access for all women and men to affordable and quality technical, vocational and tertiary education, including university' (MoEYS, 2019, p. 23). Despite this, quality and relevance to national development is a challenge. While the country needs innovators and professionals in science, technology, and innovation, only one-third of the students are enrolled in these fields. While a majority enrol in business-related subjects and many other low-cost majors in social sciences and the arts, enrolment in majors critical for creating thinkers, social innovators, and the natural sciences is low (Sok & Bunry, 2021b). Quality and relevance have been a persistent concern, although this has improved significantly. Employers have long complained about low practical skills and questionable work attitudes graduates possess (Ford, 2013; Un & Sok, 2014), and numerous tracer studies at the national and institutional levels indicate that a majority of them earn around two times that of unskilled labourers, and primarily serve frontline positions and even semi-skilled/unskilled positions (DHE, 2014, 2022). The low quality also manifests in the fact that few programs are accredited internationally and that no programs assessed based on the national QA Manual have passed the standards. Notwithstanding, access has increased significantly in absolute terms. Enrolment increased from 28,080 in 2001 to 284,599 in 2023 (MoEYS, 2024). In 2023, the gross enrolment in bachelor's degrees stood at 17.9% (MoEYS, 2024). This increase is mainly due to privatisation, with more than 90% enrolling in fee-paying programs (Sok & Bunry, 2023). Despite this progress, access is still restricted. The enrolment rate is relatively low compared to the attainment rate of secondary education, which is one of the weakest in the region (Mak et al., 2019a).

Progress in inclusion and equitable access also somewhat varies. Opportunities for all women and men have been supported by establishing many HEIs outside Phnom Penh. More HEIs have expanded throughout the country and are closer to rural communities, where indigenous and poor people live, and every province has HEIs. MoEYS's tuition fee scholarship program offered annually to high school graduates has supported thousands of underprivileged students, especially those from low-income families (20% pro-poor) and remote areas (5%) (Bunry & Walker, 2022). In addition, students with disabilities who pass the high school exit exam automatically receive the scholarship. Another significant achievement is the increasing trend in female enrolment in the past 20 years. Female enrolment had increased from 31.52% in 2001 to 52.3% in 2023 (MoEYS, 2024). Higher enrolment is observed in the associate and bachelor's degree levels, yet females account for a smaller proportion at the master's and doctoral levels and in STEM-related majors.

Equitable access in terms of wealth and geographical locations and inclusion, namely indigenous and disabled people, is also an issue. There is no data on access by wealth quintile, but more than 90% are self-sponsored (Un & Sok, 2014), indicating that higher education is a private good, putting people in poverty and lower wealth quantiles at a disadvantage. The existing database does not capture student enrolment by places of origin; however, anecdotal evidence suggests enrolment favouring students from the capital and urban areas. The Education Management Information System data shows consistently lower enrolment and completion rates for rural students in the upper secondary education level. Data on access for indigenous communities and people with disabilities is unavailable. Nevertheless, access is known to be limited.

CONCLUSION

This chapter examined issues that advance Cambodia's higher education development. Strategic, systemic reforms in the key areas discussed in this chapter are needed to make higher education serve national development and SDGs better. Such reforms will help improve academic program design and delivery, acculturate quality assurance and accreditation, and institutionalise research development. Such reforms can then generate technology transfer and innovation to address local problems. Systemic reforms needed to implement strategic goals require strategising university development, transformative university leadership, strategic human resource and financial management, and the collective commitment and goodwill of the government and leaders in the sector.

REFERENCES

Ahrens, L., & McNamara, V. (2013). Cambodia: Evolving quality and issues in higher education. In L. P. Symaco (Ed.), *Education in South-east Asia* (pp. 47–69). Bloomsbury.

Ayres, D. M. (2000). *Anatomy of a crisis: Education, development, and the state in Cambodia, 1953–1998*. University of Hawaii Press.

Bunry, R., & Walker, K. (2022). Cambodian women and girls: Challenges to and opportunities for their participation in higher education. In V. McNamara & M. Hayden (Eds.), *Education in Cambodia: From year zero towards international standards* (pp. 275–292). Springer.

Chet, C. (2009). Higher education in Cambodia. In Y. Hirosato & Y. Kitamura (Eds.), *The political economy of educational reforms and capacity development in Southeast Asia* (pp. 153–165). Springer.

Department of Higher Education. (2014). *Tracer study: Baseline report* [draft].

Department of Higher Education. (2022). *Tracer study results of five HEIs* [unpublished report].

Directorate General of Higher Education (DGHE). (2021a). *Concept paper on development of a financial management system for PAI HEIs* [research report].

Directorate General of Higher Education (DGHE). (2021b). *Concept paper on development of a human resource management system for PAI HEIs* [research report].

Ford, D. (2006). *Cambodian higher education: Growing pains* (p. 44). International Higher Education.

Ford, D. (2013). Cambodian higher education: Subprime degrees? *International Higher Education, 70*, 15–16.

Hum, C., Choi, T. H., Lo, S. K., Sok, S., & Yu, W. M. C. (2024). Aligning academic career management in the evolving landscape of Cambodian public universities. *International Journal of Comparative Education and Development, 26*(2), 95–113.

Mak, N., Sok, S., Un, L., Bunry, R., Chheng, S., & Kao, S. (2019a). *Finance of public higher education in Cambodia*. CDRI.

Mak, N., Sok, S., Un, L., Bunry, R., Chheng, S., & Kao, S. (2019b). *Governance of public higher education in Cambodia*. CDRI.

Ministry of Education, Youth, and Sport (MoEYS). (2019). *Cambodia's education roadmap 2030: Sustainable development - Goal 4*.

Ministry of Education, Youth, and Sport (MoEYS). (2024). *Education congress report for 2022–2023 and directions for 2023–2024*.

Sok, S. (2016). *Higher education governance reforms in Thailand and Malaysia and policy implications for Cambodian reform* [research report].

Sok, S., & Bunry, R. (2021a). Internationalisation of higher education in Cambodia: Toward an agenda for higher education development. *International Journal of Comparative Education and Development, 23*(3), 193–211.

Sok, S., & Bunry, R. (2021b). *Cambodian public higher education in 2040: Potential scenarios and the need for transformative leadership. Higher education in Southeast Asia and beyond.* HEAD Foundation.

Sok, S., & Bunry, R. (2023). Higher education in Cambodia. In L. P. Symaco & M. Hayden (Eds.), *International handbook on education in Southeast Asia* (pp. 1–24). Springer. Advance online publication. https://doi.org/10.1007/978-981-16-8136-3_47-1

Sok, S., Un, L., & Bunry, R. (2019). Governance in public administrative institution universities in Cambodia: Towards public autonomous universities in Cambodia? In C. D. Wan, M. N. N., Lee, & H. Y. Loke (Eds.), *The governance and management of universities in Asia: Global influences and local responses* (pp. 5–20). Routledge.

Tao, N., & Kao, S. (2023). Overview of education in Cambodia. In L. P. Symaco & M. Hayden (Eds.), *International handbook on education in South East Asia* (pp. 1–26). Springer. Advance online publication. https://doi.org/10.1007/978-981-16-8136-3_43-1

Tek, M. T., & Leng, P. (2017). How do Cambodian leaders define and perceive higher education internalisation? *Cambodia Development Review, 21*(1), 1–7.

Trost, A. (2020). *Human resource strategies: Balancing stability and agility in times of digitisation.* Springer.

Un, L., & Sok, S. (2014). Higher education governance in Cambodia. In *Leadership and governance in higher education: Handbook for decision makers and administrators* (pp. 71–94). RAABE Publishing.

Un, L., & Sok, S. (2018). *Higher education systems and institutions, Cambodia, in Encyclopedia of international higher education systems and institutions* (pp. 1–10). Springer, Dordrech.

Yates, M. A. (2004). *The 4E's leadership framework.* HEC-Oxford Executive Education.

CHAPTER 3

INDONESIAN HIGHER EDUCATION: ISSUES IN INSTITUTIONAL AND INDIVIDUAL CAPACITIES

Nurdiana Gaus

Universitas Gadjah Mada, Indonesia

ABSTRACT

This chapter aims to illustrate how Indonesian higher education (HE) has struggled to compete in the globalised world, as evidenced by the country's below-average performance in global university rankings and the Global Innovation Index, despite the significant support from the government to improve Indonesia's capacity for knowledge production. To further examine this issue, related sustainable development goals in HE (e.g. SDG 4.3) are framed within the discussion of the interrelated concepts of leadership, autonomy, quality, research, and innovation. This chapter shows that the lack of understanding of these concepts by both the government and university leaders may have affected the HE sector's ability to improve institutional capacity. A contextual background of the country's HE sector is also discussed alongside governance issues in three periods, i.e. colonialisation, post-colonialisation (Old Order regime), and the post-New Order Regime.

Keywords: Leadership; autonomy; academic freedom; innovation; world-class research; SDG

Higher Education in Southeast Asia
International Perspectives on Education and Society, Volume 49, 19–33
Copyright © 2025 by Nurdiana Gaus
Published under exclusive licence by Emerald Publishing Limited
ISSN: 1479-3679/doi:10.1108/S1479-367920240000049003

INTRODUCTION

Higher education institutions (HEIs) in Indonesia are required to produce innovative knowledge to be considered 'world-class universities' and to enhance the country's welfare and wealth (Brodjonegoro, 2020b). However, such a demand has not been accompanied by renewed perspectives and practices in managing higher education (HE) (Gaus, 2019), where, following Clark (1998), innovating and entrepreneurial universities have become the primary drivers materialising Indonesia HEIs' economic roles and achieving their global reputation. This chapter examines the efforts of the Indonesian government and HEIs to compete to become world-class universities. The following section gives a historical context of the country's HE sector.

HISTORY

Indonesian HE in the early 21st century is the product of a long history from colonisation to post-colonisation. During colonial times, although several countries were documented to have colonised Indonesia, the influence of the Dutch colonial government (1500s–1942) was most significant. During these times, particularly at the end of the 18th century, a nascent modern HE took shape by establishing some higher learning schools in Java (Nizam & Nurdin, 2013; Wicaksono & Friawan, 2011). Three higher learning institutions, the Medical (1927) and Law School (1924) in Jakarta, the Engineering Institute in Bandung (1920), and the Agriculture Centre in Bogor (1941), were founded. This higher learning was triggered by the intention of the colonial government to fill the shortage of Dutch experts in the country (Logli, 2016). These colonial-legacy institutions, then, are transformed into what is known today as Universitas Indonesia, *Institut Teknologi Bandung* (Bandung Institute of Technology), and *Institut Pertanian Bogor* (Bogor Institute of Agriculture), respectively. Indonesians comprised only 200 out of 1,000 students in 1938 (Cummings & Kasenda, 1989).

Immediately after independence and during the Old Order Regime (1945–1966), the first university, also considered a non-colonial legacy, Universitas Gadjah Mada (1949), was established (Buchori & Malik, 2004). This university was initiated by the rising nationalism in rebuilding the war-torn country (Gaus, 2019). During those periods, two private universities, the Indonesian Islamic University in Jogjakarta (1946) and the National University in Jakarta (1949), were established (Buchori & Malik, 2004). During the 1950s, Indonesian HE witnessed a significant expansion in student enrolments and the number of HEIs, both public and private, due to a dramatic increase in population. The goals of the massification of access to HE for all citizens were manifested in Law No. 61 and No. 22 in 1961, in which the need to establish one public HEI in each province in Indonesia was emphasised. As a result, there were 23 new HEIs founded, ranging from universities, institutes, and teacher training colleges (Koning & Maassen, 2012). In 1978, 44 state universities and 324 HEIs were established (Logli, 2016). The enrolment increased from 6,000 in 1950 to 184,000 in 1965 (Pardoen, 1998, as cited in Logli, 2016).

In the New Order Regime (1966–1998), HE lost its professional character as the 'republic of scholars', which entails the inherent nature of autonomy and academic freedom. Sparked by the ruling regime's worries and fears of critiques and resistance from community scholars that would have toppled its power, HE was silenced and controlled under the strict purview of the government. The HE system was completely centralised, with all decisions coming from the central command (Wicaksono & Friawan, 2011). Regardless of all restrictions and subsequent poor quality, this era marked excellent growth in the number of HEIs and enrolments of public and private, which began in the 1980s. This growth was triggered by strong economic growth fuelled by the oil-price boom during the 1980s in Indonesia (Nizam & Nurdin, 2013; Wicaksono & Friawan, 2011) as well as improved secondary school completion rates and increased demand for skilled graduates (Hill & Wie, 2013, as cited in Brewis, 2019). There were 77 public HEIs established during this period (1966–1998) and 1,449 private HEIs, with a total enrolment in HEIs of over 1,519,000 (Rosser, 2018).

Size

Since then, HEIs in Indonesia have expanded tremendously in terms of forms, organising providers, and types of subjects and degrees offered. HEIs in Indonesia are classified into six types: university, institute, school of higher learning (college), academy, community college, and polytechnic (DGHE, 2021). Regarding organising providers, HEIs are categorised as public HEIs, private HEIs, and government HEIs. The government HEIs are institutions of public HE that have ties with the government as the education provider; in Indonesia, these are called the *Perguruan Tinggi Kedinasan* and religious HEIs (DGHE, 2021). There are also HEIs defined by the types of subjects and degrees they provide. These include academic HEIs and vocational HEIs. Public HEIs are differentiated by their legal entity, which determines the degree of autonomy they hold. These HEIs are called state universities with a legal entity, Perguruan Tinggi Negeri Berbadan Hukum (PTN-BH). Public HEIs with a lower level of autonomy are classified as universities in the form of public service status (or the *Badan Layanan Umum*, BLU). In contrast, those with the lowest level of autonomy are classified as universities with working unit status (*Satuan Kerja*, SATKER). Global rankings of Indonesian universities, as reported by Times Higher Education in 2023 (THE, 2023), are ranked from 1,001+ to 1,500+. This is significantly lower than other ASEAN countries such as Singapore, Malaysia, Brunei Darussalam, the Philippines, and Thailand.

Indonesian HE has always been on the periphery (Welch, 2007), either at the global or even regional ASEAN level, despite efforts made by the government since the post-reformation era to improve the long-standing issues regarding accountability, quality, equality, equity, and relevance of graduates to workforce needs. The low gross tertiary enrolment rate (GER), which is low compared to the total population and the total number of HE population (age 19–24), has been one of the indicators. Based on the data released by the Centre for Statistics Bureau (CSB, 2024), the total Indonesian population in 2022 was 275,773,000. Of this total, the HE age population was 26,328,000. In the meantime, the total

Table 1. The Growth of HE in Indonesia Under the Ministry of Education, Culture, Research and Technology.

Years	Enrolled Students		Total	GER (Gender) (%)	
	Public	Private		Female	Male
2022	3,380,281	4,495,000	7,875,281	33.55	28.91
2021	3,200,000	4,400,000	7,600,000	33.42	29
2020	2,994,015	4,374,994	7,369,009	32.21	29.55
2019	2,982,403	4,410,761	7,393,164	28.93	31.67

Note: Data obtained from *the Ministry of Research, Technology and Higher Education, the former nomenclature of the Ministry of Education, Culture, Research and Technology* (2019) and CSB (2021, 2024).

of students actively studying in 3,107 HEIs in Indonesia as of 2022 was 9,773,311 (which includes all types of universities and subjects offered) (Indonesian Higher Education Database of PDDIKTI, 2023). The 2022 GER increased slightly to 31.16%, up from 30.28% in 2020 (CSB, 2021). GER in Indonesia is the lowest among comparable ASEAN countries, such as Singapore (91% in 2019), Malaysia (43% in 2019), and Thailand (46% in 2016) (World Bank, 2021). The suspected factors associated with this low rate are mainly attributed to economic issues and the preference made by graduates of senior high schools to work directly upon their completion of secondary studies (Kontan, 2020). Indeed, recent data from the CSB (2021) reveal that only 8.5% of Indonesians have completed their undergraduate studies. This number has remained static since 2017 with the release of data by the Survey of National Social Economy (SNSE).

In the post-New Order Regime (1998), the procedures of developing and managing HEIs have been prescribed in light of those of the World Bank and UNESCO, where decentralisation, equal access for HE to all citizens, transparency, and accountability have become guiding principles (Logli, 2016; Rosser, 2018). The integration of the Sustainable Development Goals (SDGs) as the government's obligation to fulfil human rights in Indonesia through the provision of equal access for everyone has highlighted the national target of HE in Indonesia. A particular global target of SDG 4.3 has also been included in the objectives and visions of HE in Indonesia, where equal participation of females and males will be achieved in 2030. The data in Table 1 indicates a continuously growing trend of increasing female participation in HE when compared to males, which aligns with the SDG 4.3 in Indonesia.

SDG 4.3 IN INDONESIA

In 2015, the United Nations (UN) and its member states signed 17 agendas for the SDGs, with Goal 4 focussing on quality education. To enable HEIs to achieve these SDGs, leadership, autonomy, academic freedom, and world-class basic and applied research in humanities and sciences must be prioritised (Chankseliani & McCowan, 2021). President Regulation No. 59, 2017, was enacted in Indonesia to reinforce SDG implementation. To manifest that regulation, the Ministry of National Development Planning (MoNDP) was mandated to develop a roadmap to identify issues and projections of leading SDG indicators in each goal, including its forward-looking policies to achieve the needed targets (MoNDP, 2019).

The SDG 4.3 of achieving equal access to affordable technical, vocational, and HE has been addressed, alongside several actions to help achieve the SDG 2030 targets. A range of issues around the tertiary education gross enrolment rate and the net ratio of females to males are addressed. Although nationally, data show that tertiary education has enjoyed significant gender parity in participation, there has been an issue of student disparity in terms of geographic locations and income brackets or socioeconomic conditions. To help achieve the target of a net ratio of nearly 100%, locally oriented interventions are acknowledged, considering dropout issues across gender and socioeconomic status (MoNDP, 2019).

The projected strategies and targets to improve HE's GER towards the 2030 agenda are conducted in two projections (with and without interventions). The first projection without interventions in SDG targets gives a baseline of GER's range percentage for years 2015, 2019, 2024, and 2030 at 25.26%, 32.85%, 38.32%, and 43.85%, respectively. The projected GER with interventions during the same period is at 25.26%, 33.39%, 43.86%, and 60.84%, showing an anticipated improved target for 2030 (MoNDP, 2019).

Based on the issues identified, the strategies and interventions projected by the Indonesian government are divided into two periods. For the first phase (2020–2024), projected interventions are being focused on (1) increased quality education services equal distribution and (2) strengthening the quality of vocational education and training implementation. The second phase for the period (2025–2030) includes interventions such as (1) strengthening autonomy in HE, (2) developing innovative study programmes that suit development and industrial needs, and (3) developing HE as a centre of excellence and development of science and technology (MoNDP, 2019, p. 40).

LEADERSHIP AND INNOVATION IN INDONESIAN HE

By pursuing the idea of having world-class universities, Indonesia, as an emerging economy, has engaged itself in the global competition in the tertiary education market. Almost all public and private universities express such a desire, manifested in their vision and mission statements (Rosser, 2022). Becoming a world-class university means that Indonesian universities must be able to acquire, advance, and create advanced knowledge or innovation. Strong leadership is arguably an essential prerequisite for realising such a goal (Salmi, 2009). However, issues in institutional governance, ineffectiveness, and corruption in Indonesia have impeded Indonesian universities from achieving this goal (Rosser, 2022).

Literature suggests that for universities to meet this goal of becoming world-class, they need to leave their traditional management systems and transform them to align with the market. In such a system of management, leaders are supposed to have combined expertise in management and excellent research careers

(Clark, 2001; Rhoades & Stensaker, 2017) to enable the strengthening of institutional and individual capacity to engage in world-class research and advanced training (Tierney & Lanford, 2016).

Indonesia has a distinctive model of pseudo-market-oriented policy to help transform HEIs to accomplish their goals of becoming world-class universities (Gaus, 2019). This is characterised by the decentralisation of public HEIs' governance while at the same time sustaining government control. Two forms of market-adopted policy can be discerned in the shift of the rectors' role as leaders both in public and private HEIs to one that resembles that of a CEO (Gaus, 2019), and the addition of a particular Board of Trustees (BOT) in the governing body in the PTN-BH. Rectors are assigned as managers to manage their universities' innovation systems as CEOs. This has manifested in the regulation of the Ministry of Research, Technology, and Higher Education, No.24/2019 (renamed in 2021 as the Ministry of Education, Culture, Research, and Technology or MoECRT). The arrangement of the leadership structure or the governing body for innovation management places rectors at the highest level of the hierarchy, followed by deputy rectors. These leaders function as CEOs who oversee enhancing the capacity and capability of HEs in managing the process of innovation and increasing the productivity in HEIs (MoECRT, 2019). These CEOs are also responsible for managing several forms of Innovation Management Institutes and Centres, such as the Institutes of Research and Community Services, Centres of Intellectual Property Rights, Centres for Innovation, and Centres for Business. However, questions arise regarding leaders' institutional and individual capacity to act as CEOs.

As PTN-BH is governed within market norms, their governing body has added the BOT, in which memberships are proposed and elected by the university senate (RoG, 2014). The BOT members should represent the poles of government, universities, and society. Elected names are sent to the government for endorsement and are tasked with a five-year fixed term. The Ministry of Education represents the government's interests, while professionals and businesspeople represent society's interests (Arquisola et al., 2020). Notwithstanding its top position in the hierarchy, it is interesting that the BOT has limited tasks on normative aspects that only include supervising, advocating, and authorising. More specifically, its tasks relate to the stipulation of general policy, the appointment and termination of leaders of universities, supervision and evaluation of the management of universities, and its finances (Rosser, 2022).

In general, the structure of leadership or governance arrangements in public (except PTN-BH) and private universities is made up of rectors, university senates, and a Board of Professors, as well as faculty and departmental leadership (i.e. deans, heads of department, and heads of study programmes) (Arquisola et al., 2020; Rosser, 2022).

Rectors in Indonesia are elected through a highly electoral political process where all candidates compete in ways like those of general elections (Badrun, 2021). Although public universities have de facto autonomy in electing rectors, the hands of the government remain in place, as evidenced by the composition of votes and membership in academic senates. Private universities have no government representation in their academic senates and have more autonomy than public universities in electing their rectors. However, the existence of *Yayasan* (foundations) in private universities restricts their autonomy in electing rectors. *Yayasan* has full authority to approve or disapprove the elected rectors by the university senate (Moeliodihardjo, 2014).

Except for private universities, based on the regulations of the Minister of National Education (now also known and merged into the MoECRT) No. 24, 2010, the Ministry possesses a vote of 35%, given that HEIs are under the management of the Ministry, and in order balance the internal votes in HEIs. This vote also plays a vital role in determining the final decision on who will be elected as a rector (Badrun, 2021; Kompas, 2016). As mentioned, the election of a rector is heavily influenced by politics and is comprised of candidates competing based on political savvy and lobbying, particularly in obtaining the 35% vote of the MoECRT (Kompas, 2016). The repercussion of this conduct has been the rise of putting the competed rector's position on sale, in which money will become a key determinant for success. Such a condition will potentially erode the dignity (or *Marwah*) of universities in Indonesia (Badrun, 2021), leading to the emergence of predatory senior managers who, according to Rosser (2022), are the ones that thwart the accomplishments of world-class universities. In addition, successfully securing that position would risk expanding the government's grip and control imposed on that elected rector (Badrun, 2021). Following this, the government's intervention in the election of rectors in all public universities has become one factor that may exacerbate Indonesian HEIs' failure to excel.

INSTITUTIONAL AUTONOMY AND ACADEMIC FREEDOM

Autonomy and academic freedoms are two of the primary privileges that universities require to achieve their role in society (Thorens, 1998). Even though they are interrelated, they are different in terms of their focus. Autonomy is the extent to which universities can independently make decisions without prior consent from external parties, including ministerial parties. Autonomy takes three forms: autonomy in human resource management, autonomy in financial management, and autonomy in policy implementation (Verhoest et al., 2004). As for academic freedom, individual members are granted the right to express their thoughts, ideas, concerns, and critiques to seek the truth for the development and advancement of knowledge and the improved quality of societal life (Maassen et al., 2017). Bringing together leadership, autonomy, and academic freedom may allow for the establishment of an innovative university with an entrepreneurial ethos (Clark, 2001).

As shifts have swept the landscape of the Indonesian HE sector, brought about by neoliberal ideology and the New Public Management (NPM), the internal governance of HEIs in the country has turned into that of business principles (Gaus & Hall, 2016). The governing body, particularly the BOT (only applies to PTN-BH) and rectors, have transformed akin to corporate CEOs, who run and manage their institutions resembling corporations or businesses. Considering autonomy and academic freedom, they have been widely acknowledged as an inseparable and inherent nature of HE. However, autonomy implementation is still restricted to merit-based practice. Only universities that meet pre-determined conditions will be granted full autonomy through the status of PTN-BH, going against the ideal situation wherein universities should be inherently autonomous. In other words, autonomy also depends on the government's counsel.

In the Indonesian context, the government has realised that to enable universities to contribute to the nation's advancement, universities must be granted autonomy and academic freedom. The Higher Education Law, No. 12, 2012, provides this condition. However, while autonomy and academic freedom have been built as inherent features or 'unique genetic features'(Clark, 2001) of HE, these are not free options for entire public universities to take up in the local context, these are preconditional features or statuses granted based on merit upon meeting the requirements set up by the government in eight components or indicators, such as management, human resources, finance, and professional administration, among others. Universities that meet those conditions will be bestowed with the status of public HE with a legal entity (PTN-BH). In other words, autonomy for universities is government-led autonomy or a 'regulated autonomy' (Marginson, 1997). In 2023, 21 public universities (out of 125) have been granted this status, and universities from Java Island represent the majority of these. HEIs with regulated status include, among others, the Institute Teknologi Bandung (ITB), Institut Teknologi Sepuluh Nopember (ITS), Surabaya, Institut Pertanian Bogor (IPB), Universitas Gadjah Mada (UGM), Universitas Indonesia (UI), Universitas Airlangga (UNAIR), Universitas Diponegoro (UNDIP), Universitas Sumatera Utara (USU), Universitas Hasanuddin (UNHAS), Universitas Sebelas Maret (UNS), Universitas Pendidikan Indonesia (UPI). Private universities, on the one hand, have complete autonomy and independence, specifically in academic matters that include student admissions, curricula, student evaluations, and non-academic matters, including financial management, asset management, faculty recruitment, and reports of responsibilities.

As for the PTN-BH, such institutions have complete autonomy in financial management. They can use their educational income at their disposal without prior consent from and without remitting it to the Ministry of Finance, reporting their income as non-tax state income (NTSI). Luckily, such universities can also keep income from educational ventures as part of their monetary assets. Meanwhile, non-autonomous BLU universities must report their income as NTSI and report it to the state. SATKER universities, on the contrary, must report all their income and remit it to and obtain prior consent from the Ministry of Finance before using it. With these varying degrees of flexibility in financial management, there is inevitably an unjust opportunity for SATKER universities to thrive and advance, given the tight control (Bramastia, 2020). This will eventually lead to SATKER universities being left behind in making the transformation to world-class status because they must go through complicated bureaucratic procedures to use their financial resources (Bramastia, 2020). In the case of BLU and SATKER, the argument of non-selective autonomy is forwarded. It would avoid what Clark (2001) states, wherein the government or the national system and regulation may impede the needed transformation of universities.

Nevertheless, despite the financial autonomy of the PTN-BH, much is to be desired regarding their world rankings. For instance, data released by the Times Higher Education (2023) only ranked Universitas Indonesia in the 1001-1200 band, Institut Teknologi Bandung, Universitas Airlangga, Binus University, and Gadjah Mada University in the 1201-1500 band, while the rest are in the 1500+ band. Although Indonesian universities show good performance at the regional level among ASEAN countries by successfully placing three universities amongst the top 15 best Southeast Asian universities (QS World University Rankings, 2023), given the vast number of universities in the country compared to other ASEAN countries, such achievement signals the need further to improve the performance and management of local universities.

Academic freedom in Indonesian universities is being threatened since, as discussed earlier, the MoECRT has 35% of the votes to elect rectors. This can potentially confine rectors from boldly revealing and expressing views, as they are under the government's tight control (Badrun, 2021). Such control and politicisation may lead to a poor academic culture that affects innovative knowledge production. This concern has been voiced by an economist and former Minister of Coordinator of Marine and Resources (2015), Rizal Ramli, who lamented the lack of critical voices in Indonesia's academe. He links this situation with the government's selection of rectors via the 35% vote. This is worse than Suharto's regime of the New Order, in which, despite autonomy and academic freedom being tightly controlled, remarkably indeed, rectors were not elected and determined by the then regime, so critical rectors were rife and brave enough to tell the truth by even criticising the then ruling regime (Pikiran Rakyat, 2021).

The latest case of how academic freedom may be threatened because of the control of the government in the election of rectors is exemplified by the case of double position (or *rangkap jabatan*), held by the University of Indonesia's rector, Ari Kuncoro (Kompas, 2021). Aside from his position as a rector, he also holds a position as a deputy main commissioner at one state company. While such a position is against the university's internal regulations, it went unnoticed by the public until the rector reprimanded the university's student union regarding the poster criticism on social media against President Joko Widodo (Kompas, 2021). The action indicates how leaders may stifle academic freedom. Following Marginson (1997), such a condition can compromise academic freedom, given that the constraint and apparent interest of the government prevails.

WORLD-CLASS RESEARCH AND INNOVATION

World-class research is one component that underpins the idea of a world-class university (Salmi, 2009). For Indonesian universities to become world-class, they must be able to conduct quality research and disseminate results in internationally reputable journals. It is also essential to attract and retain the best academic staff, both domestic and foreign. Unfortunately, its financial capacity has impeded attracting and hiring top-quality professors in the country's HEIs (Al-Qurtuby, 2018). Nonetheless, the research productivity of Indonesian public and private HEIs in terms of research publication in internationally reputable journals has significantly increased from 2018 to 2021, with bibliometric indicators (i.e. impact factors, h-index, and citations) applied to define the quality and productivity of academic works (Gaus & Hall, 2016).

It should be noted that despite the increase in international publications, data released by the Directorate of Research, Technology, and Community Service (DRTCS, 2022) indicated that the quality of academic staff, as seen from their bibliometric indicators, remains poor. Although the number of publications in international journals has soared, it has been dominated by papers in proceedings (Institute of Physics Publishing Conferences (IOPs)), which accounted for 60% of total publications, with the remaining (40%) as full-length journal articles. This contrasts with Malaysia, where publications in proceedings were at 30% and journal articles at 70% (MoRTHE, 2019). In addition, according to Fiantis (2019) and Macháček and Srholec (2021), Indonesian academics' publications are primarily in predatory journals, putting the country as second-ranked (out of 20) in terms of the number of predatory journal publications (Moylan & Kowalczuk, 2016), which introduces the argument of quantity versus quality in terms of research in the country. Referring to such data, it is not difficult to infer that much is desired regarding the quality of research in HEIs in the country.

Indonesian HEIs are also required by the government to collaborate with international top-ranking universities, as exemplified by other top universities in ASEAN, such as Singapore (Altbach, 2015; Altbach & Salmi, 2011; Salmi, 2009). Following this, attempts have been made at the institutional and governmental levels to encourage researchers to commit to collaborative research and improve their research skills (Indrawati & Kuncoro, 2021). To help universities in Indonesia conduct world-class research and produce innovations, the government plays its role by (1) financing research collaboration and (2) streamlining regulations to support collaboration (Indrawati & Kuncoro, 2021). Collaboration between government and individual research institutions, as well as between domestic and foreign research institutions, have been regulated by a policy launched in 2014 by the then Directorate General of Higher Education (DGHE). The results of this policy have been the increase in active participation of Indonesian researchers in international collaborative research during 2014–2019, particularly in STEM (Science, Technology, Engineering, and Mathematics) (Brodjonegoro, 2020a).

Supporting world-class research is costly and needs a developed HE system with research capability. Marginson (2013) points out the need for a strong and sustainable financial capacity for universities to compete globally. As Indonesian HEIs cannot self-fund themselves, evidence has indicated that universities highly depend on financial support from the government to enable them to conduct world-class research (Indrawati & Kuncoro, 2021). The main source of financial support for the country's research and development (R&D) still rests on the government, with little commitment from the private sector and the HEIs themselves. For instance, in 2020, the Indonesian government's expenditure on R&D was 87.68%, compared to that of business with only 7.97% and that of HE

Table 2. Gross Expenditure in R&D (by Source) in Selected ASEAN Member States.

Countries (Expenditure for the Year)	Government	Business	HE
Indonesia (2020)	87.68	7.97	3.10
Malaysia (2018)	13.41	43.92	42.57
Singapore (2017)	10.97	59.69	29.34
Thailand (2017)	5.44	80	13.85
Vietnam (2017)	21.27	73.04	5.32
Philippines (2015)	24.25	36.88	36.74

Note: Data obtained from the UNESCO Institute for Statistics (UIS) (2015).

with 3.10%. Table 2 compares Indonesia's R&D funding source against selected ASEAN countries. It should be noted that despite the significant contribution of the government to R&D expenses, the gross expenditure on research and development (GERD) as a share of GDP in Indonesia is still low compared to other ASEAN member states UNESCO Institute for Statistics (2015). In 2023, GERD as a percentage of GDP in Indonesia was only 0.3%, the lowest amongst the other five ASEAN countries in the same year as Singapore at 1.9%, Thailand at 1.1%, Malaysia at 1%, and Vietnam at 0.53% (Lowi Institute Asia Power Index, 2023).

Whilst innovative and world-class universities require diversification of sources of income through strengthening partnerships with private industries and corporations, the country's overreliance on government funding may prove a barrier to expanding and strengthening the capacity of Indonesian public and private HEIs to become world-class universities. Considering this, former Minister of RTHE/ the National Institution of Research and Innovation, Bambang Brodjonegoro, revealed that the strategic direction of research funding, or GERD, in Indonesia, is moving in the wrong direction (Brodjonegoro, 2020b). The dominant source of research funds is from the government rather than the private sector, which indicates that Indonesian universities are experiencing a lack of capacity to diversify funding, where most are still far from being self-reliant regarding resource generation.

Sadly, despite a large proportion of R&D expenditure coming from the government, the desired results remain far from expectation. Universities in the country, even the best ones, have failed to strengthen their research productivity and quality (Gaus et al., 2021). Such a reality can be seen from the poor quality of publications and below-average world rankings of HEIs, which consistently sit in the.800+ band (Times HE, 2023). Similarly, in the global innovation index (GII) for 2023, the country is ranked 61 out of 132 (GII, 2023). Nugroho (2019) pointed to several issues circumscribing the development and advancement of world-class research and innovation in Indonesia among other things:

> the lack of research ecosystem, the lack of a shared vision on the importance of research, unclear institutional design (strategy and coordination), lack of a peer review culture, rigid administrative procedures governing research funding, failure to secure funding from non-governmental sources.... (as cited in Indrawati & Kuncoro, p. 48)

The development of research practice in Indonesia is also worsened by the politicisation of research, indicated by the involvement and assignment of a political party figure into the structural posts of the Indonesian National Research and Innovation Institute (BRIN). This has concerned scholars in the country, as this would not lead to the practice of scientific autonomy (Fadilah, 2022).

CONCLUSION

This chapter examined how underdeveloped institutional and individual capacities coupled with national systems (politicisation of HE by the Indonesian government) have, to some extent, impeded attempts to produce innovative knowledge. Consequently, there has been a thwarting of the ambition to materialise the welfare and prosperity of the nation and to rank higher globally in international university assessment exercises. As a result, it is possible that the role of Indonesian HEIs as centres for enhancing national prosperity and welfare via high-quality research and supporting an SDG related to quality education will not be fulfilled. The lack of synergies between the roles of institutional and individual leadership capacities, the understanding of the true meaning and implementation of institutional autonomy and academic freedom, and the lack of funds to undertake high-level research to produce innovation are all issues that need to be considered. The evidence discussed in this chapter signals that strategies to enable Indonesian universities to achieve world-class status are run unsystematically, often aligned with imperatives coming from the government without efficient support. More supporting infrastructures and building the capacity and skills of academic staff, especially in research, are needed. Leading government policy without the necessary change and improvement in international conditions, as mentioned above, may create a 'crowding-out effect' (Gaus et al., 2021) in a sense that all financial funds allocated to support the development of research and innovation in HEIs, among others, would not produce the needed and desired results. It may be wise to consider attempts to promote changes to inhibited internal or organisational culture or 'organisational saga' (Clark, 1972) before applying some government imperatives. Despite these issues, the country's sustained growth in access to HEI is a promising future for materialising the SDG 4.3 agenda.

REFERENCES

Abad-Segura, E., & González-Zamar, M. D. (2021). Sustainable economic development in higher education institutions: A global analysis within the SDGs framework. *Journal of Cleaner Production, 294*, 126133. https://doi.org/10.1016/j.jclepro.2021.126133

Ahmad, N. F. (2020). Sosialisasi manajemen inovasi perguruan tinggi [The socialisation of the inno- vation management in higher education]. Presented at the webinar on the socialisation of Permenristekdikti (the regulation of the Ministry of Research, Technology, and Higher Education) on management innovation in higher education.

Al-Qurtuby, S. (2018, May 12). Perlukah perguruan tinggi Indonesia mengimpor dosen asing? (do Indonesian universities need to import foreign lecturers?). *Liputan6*. https://www.liputan6.com/ https://www.liputan6.com/news/read/3533418/perlukah-perguruan-tinggi-indonesia-mengimpor-dosen-asing

Altbach, P. G. (2015). The costs and benefits of world-class universities. *International Higher Education*, (33). https://doi.org/10.6017/ihe.2003.33.7381

Altbach, P. G., & Salmi, J. (2011). *The road to academic excellence: The making of world-class research universities*. The World Bank. https://doi.org/10.1596/978-0-8213-8805-1

Arquisola, M. J., Zutshi, A., Rentschler, R., & Billsberry, J. (2020). Academic leaders' double bind: Challenges from an Indonesian perspective. *International Journal of Educational Management*, *34*(2), 397–416. https://doi.org/10.1108/IJEM-10-2018-0328

Badrun, U. (2021, May 31). Aroma tak sedap pemilihan rektor dan dekan universitas negeri (bad indication of the election of rectors and deans at public universities). *Tempo*. https://kolom.tempo.co/read/1467366/aroma-tak-sedap

Bramastia, B. (2020, August 26). PTNBH ala kampus merdeka (PTNBH version Independent campuses. *Sindonews*. https://nasional.sindonews.com/read/143826/18

Brewis, E. (2019). Fair access to higher education and discourses of development: A policy analysis from Indonesia. *Compare*, *49*(3), 453–470. https://doi.org/10.1080/03057925.2018.1425132

Brodjonegoro, B. (2020a, July 10). Menristek/kepala BRIN sampaikan pentingnya kolaborasi penelitian internasional untuk peningkatan kapasitas riset dan inovasi national (The minister of research/ the head of BRIN said that internationally research collaboration can increase national research capacity and innovation). *Covid19*. https://covid19.go.id/p/berita/menristekkepala

Brodjonegoro, B. (2020b, November 12). *Dana Riset Indonesia sangat beda dengan negara lain (Indonesian research fund is highly different from other countries)*. Kabar, 24. https://kabar24.bisnis.com/read/20201112/15/1316835

Buchori, M., & Malik, A. (2004). The Evolution of Higher Education in Indonesia. In P. G. Altbach & T. Umakoshi (Eds.), *Asian Universities: Historical perspectives and contemporary challanges* (pp. 249–277). The Johns Hopkins University Press.

Chankseliani, M., & McCowan, T. (2021). Higher education and the sustainable development goals. *Higher Education*, *81*, 1–8. https://doi.org/10.1007/s10734-020-00652-w

Clark, B. R. (1972). The organizational saga in higher education. *Administrative Science Quarterly*, *17*(2), 178–184. https://doi.org/10.2307/2393952

Clark, B. R. (1995). leadership and innovation in universities from theory to practice. *Tertiary Education and Management*, *1*(1), 7–11. https://doi.org/10.1007/BF02354089

Clark, B. (1998). *Creating enterpreneurial universities: organisational pathways of transformation issues in higher education*. New York, Elsevier.

Clark, B. (2001). The entrepreneurial university: New foundations for collegiality, autonomy, and achievement. *Journal of the Programme on Institutional Management in Higher Education: Higher Education Management*, *13*(2), 9–131.

CSB. (2021). *Hasil sensus penduduk (the results of the population's census)*. https://www.bps.go.id/press release/2-21/01/21/1854/hasil-sensus-penduduk-2020

CSB (2024). Jumlah penduduk pertengahan tahun [The number of population mid year]. https://www.bps.go.id/id/statistics-table?subject=519

Cummings, W. K., & Kasenda, S. (1989). The origin of modern Indonesian higher education. In A. Philip & S. Viswanathan (Eds.), *From dependence to autonomy* (pp. 143–166). Kluwer Academic/ Lenum Publisher.

DGHE. (2021). *Higher Education Statistics 2020*. Secretary of Directorate General of Higher Education.

Fadilah, R. (2022, May 11). BRIN, kepentingan politik dan riset (BRIN the political interest and research). *Eramuslim*. https://eramuslim.com/berita/opini/brin-kepentingan-politik-dan-riset.htm

Fiantis, D. (2019, January 10). What are the barriers Indonesian researchers encountered in publishing their research in international journals? *The Conversation*. https://the conversation.com/us/topics/penelitian-42102?page+2

Gaus, N. (2019). Is state control in higher education governance always bad?: New public management and the history of Indonesian Higher Education Reform Policy. *Asian Politics and Policy*, *11*(2), 294–313. https://doi.org/10.1111/aspp.12462

Gaus, N., Arifin, J., Risna, S., Azwar, M., & Yurisna, P. (2021). Trading-off monetary rewards as reinforcers to enhance task motivation and performance of publication in academia. *Higher Education Quarterly*, 1–15. https://doi.org/10.1111/hequ.12350

Gaus, N., & Hall, D. (2016). Performance indicators in Indonesian universities: The perception of academics. *Higher Education Quarterly*, *70*(2), 127–144. https://doi.org/10.1111/hequ.12085

Indonesian Higher Education database of PDDIKTI. (2023). *The number of students in higher education in 2022*. https://pddikti.kemdikbud.go.id

Indrawati, S. M., & Kuncoro, A. (2021). Improving competitiveness through vocational and higher education: Indonesia's vision for human capital development in 2019–2024. *Bulletin of Indonesian Economic Studies*, *57*(1), 29–59. https://doi.org/10.1080/00074918.2021.1909692

Kompas. (2016, October 29). *Ini alasan mentri punya hak suara 35 persen dalam pemilihan rektor (these are the reasons why the minister owns the right of 35% votes in the election of rectors)*. https://nasional.kompas.com/read/2016/10/29/12085

Kompas. (2021, July 23). *Polemik rangkap jabatan, bungkamnya UI hingga rektor mundur dari komisaris BRI (The polemic of double positions, the silence of UI and the retreat of the rector from the commissioner of BRI*. https://nasional.kompas.com/read/2021/07/23/09544551/

Koning, J., & Maassen, E. (2012). Autonomous institutions? Local ownership in higher education in eastern Indonesia. *International Journal of Business Anthropology*, *3*(2), 54–74.

Kontan. (2020, September 2). *Jumlah siswa yang lanjut perguruan tinggi di Indonesia tertinggal jauh dari tetangga (the numbers of senior high school graduates who continue to higher education have lagged behind by those of neighbouring countries)*. https://nasional.kontan.co

Logli, C. (2016). Higher education in Indonesia: Contemporary challenges in governance, access, and quality. In C. S. Christopher, N. N. Lee, N. H. John, & E. N. Deane (Eds.), *The Palgrave handbook of Asia Pacific higher education* (pp. 561–581). https://doi.org/10.1057/978-1-137-48739-1_37

Lowi Institute Asia Power Index. (2023). *Gross domestic expenditure on R&D as a share of GDP*. Retrieved January 11, 2024, from https://power.lowyinstitute.org/data/economic-capability/technology/rnd-spending-of-gdp/

Maassen, P., Gornitzka, Å., & Fumasoli, T. (2017). University reform and institutional autonomy: A framework for analysing the living autonomy. *Higher Education Quarterly*, *71*(3), 239–250. https://doi.org/10.1111/hequ.12129

Macháček, V., & Srholec, M. (2021). Predatory publishing in Scopus: Evidence on cross-country differences. *Scientometrics*, *126*, 1897–1921. https://doi.org/10.1007/s11192-020-03852-4

Marginson, S. (1997). How free is academic freedom? *International Journal of Phytoremediation*, *16*(3), 359–369. https://doi.org/10.1080/0729436970160309

Marginson, S. (2013). Different roads to a shared goal: Political and cultural variation in world-class universities. In W. Qi, C. Ying, & C. L. Nian (Eds.), *Building world-class universities: Different approaches to a shared goal* (pp. 13–33). Sense Publisher.

Moeliodihardjo, B. (2014). *Higher education sector in Indonesia*. British Council.

MoNDP. (2019). *Roadmap of SDGs Indonesia: A highlight*. The Ministry of National Development Planning.

MoRTHE. (2019). *Increase the quality of scientific publications by enhancing the number of articles in reputable international journals, not proceedings*. MoRTHE.

Moylan, E. C., & Kowalczuk, M. K. (2016). Why articles are retracted: A restrospective cross sectional study of retraction notices at BioMed Central. *BMJ Open*, 047. doi:10.1136/bmjopen-2016-012047

Nizam, N., & Nurdin, M. (2013). Governance reforms in higher education: A study of institutional autonomy in Indonesia. In N. V. Varghese & M. Martin (Eds.), *Governance reforms and university autonomy in Asia* (pp. 85–104). International Institute for Educational Planning.

Nugroho, Y. (2019.) *Membangun ekosistem riset di Indonesia [Building a research ecosystem in Indonesia]*. Kompas. https://www.ksp.go.id/membangun-ekosistem-riset-di-indonesia.htm

Pikiran Rakyat. (2021, June 29). *Soal kebijakan rektor ditunjuk oleh presiden, Rizal Ramli: President bobot akademik pas-pasan dipilih presiden (The policy of rectors are assigned by the president, Rizal Ramli: the so so academic capacity president is selected by president)*. https://depok.pikiran-rakyat.com/nasional/pr-092133734/soal-kebijakan-rektor-ditunjuk-olehpresiden

QS World University Rankings. (2023). *QS Asia University Rankings 2023: South-Eastern Asia*. https://www.topuniversities.com/university-rankings/asia-university-rankings/south-eastern-asia/2023

Rhoades, G., & Stensaker, B. (2017). Bringing organisations and systems back together: Extending Clark's entrepreneurial university. *Higher Education Quarterly*, *71*(2), 129–140. https://doi.org/10.111/hequ.12118

Indonesian Higher Education: Issues in Institutional and Individual Capacities

RoG [Regulation of Government]. (2014). *The operationalisation and management of higher education in Indonesia*. The Government of Indonesia.

RoMoRTHE. (2019). The management of innovation in higher education. The Ministry of Research, Technology, and Higher Education.

Rosing, K., Frese, M., & Bausch, A. (2011). Explaining the heterogeneity of the leadership-innovation relationship: Ambidextrous leadership. *Leadership Quarterly, 22*(5), 956–974. https://doi.org/10.1016/j.leaqua.2011.07.014

Rosser, A. (2018). Indonesia's education system is low in quality and the underlying causes are political. *Lowy Institutes. Beyond Access: Making Indonesia's Education System Work.*

Rosser, A. (2022). Higher education in Indonesia: The political economy of institution-level governance. *Journal of Contemporary Asia.* Published online. https://doi.org/10.1080/00472336.2021.2010120

Salmi, J. (2009). *The challenge of establishing world-class universities*. The World Bank.

Statista. (2022). R & D investment share from GDP Indonesia 2020–2022. https://www.statista.com/statistics/1352919/indonesia-randd-investment-from

The Ministry of Research, Technology, and Higher Education. (2019). *The regulation No.24/2019, The management of innovation of higher education*, Jakarta.

THE. (2023). *Study in Indonesia*. https://www.timeshighereducation.com/student/where-to-study/study-in-indonesia

Thorens, J. P. (1998). Academic freedom and university autonomy. *Prospects, 28*(3), 401–407

Tierney, W. G., & Lanford, M. (2016). *Conceptualizing innovation in higher education*. https://doi.org/10.1007/978-3-319-26829-3_1

UNESCO Institute for Statistics. (2015). *UNESCO science report towards 2030*. https://en.unesco.org/sites/default/files/usr15_southeast_asia_and_oceania.pdf

Verhoest, K., Peters, B. G., Bouckaert, G., & Verschuere, B. (2004). The study of organisational autonomy: A conceptual review. *Public Administration and Development, 24*(2), 101–118. https://doi.org/10.1002/pad.316

Welch, A. R. (2007). Blurred vision?: Public and private higher education in Indonesia. *Higher Education, 54*(5), 665–687. https://doi.org/10.1007/s10734-006-9017-5

Wicaksono, T. Y., & Friawan, D. (2011). Recent developments in higher education in Indonesia. In A. Shiro & C. Bruce (Eds.), *Financing higher education and economic development in East Asia* (pp. 159–187). The Australian National University Press.

World Bank. (2021). *School enrolment, tertiary (% gross)–Indonesia*. https://data.worldbank.org

CHAPTER 4

HIGHER EDUCATION IN THE LAO PEOPLE'S DEMOCRATIC REPUBLIC

Nanludet Moxom[a] and Richard Noonan[b]

[a]National University of Laos, Laos
[b]Independent Education Consultant, Vientiane, Laos

ABSTRACT

Higher education institutions in Lao PDR are not generally performing well. Some sector goals achieved include an outcomes-based curriculum focus and gender equity. However, problems with quality are wide-ranging and complicated, with most institutions struggling to improve their quality in teaching and learning, research, community service, and quality assurance. Efforts to improve tend to be frustrated by inefficiency and unmanageability. At the heart of the problem is a lack of sufficient leadership capacity. The challenges are profound, and the need for solutions is pressing.

Keywords: Autonomy; curriculum; enrolment; finance; governance; leadership; quality; quality assurance; research; teaching/learning

INTRODUCTION

French colonial authorities in Laos paid little attention to education and gave no attention to higher education over the long period from 1893 to 1953 when Laos was a French protectorate. Following independence from France, the Royal Lao Government, with financial assistance from the West, embarked upon a significant

---

Higher Education in Southeast Asia
International Perspectives on Education and Society, Volume 49, 35–47
Copyright © 2025 by Nanludet Moxom and Richard Noonan
Published under exclusive licence by Emerald Publishing Limited
ISSN: 1479-3679/doi:10.1108/S1479-367920240000049004

expansion of the national education system. Regarding higher education, it established in quick succession a Royal School of Medicine, a Royal Institute of Law and Administration, a National School of Fine Arts, a National School of Music and Dance, and a National Institute of Pedagogy. During the late 1950s and early 1960s, it created Sisavangvong University, with affiliates that included the Royal School of Medicine, the Royal Institute of Law and Administration, and the National Institute of Education (Moxom & Noonan, 2020). These institutions were supervised by the Ministry of Education, Sports and Religious Affairs, as were regional technical colleges and teacher training colleges established in Luang Prabang, Pakse, and Savannakhet (Ogawa, 2009, p. 288). Additional higher education institutions (HEIs) established during the 1960s included the Superior Pedagogy Institute and the Buddhism Education Institute, under the authority of the Ministry of Culture.

In 1975, after more than 15 years of civil war, the Lao People's Revolutionary Party formed a communist government and renamed the country the Lao People's Democratic Republic (Lao PDR). Many existing educational structures were dismantled, and Sisavangvong University was dissolved. The higher education sector became fragmented to such an extent that no degree-granting institutions existed. Up until the collapse of the Soviet Union in 1991, young people seeking to access higher education had to go to Soviet bloc countries.

In the early 1990s, the Asian Development Bank (ADB) conducted several scoping studies on the education system and the labour market. In 1995, an agreement was reached about financing a Post-secondary Education Rationalisation Project, and *Prime Ministerial Decree No. 50/PM/95* created the National University of Laos (NUOL), which opened in 1996. NUOL resulted from a merger of 10 existing post-secondary schools and colleges in Vientiane, the national capital.

Since then, Laos's higher education sector has expanded and diversified. It now includes many different types of institutions. The four main institutional categories are (a) national HEIs, (b) regional HEIs, (c) HEIs with a provincial or community focus, and (d) specialised HEIs with a mono-disciplinary focus. The two national universities are NUOL and the University of Health Sciences. The three regional universities are Champasack University, Savannakhet University, and Souphanouvong University, each established as spin-offs from NUOL. The HEIs with a provincial or community focus include eight teacher training and five specialised teacher training colleges. The specialised HEIs with a mono-disciplinary focus are the Banking Institute, the Central Institute of Economics and Finance, the National Institute of Fine Arts, the National Institute of Justice, and the Vocational Education Development Institute. In 2022, there were, in addition, seven private higher education providers, mainly enrolling part-time students and accounting for only 16% of all higher education enrolments. There is also one small international university, Soochow International Laos, a branch campus of Soochow University in China.

The Ministry of Education and Sports (MOES) is authorised to coordinate with relevant organisations to determine detailed regulations about governance, standards, and conditions for the national higher education sector. The ministry also oversees NUOL and the three regional universities. Provincial departments within MOES, referred to as the Provincial Education and Sports Services, oversee the teacher training and specialised teacher training colleges. The specialised mono-disciplinary HEIs function under the supervision of a collection of ministries and state offices belonging to the government cabinet.

Universities in Laos generally have more academic and administrative autonomy than other public HEIs. NUOL and the University of Health Sciences, the only institutions permitted to award PhDs, have the most autonomy.

Since the early 1990s, the government has encouraged private initiatives in the higher education sector. Indeed, the *Education Law* of 2007 declared that, subject to government approval, private HEIs were encouraged (National Assembly, 2007). There used to be many more than seven private HEIs in the sector. However, in 2012, following increased concern about the quality of many HEIs, the government introduced national higher education standards regarding governance and management, human resource development, curriculum, teaching/learning effectiveness, student support services, learning environment and resources, management information systems, quality assurance, scientific research, and consultancy services. An inspection process implemented by the government resulted in the closure of many private HEIs. In 2022, private providers accounted for 9.4% of all enrolments (MOES, 2022).

In 2020, MOES outlined the organisation and management of its Department of Higher Education, assigning responsibilities to the department that included developing policies and plans for higher education development, strengthening personnel capabilities within the department and at all public HEIs, managing the higher education curriculum according to National Curriculum Standards, promoting internal quality assurance within the higher education sector, and motivating public HEIs to be self-reliant in terms of financial management and academic matters (MOES, 2020a, p. 2). The department was also made responsible for supporting public HEIs to become more internationally oriented. Although internationalisation is not mentioned explicitly in the five-year plan for MOES covering 2021 to 2025 (MOES, 2020e), the need to reach regional and international targets is frequently referenced. For instance, the National Standard Curriculum for HEIs states that the creation and development of a bachelor/master/doctoral degree curriculum must ensure 'the comparability and transferability of credits between national HEIs, and integration to the (ASEAN) region and the world' (MOES, 2020c, 2020d, 2020e).

The higher education sector's enrolment level reached 107,894 in 2012 (MOES, 2022). Since then, it has been dropping. In 2022, it enrolled 48,297 students (MOES, 2022). The gross enrolment rate in the sector was only 13.5% in 2020 (UNESCO Institute of Statistics [UIS], n.d.), which is well below the rate for most ASEAN member states. The distribution of higher education enrolments by field of study from 2018 to 2023 showed that most were in business administration and law. The second most popular field was engineering.

ACCESS AND EQUITY

The state, through MOES, provides Lao citizens with access to higher education according to their ability level. It also promotes and develops higher education to expand and strengthen quality, including scientific research, technology, and academic service to the community and society. It encourages and enables individuals and domestic and international organisations to invest and participate in higher education development (Office of the President (OP), 2020).

Regarding access and equity, educational disadvantage begins in preschool and continues through the school years and into higher education. As shown in Table 1, only 26.9% of children aged 36 to 59 months in 2023 attended kindergarten. Over one-third (38.6%) of children starting primary school in 2023 had not participated in an early childhood education program the previous year. Only 72.8% of school-age children entered the first grade of primary school in 2024. Only 37.1% of upper-secondary-age children attended a secondary school or higher in 2024.

Participation rates in upper-secondary and higher education are greatly affected by place of residence (urban/rural/remote), disabilities, socio-economic level, and ethnicity (especially in the language spoken at home and in the local community). Laos comprises people of diverse ethnic backgrounds, spread over different parts of the country. The four main ethnolinguistic groups are Lao-Tai (Lao) (62.4%), Mon-Khmer (23.7%), Hmong-Lu Mien (9.7%), and Chine-Tibetan (2.9%) (Lao Statistics Bureau, 2018). Almost 40% of the Lao population has a mother

Table 1. Some Key Statistics of Education Access.

Indicator	Definition	Percentage
Attendance at early childhood education	Percentage of children aged 36–59 months who are attending an early childhood education program	26.9
School readiness	Percentage of children attending the first grade of primary school who attended early childhood education program during the previous school year	61.4
Net intake rate in primary education	Percentage of children of school-entry age who enter the first grade of primary school	72.8
Net school attendance rate (adjusted)	Percentage of children of	
	(a) primary school age currently attending primary, lower or upper secondary school	86.0
	(b) lower secondary school age currently attending lower secondary school or higher	61.8
	(c) upper secondary school age currently attending upper secondary school or higher	37.1
Gross intake ratio to the last grade	Ratio of children attending the last grade for the first time to children at the appropriate age for the last grade	
	(a) primary school	95.0
	(b) lower secondary school	63.8
Completion rate	Percentage of children aged 3–5 years above the intended age for the last grade who have completed that grade:	
	(a) primary school	87.6
	(b) lower secondary school	56.2
	(c) upper secondary school	37.4

Source: Lao Statistics Bureau (2024).

Higher Education in the Lao People's Democratic Republic 39

tongue different from the national language, even though the official language of instruction in the education system is Lao. Young people in the early grades who do not speak Lao are much less likely to succeed academically and are eventually more likely to drop out of school (ACER, 2011).

Regarding urban–rural differences, the net attendance rate at the upper-secondary school level is 61% in urban areas, 31% in rural 'on-road' areas, and 15% in more remote rural 'off-road areas' (Lao Statistics Bureau, 2018, p. 269). Rural areas account for about two-thirds of the population (Ministry of Planning & Investment, 2016, p. 26). There are substantial differences in the tertiary gross attendance ratio (GAR) by location and wealth quintile, as shown in Table 2. The tertiary GAR is the number of students attending tertiary education expressed as a percentage of the population of nominal age enrolment in ISCED Levels 6 and 7, which in Laos is 18 to 22 years. Low upper-secondary attendance rates in rural areas and among the poorest quintiles of wealth in the community undermine equitable access to higher education.

To improve access for the marginalised, NUOL has admitted visually impaired students since 2016. They study together with mainstream students. There are some teaching-learning aids for them, such as braille texts and computer-assisted listening. However, inclusive education faces challenges. Research findings by Bouppha et al. (2021, pp. 59–63) show that visually impaired students cannot readily catch up with mainstream students regarding learning pace and performance. Lecturers do not have time to care for students with disabilities while attending to their everyday teaching responsibilities. Additionally, infrastructure, such as roads and buildings, is not 'inclusive-student friendly' because inclusive education is relatively new to Laos. Lastly, inclusive students' examination results are often given to them as an encouragement to maintain their studies with fewer challenges rather than as a reflection of their actual examination performances. Thus, teaching and learning approaches have been poorly developed for physically impaired individuals.

In terms of related government policy, one of the aims of the Education and Sports Sector Development Plan (ESSDP) is to 'establish an education fund to support disadvantaged, poor, remote, and female students' (MOES, 2020f, p. 126).

Table 2. GAR, by Location and Wealth Quintile, 2017.

Location	
National	12.6
Rural	5.5
Urban	28.8
Wealth Quintile	
First (poorest)	0.5
Second	2.9
Third	6.5
Fourth	15.2
Fifth (wealthiest)	38.7

Source: UIS (n.d.).

As of 2023–2024, quota students received a stipend of approximately US$10 per month for associate bachelor's and bachelor's degree programs. The ESSDP aims for 80% of the new intake students to be fee-paying (MOES, 2020f, p. 5), while the remaining 20% are quota students. The three categories of quota students who receive a stipend of US$20 per month from the start of their first year at HEIs are (a) high-performing upper-secondary graduates, based on their upper-secondary school leaving examination results, (b) well-performing upper-secondary graduates coming from low-income families in designated poor districts across the country, and (c) the highest-scoring scorer in the entrance examination of each faculty.

Scholarships are given to high-performing students and high- or well-performing female students from poor ethnic minority families. Charities, businesses, foreign governments, and international organisations generously provide these scholarships. For instance, during the 2023–2024 academic year, some 540 NUOL students received these scholarships. The scholarships are given for nine months, 10 months, 12 months, or until program completion, and range in value from US$20 to US$40 per month.

In 2020, MOES reported on the achievement of access and the government's efforts. According to this report, (a) early childhood education enrolment had increased across all provinces in the country, with equitable participation by both genders; (b) primary school enrolment had remained steady, with repetition rates declining; and (c) lower-secondary school enrolment had also improved, particularly for girls. These improvements were attributed to policy changes, curriculum revisions, and teacher training initiatives.

However, there is no quality measurement from ECE up to upper secondary school levels. That is, there is no apparent form of quality assurance, while, in the higher education sector, quality assurance systems are generally ineffective. Poverty and low incomes, dropout at lower levels before higher education, inadequate teaching for those with disabilities, and unemployment after graduating from HEIs are likely to result in decreased higher education participation in Laos.

The government has also ensured commitment to the SDG 2030 goals, though there is little data in terms of achievements in the higher education sector. While gender parity in enrolment has been achieved at the primary level, this has yet to be realised at the secondary level. The gender parity index (**GPI**) in literacy also remains low (in favour of males) among adults and older populations (GoL, 2021, p.40). To further address SDG 4 (Quality Education), the government has identified 40 priority districts for the most disadvantaged needing the most support. The government is also investing in teaching and research by proposed establishment of centres of excellence in (i) agriculture in Champasack, (ii) logistics in Savannakhet, (iii) engineering and tourism in Luang Prabang, and (iv) engineering and environmental studies at the NUOL (GoL, 2021, p.42).

LABOUR MARKET OUTCOMES

The gross enrolment ratio (**GER**) for ISCED Levels 6 to 8 (i.e. bachelor's to doctoral degrees) in Laos rose considerably from the early 2000s, reaching a peak in 2012–2013. The GER refers here to the total enrolment in tertiary education, regardless of age, as a percentage of the population in the five years following the upper-secondary level, covering the age range from 18 to 22. All figures here refer to bachelor's degrees or higher programs (ISCED Levels 6 to 8). The GER then declined rapidly, reaching a low in 2016–2017, then rising slowly for females but continuing to fall slowly for males. The rise from 2011 to 2012 was due to the high priority given in ISCED Level 7 (master's degree or equivalent) to expanding all levels of education (Ministry of Planning and Investment (2018).

The main reason for the decline in enrolments from 2012 to 2013 was the rapid growth in labour market demand in the industrial sector, causing many young people to no longer see higher education as the most attractive path to employment (Moxom & Noonan, 2021). In addition, the establishment of minimum standards for offering bachelor's level programs led to the closure of many programs, especially in private HEIs. A tracer study of higher education graduates between 2000 and 2012 found that 63% of respondents were currently employed, 13% were unemployed and looking for a job, 12% were unemployed but not looking for a job, and 12% were undertaking training activities or continuing their education (Duronsoy et al., 2014, p. 7).

In 2020, a report on NUOL graduates found that 67% of respondents were currently employed, 26% were unemployed and looking for a job, 6% were unemployed but not looking for a job, and 1% were undertaking training activities or continuing their education (NUOL, 2020). In 2020, in a similar tracer study conducted by Savannakhet University (2020), of the 225 participants, 41.4% were employed, 34.5% were unemployed and looking for jobs, 13.8% were unemployed but not looking for jobs, and 10.3% were training and/or continued their education. In 2020, there was a total of 10,904 students who graduated from NUOL, Champasack University, Souphanouvong University, Savannakhet University, and the University of Health Sciences (MOES, 2021). These figures show that nearly half of the graduates could not find employment. Universities may need to increase graduates' capacity for employability.

While most university graduates can find employment upon graduation, there is a shortage of graduates in sciences, technologies, and mathematics (MOES, 2018). A national lack of more sophisticated laboratory resources for these disciplines makes it a challenge to produce graduates who are readily equipped for the demands of these industries (NUOL, 2023). The increasing recognition of multidisciplinary and trans-disciplinary skills in higher education is also evident in Laos (Personal communication, November 25, 2023), despite no direct policy encouraging HEIs to apply for multidisciplinary or trans-disciplinary programs. However, the National Curriculum Standards (i.e. from associate bachelor's up to doctoral degree levels) require HEIs to develop curricula based on labour market needs (MOES, 2020c, 2020d, 2020e).

There is an opportunity for multidisciplinary or cross-disciplinary/trans-disciplinary programs if program developers have in-depth curriculum development capacity. This can also bring forth better opportunities and integration in the ASEAN region for Laotian graduates. Likewise, recognising the importance of entrepreneurship, the MOES has collaboratively developed a curriculum for an entrepreneurship course at the bachelor's degree level with NUOL in 2022, with the prospect of offering the same program through other HEIs. Furthermore, to better orient higher education to the labour market, MOES has recognised 'the linkages between education, employment and other socio-economic dimensions to guide evidence-based planning and investment' (MOES, 2020f, p. 1). It has also committed to maintaining a monitoring process for graduate employment from the four universities for which it is managerially responsible (MOES, 2020g, p. 52).

QUALITY

Quality remains of utmost concern in higher education in Laos (MOES 2019, 2022). HEIs create and develop their curricula according to the National Curriculum Standards, the qualification framework for higher education, and the current National Socio-Economic Development Plan. The curriculum must align with textbooks and teaching-learning practices, while further integration with the ASEAN region and others is also mandated (MOES, 2020b). Higher education curricula, from the associate bachelor's to doctorate levels, are framed by the Department of Higher Education. The National Curricular Standard framework covers higher education award levels. The most recent version was published in 2020. Article 5, Curriculum Structure, of National Curriculum Standard at the bachelor's degree level (MOES 2020b), indicates the requirements for approval of new curricula. Similarly, the requirements are given for approval of new at the master's degree level (MOES, 2020c) and doctorate level (MOES, 2020d).

In line with quality goals, minimum standards required for HEIs (public and private) to offer bachelor's degree programs were established in 2013 (MOES, 2013). Regulations for establishing and upgrading HEIs in accordance with the relevant laws and regulations to guarantee quality are set upon the establishment of each HEI (MOES, 2017). In 2020, the Decree on Higher Education established the country's principles, organisation, and higher education management (Office of the President (OP), 2020). The aim is to organise quality teaching and research in public and private HEIs to better meet national development needs. Higher education must encompass the *Three Characteristics of Lao Education* (i.e. scientific and modern, oriented towards national unity, and oriented towards equity) and the '*Five Domains of Lao Education*' (i.e. morality, intellectual development, aesthetics, physical education, and labour education).

Outcomes-based education has been advocated for implementation in the higher education sector since 2020. Under this approach, curriculum development heavily relies on the Bloom taxonomy (i.e. learning hierarchy and domains). Additionally, key stakeholders' inputs are also considered for program development. Moreover, teaching-learning methods, expected learning outcomes, and student assessments are all planned in rubrics. The NUOL has been at the forefront of applying OBE with related training in each academic faculty to this approach. An OBE program development guideline was also compiled and published in 2021, and currently, there are 78 graduate programs at the NUOL which have adapted the OBE approach.

Higher Education in the Lao People's Democratic Republic

For the approval of a new bachelor's degree curriculum, the ministry requires that the institution have a relevant curriculum development unit (MOES, 2020b). The curriculum should align with labour market and socio-economic needs, be in accordance with Lao Education characteristics and domains, and have bilingual program and qualification names. Graduates should have theoretical knowledge, practical skills, and research abilities. The curriculum plan must detail student intake conditions, teaching methods, and program duration. Resource requirements must be specified, including faculty, facilities, and budget. Creating a new program requires appointing a committee, conducting a needs survey, preparing a master plan, and obtaining approval from the institution's Academic Committee before submitting it to MOES. Improving an approved curriculum involves appointing a curriculum committee, with the President able to approve minor improvements covering up to 20% of subjects and unchanged credits. Significant improvements require MOES approval.

Responding to the Need for Quality in Higher Education

In response to reports that many HEIs were offering courses of low quality, national higher education standards were developed in the country and applied to all HEIs (Moxom & Noonan, 2020). Due to quality concerns, an evaluation was conducted in 54 public and private HEIs in Vientiane Capital and some public and private HEIs in the provinces in 2012 (MOES, 2014). A panel of 30 independent assessors was established, and evaluation instruments comprising 10 standards and 50 indicators were prepared. The 10 standards addressed various matters, including governance and management, human resource development, curriculum, and teaching-learning effectiveness. Despite this push for quality evaluation over a decade ago, quality remains an issue. Recently, according to MOES (2020g, p. 50), problems continuing to affect the higher education sector include: (a) universities struggling to launch new programs due to lack of qualified teachers and proper facilities, (b) graduates that are ill-equipped for the labour market due to lack of practical work experience in programs, (c) universities lacking effective self-evaluation, and (d) ineffective research findings with unclear contributions to better the Lao economy and society. Student exchange programs are also mostly one-way, with Lao students going abroad but not many international students coming to Laos. This situation is likely due to limited budgets and a lack of programs taught in other languages. As a result, Lao students have fewer opportunities to study abroad.

Internal and external assessments have been conducted in the higher education sector in line with quality concerns. For instance, in 2020, eight HEIs conducted self-assessments and five HEIs were assessed by external agencies from the MOES and the ASEAN University Network Quality Assurance (AUN-QA). These assessments concluded that, among other things, the extent of implementation of higher education development plans was insufficient, the number of new enrolments had declined compared with the number prescribed by MOES, financial autonomy remained a challenge, alongside the lack of an adequate government budget, and how academic staff members were recruited was not consistent with disciplinary needs (MOES, 2021, p. 6). Most recently, in February 2022, the quality assurance unit of the Faculty of Law and Political Science at NUOL invited ASEAN-QA experts to evaluate two programs, namely International Relations and Political Science, based on the AUN-QA framework. While MOES-QA and AUN-QA are relatively effective, the institutional quality assurance systems of HEIs in Laos are widely agreed to be limited because of inadequate personnel and institutional leadership monitoring.

The role of research is also an essential part of pushing for the quality of the country's higher education sector. In 2020, four universities under the management of MOES reported completing more than two hundred research projects – NUOL (130), Champasack (22), Souphanouvong (40), and Savannakhet (43). The University of Health Sciences, the National Justice Institute, and the Banking Institute completed 113, 2 and 2 research projects, respectively. Research projects are supported by government, industry, and international funding agencies, and 264 research papers were published in national and international journals in 2020 (MOES, 2021, p. 5).

Issues of Financing and Quality

Public HEIs receive finance from the government budget according to annual allocation plans and from grants, donations, or other funds from domestic or international sources (MOES, 2020f). Education financing from the State Budget (including ODA) was 13.1% in 2020 and 15.4% excluding ODA; this is against an Education Sector Development Plan (ESDP) 2020 target of more than 17% (MOES, 2020f, p. 4). Public national and regional HEIs submit annual budget plans directly to the Ministry of Finance. Budget plans for the other categories of public HEIs are forwarded to the respective central or local authorities. Some HEIs are partly financed for academic services, such as applied research, consulting, external training and testing, renting facilities, and developing or renting technologies.

All public HEIs are financed at least in part from student fees, but the costs for higher education in Laos are relatively low. At NUOL, for example, the bachelor's degree program fee is between US$55 and US$63 per year (NUOL, 2024). Public expenditure on education rose considerably during the early 2000s but more slowly over the past 15 years. Over the past decade, public expenditure on education represented approximately 2% of Gross Domestic Product. Tertiary education represents approximately 17% of total government expenditure on education (UIS, n.d.).

There are financial difficulties in the higher education sector. The issue of low budget for HEIs is a persistent problem. For example, one of the leading budget issues at NUOL is that faculties, offices, institutes, centres, and other directorates submit their annual budget proposals but never get the budget they requested, which undermines commitment to research, amongst other things. Furthermore, late budget delivery is a recurring problem. Consequently, funds received tend not to be spent on time and must be returned to the funding source. MOES reported that the direction of encouraging HEIs to enhance their financial and academic performances has not yet been clear and needs improvement (MOES, 2020g, p. 50). In addition, the foreign language (English) ability of staff members of the Ministry is limited, which makes them unable to form opinions and compete for assistance funding to develop the broader education sector (MOES, 2020g, p. 70). It should be noted that public HEIs, particularly NUOL, make significant earnings apart from tuition fees. These incomes are from long-term land leases and private businesses conducted on campus.

Furthermore, expense inappropriateness may also be an unrelenting issue. For example, while central-level spending in universities is relatively easy, academic faculty-level expense approvals by the institution take longer and face severe budget restrictions (Personal communication, December 15, 2022). Other related issues are the late receipt of wages for additional teaching hours due to centralised decisions. For example, before 2018, financial decisions regarding additional teaching hours in the NUOL were delegated to the faculties. However, due to a lack of transparency, decisions are now being made on a centralised level. These matters may prove detrimental to the overall push for quality teaching and research in the sector.

GOVERNANCE AND LEADERSHIP

Governance and leadership are also areas of concern for the higher education sector in Laos. Good governance can create high-performing leadership and vice versa. Higher education autonomy is relevant to governance and leadership performance. The governance structure of universities in Laos includes the university council, the president's executive board, the academic committee, and the party committee (Moxom & Hayden, 2018). Public HEIs are granted autonomy under the following conditions: (a) the government or a state instrumentality agrees; (b) the institution is distinctive and has been accredited by an external authority; (c) the institution has a governance structure capable of supporting autonomy; and (d) specific regulations have been approved concerning the conditions and standards to be maintained (Office of the President (OP), 2020, p. 9). Additionally, personnel in managerial positions at HEIs must, among other things, have the right political stance to serve the people and hold suitable qualifications for their posts. For presidents of colleges and academics, individuals must have at least a master's degree or equivalent and at least five years of working experience, while presidents of universities should have a doctoral degree or equivalent of at least five years of working experience (Office of the President (OP), 2020).

A significant issue in Laos is that public HEIs are highly centralised and lack much autonomy for making decisions about processes (how) and goals (what), particularly strategic choices. This lack of independence is partly due to deficiencies in quality, as noted above. However, quality development requires that public HEIs have more institutional autonomy. At present, though, the benefits of being autonomous are not well understood by local managers in the sector because there is a lack of meritocracy in leadership appointments, contributing to deficiencies in managerial competence (Moxom & Hayden, 2018).

The extent of accountability in institutional governance is also relatively weak (Moxom & Hayden, 2018). When accountability is weak, visions and goals are less likely to be fulfilled. One way to address this weakness is to introduce key performance indicators. However, the governance and management culture in public HEIs continues to be bureaucratic and authoritarian and dominated by rules and regulations (Moxom & Hayden, 2018). There is a lack of open discussion about goals and vision, with key management positions (e.g. deanship, presidency, etc.) approved by the Prime Minister on advice from MOES. There is a lack of transparency in the process.

CLOSING REMARKS

This chapter has provided an overview of the higher education sector in Laos, with attention given particularly to issues of enrolment, finance, curriculum, teaching-learning, research, quality, quality assurance, autonomy, governance and leadership. Quality issues in the sector are significant due largely to a lack of effective leadership. With stronger university leadership, governance mechanisms would likely align better, providing greater accountability, transparency, and competency. Eventually, university autonomy can be achieved through negotiation or communication by capable leaders. Quality issues may also be addressed by fully aligning the country's higher education sector with regional (e.g. ASEAN) and international standards. Linking financial allocations to quality priorities is also recommended, and a more decentralised approach to managing the distribution of funds would contribute to better institutional outcomes. For the moment, though, the higher education sector in Laos is making slow progress. Though there is a vision for at least one of its universities to attain standing as a high-performing ASEAN HEI, the evidence suggests that this vision is difficult to attain.

REFERENCES

ACER. (2011). Evaluation of Australia's investment in teacher development in Lao PDR. *BEQUAL*.

Bouppha, B., Vilachith, P., Anoulack, R., & Pasanchay, K. (2021). *Challenges facing visually impaired students in [at] National University of Laos*. National University of Laos.

Duronsoy, J., Vilaythong Syvilay, V., & Billany, N. (2014). *Report on tracer study on graduates' employability in LAO PDR*. Strengthening Higher Education Project. MOES.

GoL [Government of Lao PDR]. (2021). *Voluntary national review (Implementation of the 2030 Agenda for Sustainable Development)*. GoL.

Lao Statistics Bureau. (2018). *Lao Social Indicator Survey II 2017, Survey findings report*. Lao Statistics Bureau and UNICEF.

Lao Statistics Bureau. (2024). *Lao Social Indicator Survey III-2023: Key indicator report*. Retrieved June 18, 2024, from https://www.unicef.org/laos/reports/lao-social-indicator-survey-iii-lsis-iii-2023-key-indicators-report

Ministry of Education and Sports (MOES). (2013). *Minimum standards of higher education institutions*. MOES.

Ministry of Education and Sports (MOES). (2014, July). *Summary of the implementation of education and sports development plan during academic year 2012-2013 and education and sports development plan for academic year 2013–2014*. MOES.

Ministry of Education and Sports (MOES). (2017). *Agreement on approval for establishment of higher education institutions*. MOES.

Ministry of Education and Sports (MOES). (2018). *ESDP 2016-2020: Mid-term review report*. MOES.

Ministry of Education and Sports (MOES). (2020a). *Agreement on the organisation and management of the Department of Higher Education* [Serial No: 5623/MOES]. MOES.

Ministry of Education and Sports (MOES). (2020b). *Agreement on national standard at bachelor degree*. MOES.

Ministry of Education and Sports. (MOES). (2020c). *Agreement on National Standard at Master Degree*. MOES.

Ministry of Education and Sports (MOES). (2020d). *Agreement on national standard at master degree*. MOES.

Ministry of Education and Sports (MOES). (2020e). *Agreement on national standard at doctoral degree*. MOES.

Ministry of Education and Sports (MOES). (2020f). *Education and sports sector development plan 2021–2025*. MOES.

Ministry of Education and Sports (MOES). (2020g). *Summary of the implementation of education and sports sector development plan for academic year 2019–2020 and the plan of education and sports sector development 2020–2021*. MOES.

Ministry of Education and Sports (MOES). (2021). *The implementation of development plan for year 2020 and focused plan for year 2021 of higher education sector*. MOES.

Ministry of Education and Sports (MOES). (2022). *Report on the implementation of 2022 higher education development plan and 2023 focused plan*. MOES.

Ministry of Planning and Investment. (2016). *Results of population and housing census 2015*. Ministry of Planning and Investment.

Ministry of Planning and Investment. (2018). *Lao population projections 2015–2045*. Ministry of Planning and Investment.

Moxom, N., & Hayden, M. (2018). The culture of institutional governance at a university in Laos: An ethnographic exploration. *Journal of International and Comparative Education*, 7(2), 35–48. https://doi.org/10.14425/jice.2018.7.1.35

Moxom, N., & Noonan, R. (2020). Post-secondary and higher education. In R. Noonan (Ed.), *Education in the Lao People's Democratic Republic: On track for the twenty-first century* (pp. 191–216). Springer Nature Singapore.

Moxom, N., & Noonan, R. (2021). Higher education in Lao PDR: Challenges and direction. *Higher Education in Southeast Asia and Beyond*, (10), 39–43.

National Assembly. (2007, July 3). *Education Law (Revised)*. No. 04/NA. National Assembly.

National University of Laos (NUOL). (2020). *Tracer study on NUOL graduates graduated between 2015 and 2019*. NUOL.

National University of Laos (NUOL). (2023). *Teaching-learning monitoring report*. NUOL.

National University of Laos (NUOL). (2024). *Summary of fees for undergraduate diploma up to doctoral degree programs*. NUOL.

Office of the President (OP). (2020). *Decree on the law on higher education*. Number 235/GOV. Government of Lao PDR.

Ogawa, K. (2009). Higher education in Lao PDR. In Y. Hirosato & Y. Kitamua (Eds.), *The political economy of educational reforms and capacity development in Southeast Asia: Cases of Cambodia, Laos and Vietnam* (pp. 283–301). Springer Netherlands.

Savannakhet University. (2020). *Report on tracer study on graduates' employability*. Savannakhet University.

UNESCO Institute of Statistics (UIS). (n.d.). *Data for sustainable development goals*. Retrieved June 18, 2024, from https://uis.unesco.org/en/home

CHAPTER 5

HIGHER EDUCATION IN MALAYSIA

Cheong Kee Cheok

Faculty of Economics and Administration, University of Malaya, Malaysia

ABSTRACT

Higher education in Malaysia only began in 1949 with the establishment of the University of Malaya in Singapore. With independence in 1957, a new campus was established in Kuala Lumpur in 1962. Since then, Malaysian higher education has undergone several major changes. The first was the focus on affirmative action while opening up to private institutions, which heralded a new phase. Malaysia's early 21st century higher education sector can be characterised as having roughly equal numbers of students enrolled in about 120 public and 500 private institutions with the gender ratio biased significantly in favour of females. Public institutions employ more qualified academic staff, but private institutions emphasise teaching over research. The sector faces major challenges, some internal to the system while others related to the rest of the economy. Internal challenges relate to the primacy of affirmative action over merit as entry qualifications for enrolment as well as the paucity of science and technology graduates. Economy-wide challenges relate to female graduates' low participation in the labour force, attrition through brain drain, and failure to achieve technological catch-up. These factors combined conspire to ensnare Malaysia in the 'middle-income trap' the escape from which requires fundamental reform.

Keywords: Middle-income trap; private higher education; quality; STEM; university autonomy; labour force participation

---

Higher Education in Southeast Asia
International Perspectives on Education and Society, Volume 49, 49–65
Copyright © 2025 by Cheong Kee Cheok
Published under exclusive licence by Emerald Publishing Limited
ISSN: 1479-3679/doi:10.1108/S1479-367920240000049005

INTRODUCTION

This chapter reviews the history, size, and structure of the higher education sector, with a comment regarding the extent to which the UN's Sustainable Development Goal (SDG) has been achieved and a focus on the issues this sector faces that need to be overcome if its objectives are to be achieved. History is important because it is the legacy the education system has inherited today. Although lauded as 'realising a more innovation-oriented and competitive higher education system' (Campbell, 2018, p. 4), recognising their consequences, intended or otherwise, is no less important. The issues dealt with here relate to the situation in the higher education sphere and to higher education's impact on the economy at large. The review begins with an account of the history of higher education in Malaysia.

HISTORY OF HIGHER EDUCATION

Before independence as the Federation of Malaya, the British colonial administration did not contemplate educating the local population above the secondary level. Those who aspired to obtain higher education in English had to journey to Singapore, Hong Kong, or the UK. In Singapore, the King Edward VII College, a medical college, was founded in 1905 and Raffles College offered courses in other disciplines, in 1928. Further education in Malay was offered by teacher training colleges – the Malacca Training College in 1901, the Matang Training College in 1913, and the Sultan Idris Teaching College in 1922 (Rozita et al., 2011, p. 1006).

Post the Japanese Occupation, the colonial administration effected a policy change that prioritised higher and vocational education and as a consequence, the University of Malaya was established in Singapore by merging King Edward VII and Raffles College in 1949. But Malaya declared independence from British rule in 1957 and with the university's rapid growth it was decided to establish an autonomous campus in Kuala Lumpur in 1962. The original campus was then renamed the University of Singapore. For seven years, this was the only university in Malaya until the University of Science was established in Penang in 1969, followed by others.

As the result of race riots that took the lives of hundreds in 1969, the proximate causes of which was the significant income/wealth between the mainly Malays and the mostly urban ethnic Chinese, an affirmative action program, dubbed the New Economic Policy (NEP), in favour of the '*Bumiputera*' community (Literally translated as 'indigenous peoples mainly Malays' was put in place. In achieving the NEP objective of 'restructuring society', higher education was to play a major role. Under this policy rigid ethnic quotas of 55% *Bumiputera* students were imposed on almost all universities, most scholarships were given to them, a matriculation program to facilitate their entry into university, and the use of Malay as the medium of instruction for higher education in 1983 was mandated, and over time, all senior management and administration positions came to be held by *Bumiputeras* (Mukherjee & Wong, 2011, p. 132). Thus, in contrast to the elitist education system which permitted only a select few to enter university, the EP facilitated the massification of education in which higher education became accessible to those, especially from the rural areas. At the same time, in place of the University of Singapore's pursuit of meritocracy, Malaysian higher education was focussed on nurturing a national identity (Cheong & Selvaratnam, 2019). The objective of regional integration reflected the relevance of non-academic factors for HE.

As student enrolment expanded, student activism emerged. Karim and Hamid (1984) dated the rise of social and political concerns in the student movement based originally in the University of Malaya to 1967, during which year students championed specific social issues. The most prominent of these was the Teluk Gong struggle, in which Hamid Tuah led a group of landless poor to clear forest land, planted crops, and built houses. The government responded by destroying the crops and demolishing the houses, outraging the students who openly supported Hamid Tuah. Student political activism continued and in 1969, students mounted a campaign to ask Prime Minister Tunku to resign. This was to be the last straw. The government passed the Universities and University Colleges Act in 1971 which barred university students and staff from participation in any form of political activity. This was a major avenue of academic expression suppressed.

With student voices silenced, the 1980s saw no student activism, but in 1987, on the heels of the economic downturn in 1985–1986, ethnic discontent surfaced in the form of demonstrations by both local Chinese and Malays. Among other education issues, one did involve the University of Malaya, and that was a protest against the use of Malay in Chinese and Tamil studies (Liu & Weiss, 2014, p. 293). The result was 'Operation Lalang' which saw the arrest of over 100 politicians, social activists, and church members.

A parallel development in the mid-1980s was the liberalisation of higher education. From independence to the 1985–1986 recession, higher education was the monopoly of the Ministry of Education, the conventional wisdom being that the highest returns accrued to primary education (World Bank, 2000) and fiscal resources prioritised this sector. Higher education was provided overseas through scholarships and private funding.

However, the high costs of overseas higher education taxed the reduced fiscal resources, especially after the 1980s recession (Sivalingam, 2007). These constraints, together with the unmet demand for higher education by the expanded output of secondary education, and Vision 2020's objective of Malaysia becoming a knowledge economy by 2020 saw a policy shift towards private higher education. Initially, private tertiary education institutions (PHEIs) were not allowed to award degrees, forcing PHEIs to form all manner of partnerships (joint degrees, twinning programs, XXX+1 or 2, etc.). As the number of international students increased, the government recognised the potential for Malaysia to be an education hub. In 1996, the Private Higher Education Institutions Act that allowed the establishment of private universities and foreign university branches, and the upgrading of university colleges to full universities was passed. The result was an explosion of private HEIs even as the number of public HEIs were increased. As will be seen below, today, the number of private HEI students enrolled has climbed to about) the same as public HEI students. Albeit more modestly, the number of public universities also increased, together with enrolment, with

Universiti Utara Malaysia (UUM) and universities in Sabah and Sarawak established (Ibrahim et al., 2011).

Since 1996, the private HEI sector has grown with increases in the numbers enrolled and in the number of institutions to the point where some degree of oversight and quality assurance was deemed by the government to be needed. In 2004, the Ministry of Higher Education was created with responsibility for higher education and detached from the Ministry of Education. In 2007, the Malaysian Qualifications Agency Act was passed which created the Malaysian Qualifications Agency tasked with ensuring implementation of the Malaysian Qualifications Framework and also undertakes quality assurance. The Malaysian Qualifications Agency Act is the successor of the 1996 *Lembaga Akreditasi Negara* (LAN). As later sections will show, the private HEI sector has grown so large that intense competition for students has whittled away profits of private HEI institutions (Hunter, 2020) to the point that that sector's growth phase has come to an end.

THE STRUCTURE OF MALAYSIAN HIGHER EDUCATION

Malaysian higher education today is divided almost equally between the public and private sectors in terms of enrolment (Table 1). Although public HEI enrolment still outpaced that of private HEIS in 2005, private HEI enrolment has caught up with public HEI enrolment, which grew more gradually as public HEIs were established. Indeed, the number enrolled in private HEIs from 2010 has exceeded that of public HEISs every year except in 2015 and 2020 when the pandemic struck (note: this chapter will deal with figures until the initial part of the pandemic [i.e. 2020] to discount for variations caused by the emergency).

Decomposition of enrolment by gender shows females consistently outnumbering males, especially among public HEIS, with their proportions falling to just 63% in the most recent years (Table 1) (Ong, 2016). Indeed Ong (2016) noted an increasing trend in gender disparity – for undergraduates, the share of females

Table 1. Enrolment Profile of Malaysian Higher Education Students.

	Total Enrolment		Gender Distribution (M/F%)		
	Public	Private	% Public	Public	Private
2020	584,576	537,434	52.1	63.4	88.9
2019	567,635	633,344	47.3	63.8	89.4
2018	552,702	576,982	48.9	61.7	84.1
2017	538,555	565,852	48.8	61.1	92.6
2016	532,049	595,347	47.1	61.1	80.9
2015	540,638	493,926	52.2	61.2	84.3
2010	462,780	541,029	46.1	66.3	86.4
2005	307,121	258,805	54.2		

Source: Ministry of Higher Education (2005–2020).

enrolled increased from 10.7% in 1959 to 62% in 2013. In private HEIs, females still outnumber males, but not by as much, their shares being just up to 20% higher.

In total, Malaysia's tertiary enrolment rates are relatively low for its income which puts it in the higher middle-income group. Although at 43% in 2019, Malaysia's rate is higher than that of Indonesia and the Philippines, both at 36.7, they are lower than those of lower-income Thailand, at 49.3 in 2016, and China, which saw spectacular growth of tertiary enrolment equalled Malaysia's in 2015 and overtook it thereafter, to reach 53.8% in 2019. High-income countries like Korea and Singapore have much higher enrolment rates. Nagaraj et al. (2014, p. 145) noted this low proportion was attributable to significant attrition each year of secondary school among male students so that the number of eligible applicants for tertiary education was reduced.

In terms of public HEIs, expansion was gradual. From the establishment of the University of Malaya in 1962, it took more than a decade for another four universities to be established. The 1980s saw only two more universities established, although the 1990s up to the beginning of the next century saw the creation through the establishment and/or upgrading of eight more universities established in response to the rising demand for university education. Finally, the first decade of the 21st century saw the creation of the final two universities. The government designated the first 5 as 'research' universities and provided them with more research funding, 4 more were broad-based universities and the remaining 11 were designated as specialised universities. In addition to these universities, the public tertiary HEIs included 30 polytechnics and 72 community colleges as of 2015.

Private sector HEIs are made up of four types of institutions. The first group is composed of 28 private universities with several faculties awarding their degrees. Also, in existence are 22 university colleges, also able to award degrees, and sometimes in partnership with foreign universities. In addition, there are about 400 private colleges that do not award their degrees but in conjunction with foreign universities, the number of which fluctuates from time to time depending on economic conditions and ability to compete. Finally, 10 foreign university branch campuses are located in Malaysia, almost all from the UK, Australia, and Ireland, with the notable exception of China's Xiamen University (Education Malaysia, 2021; Symaco & Wan, 2017).

Apart from enrolment, a comparison can also be made concerning the staff/ student ratio. Public HEIs have a lower student/staff ratio and more highly qualified academic staff, with 57% with PhDs against private HEIs' 22.6%. The majority of the latter's staff are holders of Masters degrees. Since private HEIs are mainly focused on teaching and are profit-oriented, the hiring of Master-level academic staff is more cost-effective and not difficult to understand. The slightly larger classes in private HEIs can also be thus understood.

With the history and structure described above, it is clear where Malaysia stands concerning the UN's SDG 4.3, which are that 'by 2030 ensure equal access for women and men to affordable quality technical, vocational and tertiary education, including university education' (SDSN, 2015).

From the point of view of tertiary education, Malaysia has a way to go before reaching the enrolment levels of advanced nations, the consequence of significant attrition at the secondary school level that eroded the pool of applicants to tertiary institutions. But in terms of gender parity, this has already been achieved. As will be pointed out later, some challenges remain for the quality of higher education. Although not covered in this chapter, Malaysia's TVET system, although much improved, still has room for strengthening in comparison with Singapore's (Cheong et al., 2013).

CHALLENGES FACING HIGHER EDUCATION

The sector, particularly for public HEIs faces several challenges, some of which are internal to the system and therefore policy-induced while others impact the wider economy. We take up the first group of challenges.

Quantity Versus Quality

Since its launch in 1971, the New Economic Policy has been rigorously applied to education, signalling the primacy of reducing inequalities over meritocracy. In pursuit of this approach, the NEP has to a large extent achieved the UN's SDG4 – 'ensuring inclusive and equitable quality education...'. It did this by increasing access to HE to an expanded segment of the eligible education, and by enrolling a more than proportionate share of women. But sacrificing quality for quantity has damaged the former, as shown by the most recent results of the OECD's Program for International Student Assessment (PISA). Another international test, the Trends in International Mathematics and Science Study (TIMSS), the latest being in 2018, produced similar results for Malaysian secondary school students. Malaysian students scored well below the mean score for reading, mathematics and science, compared to their East Asian counterparts, especially China and Singapore, and developed country counterparts like the US, UK, and Canada. Since part of the output of secondary education becomes eventually input of tertiary education, the compromised quality of the former has consequences for the latter.

To the overall damage inflicted by the New Economic Policy are added policies explicitly favouring *Bumiputera* students. This took the form of quotas for *Bumiputera* students, teachers, institutions, and student loans. Quotas for secondary education fed into tertiary education, the main purpose being to increase *Bumiputra* enrolment which had been historically considerably lower than that among the *non-Bumiputera* students. The NEP was successful in reversing this imbalance not only through quotas but also through tertiary institutions like the Universiti Institut Teknologi MARA reserved for *Bumiputera* students, and through skewing the enrolment quota heavily in favour of *Bumiputera* students, as with the National University of Malaysia. It is no wonder that Mukherjee et al. (2011, p. 41) reported that *Bumiputera* enrolment in public universities between 2005 and 2008 was over 80% of total enrolment and their share of scholarships to local public and foreign universities for the period 2000–2008 even higher at 87% and 73% respectively (Mukherjee et al., 2011], p. 92).

Higher Education in Malaysia

How can such large numbers of *Bumiputera* students be admitted? Tan (2012) points to the government setting up parallel tracks in the secondary school system, with one track, mainly for *Bumiputera*, virtually guaranteeing admission to universities (Cheong et al., 2011, p. 177; Loo, 2012], p. 223; Pak, 2013) while the other, for non-*Bumiputera* students, have to do well in the competitive *Sijil Tinggi Persekolahan Malaysia* (STPM) (Malaysia Higher School Certificate) examination to gain entry to public universities. Other schools/colleges set up for *Bumiputera* students, such as residential schools and MARA junior science colleges also allow their students to bypass the more rigorous STPM route to university admission. Qualitative differences between *Bumiputera* and non-*Bumiputera* students are thus built into the system of education progression at the tertiary level.

One outcome of affirmative action implemented through the NEP is that the differences in input (enrolment) will not lead to a level playing field when it comes to performance in and assessment at university. Rappa and Wee (2006) tabulated first-class honours degrees awarded to graduates in three universities for the period 1994 to 1999. Despite the *Bumiputera* students being in the majority, they accounted for fewer than a quarter of the recipients of first-class honours degrees at the University of Malaya, and almost always fewer than 10% in Universiti Teknoloji Malaysia and Universiti Utara Malaysia.

A second outcome of differential university entry requirements is differences in subjects pursued. The majority of students granted easy entry were clustered into 'soft options' in humanities and social science programs. This situation is not helped by many *Bumiputera* graduates' expectations to be absorbed into the civil service.

Table 2 shows the major study disciplines which count an overwhelming dominance of female students. They are education, the humanities, and social sciences.

Table 2. Study Subjects in which Female Students Predominate, 2010–2020.

	Education		Humanities		Social Science	
	No. of Males	% Males	No. of Males	% Males	No. of Males	% Males
Public HEIs[a]						
2020	10685	27.0	17120	35.2	57387	30.8
2019	10011	26.8	16569	34.0	55406	30.7
2015	10244	27.0	16175	34.2	50530	30.3
2012	13303[b]	27.3	16851	37.2	59930	32.5
	No IPTS		19074/49544		70935/220800	
Private HEIs						
2020	5585	13.6	23845	49.8	91701	42.6
2019	6453	14.6	29240	49.8	106138	42.4
2015	8088	22.4	18603	45.9	76490	40.2
2012	No private HEI		2223	51.9	11005	30.2

Source: Ministry of Higher Education (2012–2020).
Notes: [a]Public universities only.
[b]Figures apply to public universities only. Education was not offered by private HEIs.

Especially in education, male students in public HEIs count for only a quarter of students enrolled; for private tertiary education, for which this subject was not taught even as late as 2012, the proportion was even smaller, making education a subject primarily for females. Among public universities, the humanities and social sciences are also female-dominated, with females accounting for two-thirds of the enrolment. The imbalance is less severe in private HEIs, with no ethnic quota applied to enrolment, and humanities enrolling nearly equal proportions of either gender. For both public and private HEIs, the social sciences attract by far the largest numbers of students.

A third and negative outcome is that many non-Bumiputera students who might have been admitted to public universities on grounds of merit are now denied the opportunity. Others fortunate to be admitted may also face the prospect of not being able to study for the subject areas of their own choice. These students then provide the clientele for the growing private tertiary education sector. However, the much higher tuition fees charged by the private HEIs deprived poor non-Bumiputera households of the opportunity to access higher education. Affirmative action based purely on need might have remedied the situation. Not, however the NEP. The argument is that the need to pay attention to ensure regional balance may lead to meritocracy being made a lower priority. But again, the latter is not an inevitable outcome since meritocracy can function within a regional space.

The NEP, in segregating student intake, has brought about imbalances within the public HEIs and outside them, first by skewing the choice of subjects taken by students, and second by promoting inadvertently the growth of private HEIs. To the extent there is virtually no means for transfer between the public and private HEIs, the NEP has created silos of higher education provision in the same country.

Shortage of STEM Graduates

A corollary of the skewed preference for social science and humanities subjects is the shortage of science, technology, engineering and mathematics (STEM) graduates. This has raised concerns among commentators about the country's ability to compete internationally especially when technology in areas such as robotics, artificial intelligence (AI), and the Internet of Things (IoT) have been extensively used in industry. Taking the ratio of graduates in 'Science, Mathematics and Computing' and 'Engineering, Manufacturing and Construction' to the total number of graduates, a percentage of around 25% is arrived at, much lower than technology-enabled countries like Singapore with 34.9% and Germany's output of STEM graduates (McCarthy, 2017). Having a majority of female students would not have helped. Most of them would have taken non-STEM subjects, abetted by the easy, and for Bumiputera students, access to government loans and scholarships.

A different metric paints an even less rosy picture, however. The PISA test (OECD, 2018) shows Malaysian secondary school students performing poorly in mathematics and science. Low standards in science at secondary levels inevitably translate into compromised student quality at the tertiary level.

Ibrahim (2015) blamed 'parents not positive about the science profession, ineffective science teachers, poorly equipped laboratories, almost non-existent laboratory experiments, examination questions that require less thinking skills ...' as reasons students have no interest in STEM subjects. Than (2021, p. 16) cites several other reasons for the lack of interest. The first is the perception that STEM subjects are more difficult than other subjects. Starting salaries are also not appreciably better than other graduates. As a result, unemployment among STEM graduates is not appreciably lower than for other graduates. For instance, a recent (2020) tracer study conducted by MOHE found unemployment rates of science, mathematics and computing graduates, and engineering, manufacturing and construction graduates at 14.7% and 13.5% respectively, not appreciably lower than the overall graduate unemployment rate of 15.6%. Other reasons cited are weaknesses in the country's TVET system and the lack of university-industry linkage. She also blames the ministry's over-emphasis on publications that boost university rankings but neglect patenting efforts.

Other commentators have not been less critical. Nasa and Anwar (2016) voiced their concern that Malaysia is producing too few STEM graduates. The then Minister of the Energy, Science, Technology, Environment and Climate Change Ministry expressed concern about waning interest in STEM studies (Malay Mail, 2019).

Manaf et al. (2018, p. 26) explained this performance gap in terms of both demand and supply. On the demand side, there is a general lack of interest in STEM subjects while on the supply side, the learning material and teaching strategies leave much to be desired. Specifically, they argued that the perceptions of both parents and students that STEM subjects are harder to learn than other subjects. Furthermore, teaching had focused on content instead of on application. Thirdly, lack of interest had also been attributed to variation in the quality of teaching, whereby a teacher-centric approach discouraged student questions.

Given the shortage of STEM graduates, there should have been a scramble for them or pleas for more such graduates from tertiary institutions. Yet the industry has been relatively muted and there have been even reports of STEM graduates remaining unemployed for months (for instance Chin, 2019). What explains this situation? A likely explanation is that despite all the buzz about development, Malaysia still relies on a cheap labour low-technology production model that can make do with the existing supply of STEM graduates or fully utilises only a part of the STEM output. But that has consequences for the country's sustained growth. Those unsuccessful in obtaining employment would have moved to non-STEM jobs or leave the country in search of employment (Than, 2021, p. 162).

Lack of University Autonomy

With the NEP also came the government's growing intolerance of dissent in the form of student activism on issues of social injustice, especially in light of the race riots of 1969. The Universities and University Colleges Act of 1971 marked the end of university autonomy that was enjoyed by the University of Malaya since its establishment in 1962 and the beginning of state intervention and deepened with each amendment of the Act Concerned that student activists might, under cover of autonomy, oppose the government's policies, the 1975 Amendment saw the government take full control of the universities. The 1995 Amendment paved the way for the universities' corporatisation while conferring some autonomy, such as establishing companies, 'full corporatisation was never entirely permitted with university governance and leadership remaining heavily dependent on the Ministry of Education' (Morshidi et al., p. 93). The Private Higher Education Institutions Act 1996 empowered the setting up or upgrading of private HEIs to full universities but designated them as for-profit enterprises under the supervision of the Registrar General. Today, university autonomy remains more rhetoric than substance (Wan, 2017, p. 17).

Why the reluctance to confer autonomy? Morshidi (2010) attributes the refusal to let go to political uncertainties, but this cannot characterise the entire period since the 1970s. Ross (2019) explains the lack of education reforms in terms of 'legislative complexity and political naivety'. As an interventionist state, both politicians and bureaucrats may find it difficult to relinquish control and tolerate dissent. Whatever the motivation, this lack of autonomy stifles both academic freedom and upsets the long-established balance between them in terms of high-quality graduates, research, publications, intellectual output, and societal outreach. In making a plea for university autonomy, Wan et al. (2020, p. 99) concluded:

> [...] some (civil service) hostilities have eroded the academic values, cultures and practices, and shaped the university into a disinterested custodian of knowledge. This means ... resisting attempts to transpose the higher education landscape as merely training grounds for skilled workers, journal-paper churning factories ... with no higher purposes directly towards humanity ....

Other calls have been made for an independent, truly autonomous higher education system (Hunter, 2019). The World Bank (2013, p. 69) which concluded that Malaysia has one of the most centralised education systems in the world, showed empirically that decentralisation of decision-making improved students' outcomes. Quite apart from issues of accountability, this provided the strongest rationale for autonomy.

The above are issues related to Malaysia's system of higher education. For its part, the government has sought to address some of these issues through its Education Blueprint 2015–2025 (Ministry of Education, 2013). Its efficacy remains to be seen, with challenges not only in program design but also in implementation. But higher education also has impacts on the rest of the economy. These impacts, mostly unfavourable, we turn to next.

HIGHER EDUCATION'S IMPACT ON THE ECONOMY

The output of higher education impacts the transition to the world of work. First, the considerable drop-out from as early as secondary school that reduces enrolment in higher education results in an under-qualified workforce. In pinpointing problems with Malaysia's education, it is reported that 80% of the country's workforce is educated only up to secondary level (NEAC, 2010, p. 42).

Even this modest human capital base has further been depleted by outmigration of skilled labour, many of whom educated up to tertiary level with few returnees. The NEAC Report (2010, p. 42) continued:

> A disastrous exodus of human capital has flowed from the perception that in Malaysia's labour markets, rewards have historically not been commensurate with skills, achievements, and merit. Perhaps half a million talented Malaysians now live and work outside the country – 50% of them educated up to tertiary level, all embodying valuable skills no longer available to contribute to economic development in the country.

Among the graduate workforce in Malaysia, there are many complaints about the mismatch of skills learned by Malaysian university graduates and those demanded by industry, principally in soft skills – including confidence in job interviews, communications, and problem-solving skills (Abdul Kadir et al., 2020; Cheong et al., 2016). One survey (Cheong et al., 2016) found employers finding graduates from private HEIs performing better than graduates from public HEIs, on account of their better command of English, with both groups behind graduates from foreign university campuses. Among female graduates, the fact that they tend to congregate among lower-paying occupations represents both conscious and voluntary gender discrimination as well as underutilised human capital. But the most significant impact on human capital lies in females' low participation in the workforce, a subject to which we next turn. Needless to say, these quantitative and qualitative deficits will restrain Malaysia's long-term growth and compromise its competitiveness against rapidly improving neighbours like Indonesia and Vietnam.

Low Female Labour Force Participation

The contribution of the country's human capital to economic development depends not only on how many are educated, but the responsibility also which falls upon the education system, especially higher education, and how well they are educated. It depends also on how many of those educated find employment and the type of jobs they take up, which are the role of the labour market.

In the transition from education to work, a gender ratio favouring females has not translated into greater female participation in the workforce. A feature of Malaysia's labour force is its low female labour force participation rate (FLFPR). Despite recent gains in the FLFPR of about 8% between 2010 and 2017, Malaysia's FLFPR, at 38.6 in 2019, is lower than all its ASEAN peers, particularly its neighbours Vietnam, at 47.9, and Thailand, at 45.7, both in the same year, according to the World Bank database. This is especially the case for female graduates. The Department of Statistics (DOSM), reporting on a 2018 tracer study of tertiary education graduates, revealed that an alarming 62.8% of female graduates were outside the labour force compared with 37.2% of male graduates (DOSM, 2019). And they are unlikely to enter the labour market in a later phase of their lives. This is because the lower FLFPR is also manifested in there being a 'single peaked' phenomenon, dropping off during the prime ages of 30 to 54 while males worked throughout their prime ages 25 to 54 (KRI, 2018, p. 81). This pattern of FLFPR, which has remained unchanged up to the present, stands in sharp contrast to the situations in Korea and Japan where women re-entered the labour force after marriage and childbearing (Schmillen et al., 2019, p. 39).

This meant that despite the extension of the retirement age for adults from age 55 to 60 in 2013, fewer than 40% of women aged 55 to 59 continued to participate in the labour force. Given the greater presence of females in the country's school system and hence their higher education attainment, their non-participation in the labour force especially during the prime ages represents significant underutilisation of the human capital the government had expended considerable effort and resources to nurture.

Greater female participation in the labour force is also important given the progressive ageing of Malaysia's population. This has implications for both the labour force as well as those outside it. For the labour force, an ageing population means a gradual diminishing of the pool of workers as many, on reaching retirement age, retire or are unable to work further, increasing the dependency burden. Fewer people in the workforce have to support more dependents.

Outside the labour force, an obvious implication is the progressive increase in the old-age-dependent population that needs to be supported by a smaller proportion of the working population. The implications for female LFPR are unclear. On the one hand, as caregivers, females may have to spend more time at home caring for elderly members of their families. On the other, women may be forced to re-enter the workforce to support their families, so in the absence of social protection institutions (Chan et al., 2010), more women at work will not only increase the size of the workforce but also ensure better burden-sharing in the care of the aged and ageing. A less obvious implication is the ageing of the workforce itself. A negative consequence of this is a negative perception that may lead to discrimination against the ageing workforce (Anisah et al., 2018, Chan & Jariah, 2007).

Shift to Services

Graduate tracer studies reported that most of the new graduates found employment in the services sector. For instance, graduate statistics released by DOSM for 2019 show by far the largest number of graduates employed in the services sector (78.8%), with the manufacturing sector running a poor second (12.7%). If construction were included in services, it would have augmented that sector's share by 5.3%. The bias in favour of social science specialisations among graduates explains this phenomenon. In addition, the government's absorption of many graduates into government service, which has swelled to 1.4 million persons out of a population of about 30 million, is among the largest in the world.

The growing role of the services sector has been evident nationwide over the recent decade. In 2010, the services sector accounted for nearly 50% of Malaysia's GDP; by 2019, it had surpassed 55% while the industry shrank from 40% to 35%. The services sector has been characterised as generating the highest value-added in general and hailed by many, including those in government (e.g. Borneo Post Online, 2014). Indeed, in proclaiming that the 'services sector (is) to drive (the)

Higher Education in Malaysia

Malaysian economy', the Malaysian External Trade Development Corporation (MALTRADE) noted optimistically that 'the services sector ... remains a key driver of growth in the Malaysian economy' (MALTRADE, 2016). Whether its growth has indeed been beneficial to Malaysia depends on the manner and sources of this growth.

At the same time, emerging private sector businesses that employ new technologies such as the IoT, AI, and robotics are finding Malaysia not particularly attractive, with its continued, and with no major measures to lessen, reliance on low-skilled labour, and unable to move up the value chain. The country continues to be handicapped by a shortage of a technological workforce and STEM graduates from higher education. Furthermore, with no clear coherent policy to promote technological diffusion, foreign firms investing in Malaysia have no incentive to transfer technological expertise to local companies, which may in any case not be technologically equipped to take advantage of it.

CONCLUSION

A review of Malaysia's higher education system shows it to have achieved notable success in at least one area – to increase access to many who might have missed the opportunity. By doing so, it has increased enrolment in higher education, especially for females. However, by implementing the New Economic Policy, many non-Bumiputera students who would have qualified on merit are denied access to public universities. The unintended consequence is the rise of private-sector higher education. As for those admitted into public universities, different entry qualifications have resulted in a preference for 'soft' specialisations at the expense of STEM subjects. Two lessons can be drawn from this review. First, combining objectives – academic excellence with redistribution through affirmative action – have suboptimal outcomes, especially for academic quality. Second, control can be exercised over input or output, but not both. And manipulating input quality compromises that of output.

But higher education also has major impacts on the rest of the economy – from the school-to-work transition to industrial innovation and the pace of economic growth. In terms of the school-work transition, the larger number of females enrolled in higher education combined with their high dropout from the labour market exaggerates the underutilisation of the country's human capital. The small number of STEM graduates hampers the upgrading of industry which is also saddled with industry's and government's reliance on a low-skill, low-wage model. This has accelerated premature de-industrialisation, setting the stage for the country being ensnared in the 'middle-income trap', when a country has reached middle income, is unable to advance to developed country status because it lacks the technology to compete with countries in the higher development ladder, but is threatened competitively by countries lower down the development ladder which are endowed with lower-cost. The lesson here is that focusing exclusively on numbers without regard for the quality of human capital runs the risk of driving the country 'down the low industrialisation road' (Rasiah et al., 2015, p. 77).

Finally, it bears remembering that Malaysia is among the most lavish spenders on education; government expenditure on education as a share of GDP peaked at 7.5% and above between 2001 and 2003, the highest in Asia before dipping in 2006, then peaking again in 2009 and staying high and staying above 5% until 2014, moderating to just over 4% thereafter (World Bank databank). Spending on tertiary education as a proportion of total expenditure on education, at 21.3% in 2018 was higher than its regional peers except Singapore. This spending has dramatically improved access but at a qualitative cost, both within and outside the higher education system. The question to ponder is: Have the resources been cost-effectively expensed? The World Bank (2013, p. 64) believes that they are 'inefficiently allocated' based on two metrics – education expenditures are above average for countries participating in PISA while performance was well below average, and learning outcomes, as measured by PISA and TIMSS also declined while expenditures increased between 2003 and 2013.

Finally, the story of Malaysian higher education would not be complete without documenting the coronavirus that swept over all countries in 2020. This pandemic has resulted in Malaysia as well as other countries imposing lockdowns that not only brought academic life to a near standstill but also severely impacted economic activities. In academic life, Sia and Adamu (2021) noted that the immediate impact of the pandemic was first to end all face-to-face interaction in the HEIs, and second to migrate all instruction online. But given the rapid spread of the virus, all HEIs were caught in varying degrees of unpreparedness. A third impact is the revenue lost because, with fights disrupted, international students are unable to attend HEIs, especially private (Choong, 2020). HEIs have responded by shifting courses and meetings online using a variety of platforms. This has posed challenges both to students and staff in that they are not familiar with this mode of interaction and have to use these platforms with almost no lead time or training. Another challenge is the digital divide between relatively well-connected West Malaysia and underdeveloped East Malaysia. COVID-19 offers HEIs new ways of teaching and learning that were not available to them before. These are likely to impact more private HEIs. For public HEIs which are tightly controlled by the ministry, how much they change will depend on the ministry's buy-in of these innovations.

REFERENCES

Abdul Kadir, J. M., Naghavi, N., Subramanian, G., & Abdul Hamid, N. A. (2020). Unemployment among graduates: Is there a mismatch? *International Journal of Asian Social Science, 10*(10), 583–592.

Academy of Sciences Malaysia. (2021). *Science outlook 2020: Unlocking the future.*

Anisah, A. H., Aliza, A. H., & Fadilah, P. (2018). Ageing workforce – A challenge for Malaysia. *Journal of Administrative Science, 15*(3), 1–13.

Borneo Post Online. (2014, August 18). *Service-s sector may contribute more to Malaysia's GDP growth.* https://www.theborneopost.com/2014/08/18/services-sector-may-contribute-more-to-malaysias-gdp-growth/

Buchholz, K. (2020, September 16). Where most students choose STEM degrees. *Statista.com*. https://www.statista.com/chart/22927/share-and-total-number-of-stem-graduates-bt-country/

Campbell, J. K. (2018). The trimella of Malaysia's higher education. *International Journal of Technology Management and Sustainable Development, 27*(1), 3–24.

Chan, Y. F., Laily, P., Jariah, M., & Hamid, T. A. (2010). The future of the Malaysian older employees: An exploratory study. *International Journal of Business and Management, 5*(4), 125–132.

Cheong, K. C., Hill, C., Fernandez-Chung, R., & Leong, Y. C. (2016). Employing the 'unemployable': Employers' perceptions of Malaysian graduates. *Studies in Higher Education, 41*(12), 2253–2270.

Cheong, K. C., Kuppusamy, S., Lee, H. A., & Abdilah, N. (2013). *Malaysia workforce development: SABER country report*. World Bank.

Cheong, K. C., & Selvaratnam, V. (2019). Legacy in education. In R. Rasiah & K. Salih (Eds.), *Driving development: Revisiting Razak's role in Malaysia's economic progress* (pp. 157–190). University of Malaya Press.

Cheong, K. C., Selvaratnam, V., & Goh, K. L. (2011). Education and human capital formation. In R. Rasiah (Ed.), *Malaysian economy: Unfolding growth and social change*. Oxford University Press.

Chin, C. (2019). Disheartened engineers leaving the field. *The Star*, February 17. https://www.thstar,com.my/news/nation/2019/02/17/disheartened-engineers-leaving-the-field-grads-hampered-by-lack-of-technical-knowhow-and-communication/

Choong, J. (2020). Study shows Covid-19 could devastate private universities as students delay studies to brace for looming recession. *Malay Mail*, May 9. https://www.malaymail.com/news/malaysia/2020/05/09/study-shows-covid-19-could-devastate-private-universities-as-students-delay/1864519

Department of Statistics, Malaysia (DOSM). (2019, December 12). *Graduate statistics 2018*. https://www.dosm.gov.my/

Education Malaysia. (2021). *Malaysia higher education in brief*. Education Malaysia Global Services. https://educationmalaysia.gov.my/malaysia-higher-education-in-brief/

Gill, I. S., & Kharas, H. (2007). *An East Asian Renaissance: Ideas for economic growth*. World Bank.

Hunter, M. (2019). Malaysia's public universities falling behind. *Asia Sentinel*, September 9. https://murrayhunter-substack,com/p/malaysian-public-universities-falling

Hunter, M. (2020). The collapse of Malaysian private universities (updated). *Asia Sentinel*, April 2. htpps://murrayhunter-substack.com/p/the-collapse-of-malaysian-private

Ibrahim, A. (2015). Science education in Malaysia needs urgent overhaul. *New Straits Times*, July 27. https://www.nst.con.my/news/2015/09/science-education-malaysia-needs-urgent-overhaul.

Ibrahim, R., Muslim, N., & Buang, A. H. (2011). Multiculturalism and higher education in Malaysia. *Procedia Social and Behavioral Sciences, 2011*, 1003–1009.

Karim, H., & Hamid, S. N. (Eds.). (1984). *With the people: The Malaysian Movement 1967–1974*. Institiut Analisa Sosial.

Khazanah Research Institute (KRI). (2018). *Part 2: The Malaysian Workforce – A changing landscape*. KRI.

Liu, J., & Weiss, M. L. (Eds.) (2014). *Routledge handbook of contemporary Malaysia*. Routledge.

Loo, S. P. (2007). Schooling in Malaysia. In E. A. Postiglione & J. Tan (Eds.), *Going to school in East Asia* (pp. 207–227). Greenwood Press.

Malay Mail. (2019). Ministry: Waning STEM student numbers concerning. *Malay Mail*, September 27. htpps://www.malaymail/news/Malaysia/2019/09/27/decline-in-students-opting-for-stem-subjects-concerning/1794928

Malaysian External Trade Development Corporation (MALTRADE). (2016, December 9). *Services sector to drive Malaysian economy*. https://www.maltrade.gov.my/en/146-press-releases/press-releases-2016/3720-services-sector-to-drive-malaysian-economy.

McCarthy, N. (2017). The countries with the most STEM graduates. *Forbes*, February 2. htpps://www.forbes.com/sites/niallmccarthy/2017/02/02/the-countries-with-the-most-stem-graduates-inforaphic?sh=37986995

Ministry of Education, Malaysia. (2013). *Malaysia education blueprint 2015–2025 (Higher Education)*. Ministry of Education.

Ministry of Higher Education, Malaysia. (2005–2020). *Statistics of higher education*. Ministry of Higher Education.

Morshidi, S. (2010). Strategic planning directions of Malaysia's higher education: University in the midst of political uncertainties. *Higher Education, 59*, 461–473.

Mukherji, H., & Wong, P. K. (2011). The National University of Singapore and the University of Malaya: Common roots and different paths. In P. G. Albach & J. Salmi (Eds.), *The road to academic excellence*. World Bank, Washington DC.

Nagaraj, S., Goh, K. L., Cheong, K. C., Tey, N. P., & Jani, R. (2014). Gender imbalance in educational attainment and labour dynamics: Evidence from Malaysia. *Malaysian Journal of Economics (Special Issue), 51*, 127–145.

Nasa, A., & Anwar, Z. (2016). Too few STEM students. *New Straits Times*, May 23. https://www.nst.com.my/news/2016/05/14/147260/too-few-stem-students

Norzaini, A., & Doria, A. (2021). A critical analysis of Malaysian higher educations' response towards Covid-19: Sustaining academic program delivery. *Journal of Sustainability Science and Management, 16*(1), 70–96.

OECD. (2018). *PISA 2018 Results*. OECD.

Ohno, K. (2013). *Learning to industrialize: From given growth to policy-aided value creation*. Routledge.

Ong, K. M. (2016). Why the lower intake of males in public universities. *Malaysiakini*, May 30. https://www.malaysiakini.com/news/343444

Pak, J. (2013). Is Malaysia university entry a level playing field? *BBC News*, September 2. Retrieved May 1, 2017, from https://www.bbc.com/news/world-asia-23841888

Rappa, A. L., & Wee, L. H. A. (2006). *Language policy and modernity in Southeast Asia: Malaysia, the Philippines, Singapore, and Thailand*. Springer.

Rasiah, R. (2015). Is Malaysia facing negative deindustrialization? *Pacific Affairs, 84*(4), 714–735.

Rasiah, R., Crinis, V., & Lee, H. A. (2015). Industrialisation and labour in Malaysia. *Journal of Asia Pacific Economy, 20*(1), 77–99.

Ross, J. (2019). Dreams of Malaysia higher education reforms falter. *World University Rankings*, December 18. https://www.timeshighereducation.com/news/dreams-malaysian-higher-education-reform-falter

Schmillen, A. D., Tan, M. L., Abdur Rahman, A., Shahrul Natasha, H., & Sandig, W. N. (2019). *Breaking barriers: Toward better economic opportunities for women in Malaysia*. World Bank Group.

Sia, K. M., & Adamu, A. A. (2021). Facing the unknown: Pandemic and higher education in Malaysia. *Asian Education and Development Studies, 10*(2), 262–275.

Sivalingam, G. (2007). *The privatization of higher education in Malaysia*. Forum on Public Policy Online, Oxford Roundtable, Kuala Lumpur.

Sustainable Development Solutions Network (SDSN). (2015). *Indicators and a monitoring framework for sustainable development goals: Launching a data revolution for the SDGs*. United Nations.

Symaco, L. P., & Wan, C. D. (2017). Development of higher education in Malaysia: Issues and challenges. In M. Samuel, M. Y. Tee, & L. P. Symaco (Eds.), *Education in Malaysia: Development and challenges*. Springer.

Talib, Z. A., Baqiah, H., & Tayeb, Y. A. (2018). Current status and trends of Science, Technology, Engineering and mathematics (STEM). In Z. A. Manaf & Z. A. Talib (Eds.), *STEM Education in Malaysia*. Ministry of Higher Education.

Tan, Y. S. (2012). Democratization of secondary education in Malaysia: Emerging problems and challenges of educational reform. *International Journal of Educational Development, 32*, 53–64.

Tham, S. Y., & Kam, A. J. Y. (2019). Exploring the trade potential of the DFTZ for Malaysian SMEs. *Trends in Southeast Asia No. 3*. ISEAS.

Than, L. L. (2021). *The role of R&D and research universities in patenting and scientific publications: A study of Malaysia*. [PhD Thesis, University of Malaya].

Wan, C. D. (2017). *The history of university autonomy in Malaysia*. IDEAS Policy Paper 40, May.

Wan, C. D., Morshidi, M., & Razak, D. A. (2020). Academic governance and leadership in Malaysia: Examining the national higher education strategic initiatives. *Journal of International and Comparative Education, 9*(2), 91–102.

Wong, C.-Y., & Fung, H.-N. (2019). Caught-in or breaking-free from the middle-income trap: The case of Malaysia. *Seoul Journal of Economics*, *31*(1), 1–22.

World Bank. (2000). *Public expenditure: Managing the crisis: challenging the future*. Report number 20371-MA, World Bank.

World Bank. (2013, December). *Malaysian economic monitor: High performing education*. World Bank.

World Bank. (2021, June). *"Weathering the surge", Malaysian economic monitor*. World Bank.

CHAPTER 6

HIGHER EDUCATION IN MYANMAR: COUP, CONFLICT, AND EDUCATIONAL CRISIS

Mark Brown

Independent Analyst, UK & Myanmar

ABSTRACT

The higher education (HE) sector in Myanmar is currently in a fragile, backward-looking state. Its fragility is due to the 2021 coup with its consequent civil disobedience movement, continued conflict between the military and people's defence force, the junta's spurious delivery of a post-Covid and post-coup education system, and the junta's apparent abandoning of the previous civilian government's progress with the National Education Strategic Plan. It is backward-looking because the current junta, like previous juntas in Myanmar, use education as a tool for military propaganda and to populate the education system with civil servants that are loyal, or at least supine, to the military. The task of this chapter is to provide an overview of HE in Myanmar and how its current condition aligns with Sustainable Development Goal 4.3. This task is contextualised by considering the role of universities in the history of sociopolitical uprisings in Myanmar. Universities as theatres of communicative action have been and continue to be spaces of public resistance. This resistance and its accompanying vertical tension continue to shape the physical constitution of universities and the delivery of HE in Myanmar.

Keywords: Myanmar/Burma; higher education; students; resistance; precarity

---

Higher Education in Southeast Asia
International Perspectives on Education and Society, Volume 49, 67–89
Copyright © 2025 by Mark Brown
Published under exclusive licence by Emerald Publishing Limited
ISSN: 1479-3679/doi:10.1108/S1479-367920240000049006

INTRODUCTION

This chapter considers the higher education (HE) sector in Myanmar at a critical juncture. The military coup in February 2021 resoundingly changed the education landscape in Myanmar. The administration of public services has, for a number of reasons and including education, been severely impacted by the junta. The hard-won gains in HE over the previous 10 years (2011–2021), spurred by the Comprehensive Education Sector Review (CESR) and achieved through the problematic yet visionary National Education Strategic Plan (NESP), risk being irrevocably undone. The result is that the HE sector risks backsliding into pre-transition disrepute.

To come to terms with this situation, the next (second) section outlines the important role that universities have played over the past century as spaces of student resistance and communicative action. HE has always been a milieu of revolution in Myanmar, so it is not insignificant that consecutive military juntas have sought to suppress dissent through structural and physical violence. The third section then illustrates the size of the HE sector. This is important to appreciate the bureaucratic system, outlined in Section four, which illustrates the structure and lines of accountability in HE in Myanmar. The nature of this centralised system and its hierarchical structures defines the successes achieved in the 2011–2021 years of quasi-civilian governance, since those successes are precisely departures from the previous junta's system. Those successes are pointed to in Section five and are the basis for the claims in Section six regarding the direct impact of the current conflict on the HE sector both domestically and regionally in the context of ASEAN. This conflict context informs Section seven's focus on Sustainable Development Goal 4.3, paying particular attention to matters of access, equity, and quality from policy to classroom. Myanmar's HE sector has great potential, as do the youth of Myanmar. The long shadow cast by the military coup stunted that potential. It remains unclear when conditions will change to enable that potential to begin to flourish once more.

HISTORY OF HE IN BURMA/MYANMAR

The history of education in Myanmar can be categorised into a number of periods: dynastic (pre-1885), colonial (1885–1948), independent parliamentary (1948–1962), socialist-military (1962–1988), nominally market-based military (1988–2011), 'disciplined' democratic (2011–2021), and the current military junta period (2021–current). In pre-colonial Myanmar (proximately, the Konbaung dynasty), education was widespread, generated a high rate of literacy, and was facilitated primarily by the Sangha (community of Buddhist monks). This excluded women on religious grounds, though a comparatively small amount of lay schools that catered for women did operate (Ikeya, 2011, p. 30; Kaung, 1963, pp. 32–33; Schober, 2011, p. 49). While monastic teaching involved elementary, intermediate, and advanced levels (Ikeya, 2011, p. 166; Khammai Dhammasami, 2018), it did not include HE as conceived today. The beginnings of contemporary HE in Burma began during the British colonial period with the founding of Rangoon College in 1878, later constituted as Rangoon University in 1920 (Kaung, 1963, p. 109). Precipitated by colonial imposition, the university act that established Rangoon University was immediately the source of nationalist contention, prompting a student strike four days after the passing of the act, thus establishing university students as a "potent force in national politics" (Smith, 1999, p. 49).

This point is worth noting with some detail. Since the 1920s, a tradition of student activism has been at the forefront of political protest in Burma (Myanmar) (Boshier, 2018, p. 233; Smith, 1999, p. 202). Over the past century of turbulent socio-political and economic events, university student activism in Burma (Myanmar) has occurred in waves, starting in 1920 with the reaction to the university act. Significant demonstrations can also be noted in 1936, due to the expulsion of Aung San and U Nu from Rangoon University; in 1962, due to post-coup hostel restrictions, resulting in the military bombing of the student union building; in 1974–1976, prompted by the military's mishandling of U Thant's funeral; in 1988, in response to the economic crises of the 1980s and Ne Win's remarks on the prospect of a multi-party government subsequent to his resignation; in 1996, in response to police violence; in 2007, owing to the military's economic mismanagement, resulting in demonstrations that included the Sangha and being labelled a 'saffron revolution'; in 2014, in response to discontent with the 2014 National Education Law; and in 2021, in response to the military's undertaking a coup of a democratically elected civilian government (Hong & Kim 2019; Steinberg, 1981; Smith, 1999). The role of universities in Myanmar's public sphere is therefore prominent, as is the continuing reemergence of student activism and the communicative action that it exemplifies. These are recurring themes throughout this chapter.

Returning to the timeline of HE in Myanmar, subsequent to independence from the British administration, yet somewhat continuous with it, the independent parliamentary period implemented policies that ensured education remained within the purview of the governing administration rather than the Sangha as it had traditionally been (Cheesman, 2003). The prior colonial administration had instituted a tiered system of education involving local vernacular and Anglo-vernacular schools – a system that created social cleavages due to the limited accessibility and affordability of English-speaking schools that served as channels for administrative careers in the colonial system. Subsequently, the newly formed parliamentary government implemented the 1951 Private Schools Registration Act, which continued social divisions by providing options for schooling in English, religious education, and academic education, thereby entrenching access issues in terms of private and public schooling, language of instruction, urban–rural access, and gender (Shah & Lopes Cardozo, 2019, pp. 68–69).

The 1962 military coup brought about the socialist-military era of Ne Win's Revolutionary Council and the BSPP (Burma Socialist Programme Party). The Union of Burma University Education Law was implemented in 1964, subsequently nationalising the education sector in 1965, replacing English with Burmese as the language of instruction, and emphasising science and vocational education with a view to modernisation (Shah & Lopes Cardozo, 2019; Steinberg, 1981).

During this period, education planning was ill-conceived, to say the least. Yangon and Mandalay Universities had their technical faculties (e.g. medicine, engineering, economics, education, agriculture) excised and relocated as institutes, with these two domestically prestigious universities renamed as arts and science universities teaching arts, science, and law (Allot, 1985, p. 142; James, 2005, p. 100; Welch & Hayden, 2013, p. 4). When the 1973 University Education Law came into effect, HE became increasingly fragmented, and this structure remains in place today (Kyaw Yin Hlaing, 2007, p. 166; Win Min, 2012, p. 201). Additionally, during the socialist-military era, schools were built in urban and rural areas, but teachers received poor training and remuneration; a lack of international collaboration meant that advances in international learning were not represented in Burmese textbooks, thereby hindering intellectual growth in HE (Aung Kin, 1983, p. 92; Lall, 2016, p. 160); the infamous rotation system was implemented to ensure that ethnic teachers were not posted in their mother-tongue communities, instead posting Bamar Burmese-speaking teachers in rural areas with a view to Burmanising ethnic populations (Cho & Gilbert, 2021, p. 222); and all this is not to mention economic ineptitude in the form of three demonetisations (Turnell, 2009).

HE in Myanmar then entered a notoriously problematic period with the 1988 transition from Ne Win's BSPP era to the military era of the SLORC (State Law and Order Restoration Council), later rebranded in 1998 as the SPDC (State Peace and Development Council). Universities during this period experienced prolonged closures. In response to the 1988 uprising, the military junta (SLORC, later SPDC) periodically closed all universities for between five and seven years in the 1990s, with Myanmar's flagship University of Yangon closed for 10 out of 12 years during this period (Lall, 2016, p. 164; Myat Mon, 2000, p. 49). The spatial dimension of HE delivery becomes important at this point. The prolonged and intermittent university closures during the 1990s and early 2000, together with the junta's semiurban and rural proliferation of technical institutes at the expense of comprehensive universities (Win Min, 2012, p. 201), and the implementation of its infamous 'distance education' (DE) model of university studies in 1992 (Yangon University of Distance Education for lower Myanmar) and 1998 (Mandalay University of Distance Education [MUDE] for upper Myanmar), resulted in a widely dispersed student body. This institutional arrangement demonstrates the military's distrust of the student body due to the tendency of student organisations to generate civic challenges to the conservative military establishment. These dispersed institutional arrangements (university closures, proliferation of technical institutes, and DE) when combined with chronic underfunding resulted in HE in Myanmar languishing. In this context, curricula and syllabi remained outdated due to international isolation and a disconnect between teaching and research (Lall, 2020, pp. 134–136). A hierarchical, militaristic 'command and control' ethos dominated, and continues to dominate, the HE sector (Welch & Hayden, 2013, pp. 5, 19).

After years of closure, the University of Yangon reopened its doors to a limited number of daytime undergraduate students in 2013 (Wa Lone & Sandar Lwin, 2014). At this point, a transition was underway from direct to indirect military governance via the election of a nominally civilian government (comprised largely of retired military personnel, headed by former general and then civilian president Thein Sein). HE in this disciplined-democratic period (2011–2021) benefited from a multilateral Comprehensive Education Sector Review (CESR) in 2013, followed by the drafting of a National Education Bill in 2014, which prompted significant student demonstrations and was amended and passed into law in 2015, and from which the National Education Strategic Plan (NESP) was ultimately devised (Brown & Hung, 2022; Lall, 2016, pp. 168–175; Metro, 2017). It is in this political space that the National League for Democracy (NLD) was elected in 2015 and assumed office in 2016. During this period, in which a genuinely civilian political party occupied the executive branch for the first time since the post-war period (though still under the tutelage of the military per its 2008 constitutional mandate), the HE sector began to experience significant changes owing to the NESP's five-year roll-out (2016–2021). The Ministry of Education's (MOE's) new policy body – the National Education Policy Commission (NEPC) – started to establish its committees (on which see below) and implement institutional autonomy for selected universities in Yangon and Mandalay Regions. Although a politically fraught period for the NLD and Aung San Suu Kyi as State Counsellor, the HE sector was nevertheless increasingly open to international collaboration and development of HE pedagogy, research, and digital infrastructure. The HE sector also experienced a decentralising shift in policy development away from the MOE and towards the NEPC as accountable to parliament, enabling 16 universities to be granted institutional autonomy in September 2020, months before the 2021 coup.

The current post-2021 military junta period was initially impacted by the Covid-19 pandemic, starting in early 2020 and continuing through 2022. In this respect, the previous civilian government had a response and recovery framework that served to address and ameliorate the impact of Covid-19 on HE (Brown, 2022). However, since February 2021 by far the biggest shadow cast over HE, and indeed the entire education system in Myanmar, is the current coup. Schools throughout the country barely operated in the months subsequent to February 2021. Schools were briefly open at the beginning of the new academic year in June 2021, but this opening was swiftly aborted ostensibly due to Covid-19 concerns but in reality due to low student and teacher turnouts because parents worried for their children's safety (threats from military-aligned personnel towards parents were widely reported) and a large proportion of teachers as public servants aligned with the civil disobedience movement (CDM) (Frontier, 2021b, 2021d). University students played a prominent role in the mass public protests that responded to Min Aung Hlaing's coup. In the period immediately following the coup, protests were large, vocal, and populated by all demographics. As protests swelled, the military began to crackdown with arbitrary shootings, arrests, torture, scorched earth tactics, extortion of civilians, disappearances, people smuggling, and martial law with its multiple dimensions of fear-inducing stratagems (Frontier, 2021a, 2021c, 2021e; Irrawaddy, 2022; Ye Myo Hein 2022). Myanmar's youth and university students figured prominently in resistance to the coup, for it was their futures at stake.

From 1920 through to 2021, universities in Myanmar have served as forums for public discussion and theatres of communicative action. Universities in

Myanmar have a long history of providing a space for higher learning that also risks destabilising established social-military powers. Currently, history appears to be reverberating through time. The 1988 generation of student activists defied the military by protesting against military economic incompetence and for democratic change. The current generation of students once again defy the military, this time by protesting for democratic continuity and against the military's quashing of civilian democratic governance, which is a structure of governance the military itself designed by constitutional fiat. Based on the 2008 constitution that it unceremoniously smuggled into effect, the SPDC subsequently undertook a political transition in 2011–2012 that first ushered in the military's proxy civilian government (the USDP – Union Solidarity Development Party) and then watched as a genuinely elected civilian government (the NLD) formed in 2015–2016. This transition – sometimes referred to as a process of democratisation, but in reality being a process of military tutelage, or praetorian guardianship (Egreteau, 2016) – created a short-lived civic space for today's students to experience far greater access to international education than had previously occurred. This military tutelage, or 'disciplined democracy', provided a public space that fostered student antipathy towards unsanctioned autocratic command and, conversely, a sensibility for the civic, participatory values associated with universal suffrage. The 2021 coup was not well received, and conflicts continue throughout the country.

HE in Myanmar, already impacted by Covid-19, has been operating as a shadow of its former self since the 2021 coup. Universities began reopening in January 2022, though the response by teachers and students was predictably underwhelming. Up to 70% of HE students, numbering in the hundreds of thousands, are reported to have abandoned their studies (Frontier, 2023; Padone, 2023; RFA, 2024a). As a result of this, many pre-2021 students have not yet and perhaps will not ever graduate, lending to a double-edged precarity. On one hand, the economic prospects for non-graduates can be expected to be less optimal than that of graduates. On the other hand, these former students are likely to fit the criteria for the junta's newly introduced compulsory military conscription (Frontier, 2024; Irrawaddy, 2024b). For students who remain, attending school in a context of civil war brings different challenges, such as attempting to learn as military personnel occupy campus grounds and being caught in the crossfire between the junta and the People's Defence Force (PDF; the military arm of the exiled National Unity Government [NUG], formed by the Committee Representing the Pyidaungsu Hluttaw, comprised of members who were democratically elected to parliament in the 2020 election), as happened at the University of Kalay (Padone, 2024; RFA, 2024b).

SIZE OF HE IN MYANMAR

Drawing from pre-2021 figures, HE institutes in Myanmar are administered by the MOE and seven other institutionally relevant ministries. The MOE oversees 134 HEIs, with the remaining 40 overseen by other ministries, resulting in a fragmented total of 174 HEIs (CHINLONE, 2018). The immediate administrative body for HEIs is the Department of Higher Education. Although accurate student enrolments are difficult to obtain, the Ministry of Planning and Finance (MPF) provides an indication. In the 2017–2018 academic year, 131,074 students were reported as enrolled in on-campus 'professional' universities (technical or vocational institutes such as medicine, pharmacy, economics, etc.), while 800,106 students were enrolled in 'non-professional' universities (i.e. arts and sciences universities, including but not exclusive to the domestically prestigious Universities of Yangon and Mandalay) (MPF, 2018, pp. 159–181). The DE system, which increases the fragmentary nature of Myanmar's HE, accounts for 64% (i.e. 515,002) of arts and sciences university enrolments (MPF, 2018, p. 179). This remote learning system is not online-based learning, but rather, learning in absentia where science students attend campus on weekends for five months out of the year, while arts students attend for a frenetic 10 days of cramming before exams at the end of the academic year (Win Min, 2012, p. 200). The DE system is facilitated by the Universities of Yangon and Mandalay, which are accordingly named Yangon University Distance Education (YUDE) and MUDE. With nearly two-thirds of student enrolments in arts and sciences universities, and over half of student enrolments (55%) in the HE system as a whole in the 2017–2018 period, the DE system figures prominently in terms of numbers, notoriously in terms of education delivery, and conspicuously in terms of its geographically dispersed mode of delivery that inhibits collective student action.

To see these numbers in context, it is worth briefly noting attrition and retention rates from primary school through to middle school on to high school. Success progressing through this basic education system is the only pathway to access HE in Myanmar. The basic education system has been transitioning from a 5-4-2 structure of primary, middle, and high school (where the first year was designated as kindergarten, grade one effectively being the second year in the 5-4-2 system, amounting to a 10-year grade system), to a 5-4-3 structure (where kindergarten is not included, thus amounting to a 12-year grade system) under the NESP. It is therefore difficult to accurately calculate attrition and retention rates. However, by averaging enrolment rates between the five-year 2013–2014 and 2017–2018 academic years, we can approximate attrition and retention rates in Myanmar's basic education system in order to note how these numbers might influence HE enrolments. For example, in that five-year period 53.8% of students on average progressed from primary to middle school, and of that percentage, 31.3% on average progressed from middle to high school, which results in 16.8% of students successfully progressing from primary to high school. Since the average matriculation pass-rate for that period was 33.19%, this means approximately 5.6% of the age-relevant student population were eligible for university (see Table A1, MPF, 2018, pp. 159–181).

Based on the MPF's figures averaged over the above five-year period, the 16.8% retention rate from beginning to end of the basic education system is disconcerting. This is compounded by the reported numbers indicating that the vast majority of university-age youth do not have access to HE. This issue may appear to be addressed when noting that in the same five-year period student enrolments in university grew by 62.9% from 571,607 to 931,180 (see Table A2, MPF,

2018, pp. 159–181). However, the number of teaching and research staff during this period did not experience the same increase (see Table A3, MPF, 2018, pp. 159–181). Owing largely to a 27.1% increase in teaching and research staff in the 2014–2015 academic year, subsequent years contracted in almost equal measure, resulting in a more modest 38.6% increase in teaching and research staff over that five-year period. The result of this rapid growth in student numbers and stalled growth in teaching and research staff (that idled through the three academic years subsequent to 2014–2015), is that the teacher–student ratio worsened from 32.2 to 37.8 students per teacher/researcher from 2013–2014 to 2017–2018 (see Table A4, MPF, 2018, pp. 159–181). This stagnating teacher recruitment coupled with rapid inflation of student enrolments created a situation in which Myanmar's HE experienced 'stagflation' (to borrow a term from economics), the result of which can only be a diminished quality of educational outputs.

This stagflation in Myanmar's HE delivery is, in part, a result of education being allocated 1.92% of GDP in 2018 and 1.93% of GDP in 2019 (UNESCO, 2020). This is the lowest percentage of GDP allocated to education in the Southeast Asia region, with Cambodia allocating 2.2%, Viet Nam 4.2%, and Malaysia 4.5% (Brown & Hung, 2022; UNESCO, 2020). In the 2017–2018 financial year, the education sector received 7.75% of the national budget, from which 77% was dedicated to the Department for Basic Education and 17% to the Department of Higher Education, which equates to approximately 1.42% of GDP invested in basic education and 0.32% of GDP being invested in HE (Brown & Hung, 2022; UNICEF, 2018, p. 7). From this, it is reasonable to suggest that a greater investment in recruiting, training, and growing the volume of teachers and researchers will begin to address stagflating teacher–student ratios and slowly improve the educational outcomes of HE in Myanmar. However, the current political instability caused by the military coup, which resulted in widespread civil disobedience (notably from students and teachers) and civil war, ensures that 'education as normal' is not a current reality.

BUREAUCRATIC STRUCTURE OF HE IN MYANMAR

Before the 2021 coup brought socio-political and economic turmoil to the country, largely halting the delivery of public HE, the HE sector was both growing in terms of student enrolments and undergoing significant restructuring in terms of bureaucratic administration. It is currently unclear to what extent these relatively new bureaucratic structures remain. Prior to the National Education Law (2014, amended in 2015), the HE sector was determined by the 1973 University Education Law and accordingly administered by the Universities Central Council (UCC) for policy and administration, and the Council of University Academic Boards (CUAB) for academic affairs (Hayden & Martin, 2013; Welch & Hayden, 2013). Highly centralised in name and function, these councils were also chaired by the Minister for Education. In 1991, the Myanmar Education Committee was established to oversee the councils and coordinate the national education system.

This committee was later rebranded as the National Education Committee (NEC) in 2011 and was also chaired by the Minister for Education (Welch & Hayden, 2013). In 2014, the National Education Law (2014) prompted critical unrest from students and teachers' unions, who took to the streets to voice their concerns about the lack of institutional autonomy and the remaining centralised, top-down nature of education administration (Lall, 2020; Metro, 2017). This resulted in minor amendments to the 2014 iteration, and the implementation of the 2015 National Education Law (Joliffe & Speers Mears, 2016). From this new legal instrument came the National Education Policy Committee (NEPC), which was effectively an amalgam of the dissolved NEC, UCC, and CUAB, though the NEPC may be different insofar as it collaborated with the MOE yet reported to parliament, thus potentially achieving some semblance of independence (Myo Kywe, 2020).

From the NEPC stem the Rectors' Committee (RC), the National Accreditation and Quality Assurance Committee (NAQAC), and the National Curriculum Committee (NCC). Collectively, these committees functioned to develop HE policies and coordinate HE activities among Myanmar's 174 HEIs (Myo Kywe, 2020). These committees had an active role in Myanmar's HE reforms, including moves towards selective institutional autonomy, which was officially implemented for sixteen HEIs in Yangon and Mandalay Regions in September 2020 (Thet Zin Soe, 2020). However, as a result of the military coup in February 2021, the NEPC was reported to have been suspended (possibly dissolved) in May 2021, which presumably includes the suspension of the RC, NAQAC, and NCC. By 2024, the operational status of these relatively new committees remains unclear, and it appears that all educational matters have regressed and recentralised back to the MOE per the appointment of the military-aligned Nyunt Pe as education minister of the military's State Administrative Council (Irrawaddy, 2021). The remaining bureaucratic organisation of HE in Myanmar therefore begins with the MOE and relevant institutional ministries, flowing down to the Department of Higher Education, with the (suspended, possibly dissolved) NEPC and its committees (RC, NAQAC, NCC) as coordinating policy adjuncts, down to the individual HEIs and their administration.

2011–2021 ADVANCES IN MYANMAR'S HE SECTOR

Though troubled through much of its history, HE in Myanmar nevertheless experienced a great deal of international exposure and investment in the 2011–2021 period. Somewhat ironically, this dramatic opening of the educational space was due to the previous junta's transition to a tutelary quasi-democratic structure of governance that courted multilateral education projects that expressly embedded international education practices designed to improve Myanmar's education sector (e.g. multilateral projects like the CESR, NESP, Strengthening Pre-Service Teacher Education in Myanmar, and JICA's Curriculum Reform for Basic Education project). Advances made during this period include, for example, the production and implementation of the NESP, some semblance of decentralisation, a preliminary move towards selective institutional autonomy, and growth in education colleges in terms of both enrolments and the professional degrees and training offered.

As the culmination of the multilateral 2013 CESR (Welch & Hayden, 2013) and the tumultuous National Education Law 2014/2015, the NESP is replete with lofty goals and ambitious targets for its modest five-year timeline. For HE, the goal was to elevate the HE sector in terms of: (1) governance and management, (2) quality and relevance, and (3) access and equity (MOE, 2016, pp. 188–202). Governance and management upgrades focused on engaging with international best practices, establishing an institute for HE (i.e. NIHED, the National Institute for Higher Education Studies), a quality assurance agency (NAQAC), augmenting governance through university charters and councils, and implementing institutional autonomy and accountability. Quality and relevance initiatives included establishing research funds and research centres, developing policies and strategies for world class HEIs, upgrading facilities, improving online learning and the effectiveness of the DE system, and enhancing staff through professional development. Access and equity concerns were directed towards providing a quality learning environment and enabling greater access via tuition waivers and scholarships.

Achieving these deliverables in five years was a monumental task. Successfully delivering all targets was significantly hampered by at least two factors: an unclear strategic plan (logical framework); and tension between the state-shrinking, globalising ethos of neoliberal policies via international partners on one hand, and local commitments to social justice issues, broadly speaking, on the other hand (Kandiko-Howson & Lall, 2020; Lall, 2020). Regarding the first hurdle, the programme for transformational HE adjustments is logical, but far from intuitive for frontline stakeholders. This is due to admirable but vague strategies that are accompanied by open rather than specific endline targets, which involve strategies constituted by tasks that lend to exclusion rather than inclusion. For example, regarding the strategy to 'improve the quality and relevance of higher education' (MOE, 2016, pp. 192–197), one outcome of which is that 'academic staff deliver effective teaching and undertake quality research' (p. 197), there are no corresponding skills-based indicators that function as targets to be achieved. Regarding the second hurdle of incompatible policy frameworks – incompatible in terms of the underlying logics of neoliberalism and social justice (Lall, 2020, pp. 10–11, 274) – neoliberal policies tend to exacerbate economic class divides, which is contrary to the strategic plan's call for greater equality. For example, the third HE strategy of the NESP seeks to expand equitable access to education regardless of socio-economic background (MOE, 2016, pp. 196–197). Compared to the first two strategies of governance and quality, this strategy is significantly underpopulated in terms of components, outcomes, and targets. What is more concerning is that this strategy is framed in terms of poverty, with scant attention to rural geography and no mention of ethnic mother-tongue languages. In addition, there is a shift in terminology between outcome and indicator statements, where outcomes capture equity in terms of socio-economic background

Higher Education in Myanmar: Coup, Conflict, and Educational Crisis 77

while indicators refer to underprivileged and disadvantaged backgrounds – this terminology remains undefined. In short, what is notable by its absence is any explicit mention of equal access for students from ethnic minority and/or rural and geographically remote backgrounds. The shift in terminology lends to conceptual vagueness in the HE strategy, leaving policy development open to political manoeuvring, and allowing for established local elites to consolidate their holdings (cf. Ford et al., 2016).

Returning to the remaining advances, a degree of decentralisation occurred with the NEPC as a policy-focused body whose line of accountability was, according to the then chairman of the NEPC, to parliament rather than the MOE (Myo Kywe, 2020), which is a bureaucratic schema quite distinct from the BSPP and SPDC eras. Nevertheless, though unclear at the moment, it appears that the NEPC is no more, meaning the MOE or a related committee will again set the policy agenda. Similarly, the selective institutional (partial) autonomy granted to 16 HEIs in September 2020, while consistent with neoliberal policymaking, was still a significant development from generations of institutional and bureaucratic stagnation in Myanmar's tertiary sector, and as such promised change, the results of which were to be determined. Yet, again, as a result of the coup this move towards institutional autonomy is now under question. If past practices of junta clampdowns on universities after student protests are any guide, then we can expect such restrictive actions to be repeated. The question is if such restrictions will also apply to the governance and management of these newly autonomous HEIs. It is no longer the results of institutional autonomy that are to be determined, but the very institutional autonomy that was granted in 2020. Finally, regarding education colleges, with HEIs effectively closed until early 2022, and this combined with the impact of COVID-19, attendance rates can be expected to have dropped. The degree structure, specifically the newly minted four-year college degrees that resulted from the NESP, may remain in place. However, the impact of the civil disobedience movement on the administration of these colleges also remains to be seen.

HE IN A CONFLICT CONTEXT

Education is political, and in few places is this more evident than in Myanmar, where power politics (*ana shin nain ngan ye*) reign. Public notices declared that selected universities reopened in early January 2022 (for example, in the military's propagandist *Global New Light of Myanmar*), yet reports indicate that attendance was low on the part of students and teachers due to the CDM (Frontier, 2022; Mizzima, 2022; Naw Say Phaw Waa, 2021, 2022). The CDM is no small matter for a number of reasons, perhaps most notably because teachers as public servants in Myanmar are generally expected to not engage in political activities (Walton, 2017, p. 65). Public servants are expected to be non-partisan in their service to the state (a virtue that the military also claims for itself, implying that party politics is beneath the self-appointed guardians of the country). This makes it deeply symbolic that teachers – who occupy an exalted status in

Burmese culture yet receive strikingly low remuneration – actively side with students to protest against the military coup (alongside many other public servants, such as nurses, who started the CDM, doctors, etc.). In response to the CDM and teachers' strikes, the junta is widely reported to have arrested teachers, and if targeted civil servants were not found, the junta then arrested family members in order to coerce strikers to step forward and hand themselves in. In addition to this, a swathe of teachers (from primary to tertiary) were suspended. In May 2021 Reuters reported over 125,000 had been suspended, including 19,500 HE staff (Reuters, 2021). To fill this gap left by the CDM exodus, it was reported that the junta then hired unqualified day-wage teachers aligned with the military junta, resulting in (and reverting back to) a 'fake education' (Frontier, 2021b). Universities as spaces of the public sphere continue their history of challenging central command dictates; likewise, the military maintains its zero-sum attitude by being unwilling to acquiesce to the public's voicing its demands (Selth, 2021, p. 34). The long-running saga of polarised power dynamics in Myanmar continues, at the cost of the education system.

With Myanmar's conflict zones having now spread inward from periphery ethnic areas to heartland Bamar areas, the ethnicity-based civil wars that have made Myanmar's politics infamous over the past 60 years (e.g. Smith, 1999, 2018) are now endemic throughout the country. But this time the glue that binds opposition is a shared national, possibly even federal, purpose to provide armed resistance to the junta. Ethnic armed groups that continue to resist the junta are joined by various regional iterations of the PDF. Both of these sets of groups are destinations for students who want to increase physical pressure on the junta. Ethnic armed groups have a long history, while the PDF is a new military wing of the exiled NUG. This conflict context, combined with the CDM and a deep mistrust of the junta, creates a difficult situation for parents and students who want to continue their education. With a premium placed on education in Myanmar, and with parents playing a significant role in the educational choices of their children, including university students, families have been confronted with a jarring dilemma of either attending school under the junta and thus tacitly supporting the coup, or foregoing their education and accordingly jeopardising their future earning power. 'I feel so much guilt for going to the school while my friends are boycotting', laments one student, 'They might think I've become one of those who support the junta killing people. When I run into my friends on the way to school, I want to stop existing' (Frontier, 2022). With expectations that exams and assessments will be easier due to the junta's desire to attract and pass students with little regard for actual literacy and skills, the lure is real and the burden of choosing is a heavy one. On the other hand, there are options for alternative education in the form of ethnic schools for basic education (Nu Nu Lusan & Fishbein, 2021); the NUG is also creating a parallel system for basic and HE (Metro, 2021; Myanmar Now, 2021); and remote, online HE services are also available, though these schools are typically anchored in international institutions, making their accreditation problematic in Myanmar's current education system, not to mention additional difficulties accessing content and classes via unstable internet and power supplies.

Higher Education in Myanmar: Coup, Conflict, and Educational Crisis

This fraught nature of HE in Myanmar subsequent to 2021 has regional implications. Notably, part of the NESP's agenda for HE reform was raising the standard of Myanmar's HE to 'ASEAN and regional standards' (MOE, 2016, p. 188). To that end, in the 2011–2021 period of education reforms, HE in Myanmar slowly became involved in ASEAN mobility schemes for staff and students. Though credit transfer systems are relatively new for Myanmar (Hotta, 2020, p. 169), a small number of universities have been engaged in schemes, such as the EU Grant funded SHARE project and the ASEAN University Network (AUN, now ASEAN +3, i.e. plus China, South Korea, and Japan) student exchange program. Other prominent schemes include University Mobility in Asia and the Pacific (UMAP), which has a number of multi-lateral and bi-lateral programs and covers 36 countries in the region; and SEAMEO-RIHED's ASEAN International Mobility for Students (AIMS) scheme, which focuses on 8 countries in the southeast Asia region. Thirteen universities in Myanmar – all from the major metropolitan regions of Yangon and Mandalay, thus clearly excluding universities in rural areas (namely, ethnic States) – have been involved in AUN's program. The University of Yangon, Yangon University of Economics, and University of Mandalay, all prestigious universities in Myanmar, figure prominently in the AUN initiative (AUN, 2020). In this ASEAN context, using the 2017–2018 academic period in Myanmar as a basis for comparison, in which 931,180 students were enrolled, just 8,328 students (approximately 0.9% of students) were reported as outbound. Of those students, 2,323 (27.9%) were destined for the ASEAN region, of which 1,896 (82% of the ASEAN aggregate, and 23% of the total outbound) were bound for neighbouring Thailand (Chao, 2020). A sharp reduction in university enrolments can be expected for some time in response to the military coup in Myanmar – due to the tradition of student revolution in Myanmar, and because students continue to resist. This, together with stiff diplomatic relations regionally and sanctions implemented internationally against coup leaders, means the internationalisation of Myanmar's HE sector can be expected to shrink.

SDG 4.3 IN THE JUNTA'S SYSTEM

We are now in a position to consider how Myanmar's HE sector has progressed in terms of sustainable development goal 4.3: To ensure equal access for all women and men to affordable and quality HE. The focus here is on access, equity, and quality.

As we have seen, universities in Myanmar are spaces of physical and social resistance. This makes them destinations for dissent and targets of state sanction. In this way, there is constant friction between emerging participatory desires and established hierarchical dictates. Universities in Myanmar are active pieces in the political strategies of established elites. This is perhaps most obvious with the splitting of existing universities in order to establish new universities, typically in semi-urban or rural locations. With students widely dispersed, so too is emerging dissent, effectively weakening the collective voice of student opposition. The advent of the DE system in the mid-1990s, which required minimal campus attendance, meant student relations were further thinned and collective voices dissipated. This is the Janus-faced nature of access to HE in Myanmar. Access is made available through widely dispersed institutions and remote programs of notorious quality, yet this disparate access weakens the unity (*nyi nyut chin*) of emerging communicative rationality and subsequent public action that may develop by way of student organisations. Such communicative potential has been strategically deconstructed and bureaucratised by previous military juntas.

Set against this backdrop of strategic control, and in a context where students may be inclined to 'ghost enrol' at university to circumvent new conscription laws, three salient challenges emerge for students wishing to access HE: cost for rural students, the (now presumably defunct) prospect of sixteen autonomous HEIs, and structural and cultural violence limiting persons with disabilities (PWDs). First, compared to their urban classmates, the relative cost for rural students is far more onerous. For example, compared to Myanmar's major commercial metropolis, Yangon, the experience of multidimensional poverty in rural areas such as Rakhine State and Ayeyarwaddy Region is, respectively, 4.4 and 3.4 times higher. Shan State and Kayin State are close behind, experiencing poverty at a rate of 3.4 times higher than Yangon (OPHI, 2019). Add to this costs such as course fees, textbook fees, dormitory fees, 'tuition' class fees, travel from hometowns and villages to university campus, separation from family, and the opportunity cost incurred by families, all make attending university significantly more prohibitive for rural students (Brown and Hung, 2022).

Second, if it were the case that institutional autonomy were to continue for the 16 universities granted limited autonomy in September 2020 (Thet Zin Soe, 2020), then a two-tiered system of HE would then be established. Such neoliberal reforms afforded to a select group of institutions in the central lowlands of Myanmar were a continuation of Myanmar's ethnically demarcated domestic geopolitics. The geographical exclusivity of this shift towards institutional autonomy is unfortunate yet hardly surprising given previous juntas' controlling and Burmanising design of the rotation system of teachers (Heslop, 2019; South & Lall, 2016) and the privileging of ethnic Bamar demographics (Walton, 2013). The ramifications of this move were potentially stark. In rural and ethnically demarcated states, the prevalence of multidimensional poverty is significantly higher than in urban lowland centres (e.g. over 30% of people in Rakhine and Shan States are recorded as experiencing severe poverty, compared to 4.6% in Yangon; OPHI, 2019). Combine this with the fact that 48.1% of Myanmar's richest quintile attend tertiary education while only 1.2% of the poorest quintile attend (UNESCO, 2020), plus the strikingly low retention rate of students traversing the basic education system (MPF, 2018, pp. 177–181) – which is due in part to mother-tongue language challenges for students in ethnic highlands – and a 33% matriculation rate of students who do complete their basic education, all amount to access being unbalanced in terms of income, geography, and ethnicity.

Third, PWDs experience significant structural and cultural challenges. Where structural violence refers to social injustice in terms of inequality and the weakening of communicative action (Galtung, 1969; Habermas, 1987), and cultural violence refers to the ideology that enables and legitimises structural violence

(Galtung, 1996, p. 196), PWDs must overcome significant constraints to access HE. To begin, the World Health Organization (WHO) reports that on average 15.3% of the global population experience some form of disability (2011, p. 30). Yet Myanmar's Department of Population (DOP) has reported that only 4.6% of Myanmar's population experience some form of disability (2017, p. xiv). In the context of this modest 4.6%, the DOP also reports that children with disabilities (CWDs) count for 1.2% of the primary school population and 1.3% of the middle school population (DOP, 2017, p. 50). With these small numbers on one hand, and the singular matriculation route to HE on the other hand, access to university for PWDs is exceedingly difficult. This is due, in significant part, to cultural beliefs that malign PWDs and result in systemic inadequacies. For example, Ko Htay Aung notes that 'the main problem for CWDs to access their rights to education is the social barriers, not their impairments', going on to say that 'our Myanmar society should remove physical, attitudinal, cultural and institutional barriers, rather than focusing on impairments' (2020, p. 32). An example of such a social barrier is the common attitude among parents of CWDs that education for their disabled child is redundant due to a lack of subsequent employment options; while a common attitude of teachers is that they do not want to take responsibility for CWDs (Ko Hyat Aung, 2020, pp. 32, 33). Supplementing this are local cultural beliefs that disability is a matter of 'karma' (*kan*) or 'fate' (ECDC, 2015). In combination, these attitudes and beliefs tend to result in a degree of complacency regarding the support offered to PWDs, which goes some way to explaining the lack of physical infrastructure required for PWDs to access and navigate school grounds, and the lack of teacher training provided for teachers to include CWDs in the classroom (Waite, 2015, p. 392).

Equity issues can also be noted regarding the matriculation scoring system used for students to apply for certain university courses, and the consequences for young people who find their options limited due to economic, geographic, and/or ethnic circumstances. Regarding the matriculation scoring system, it is both widely acknowledged and publicly declared that certain degree programmes require female students to achieve a higher score in their matriculation results compared to their male counterparts. For example, Eaint Thet Su (2019) reports that entrance into medical school for males requires a score of 490 (out of a total of 600) while females need to score at least 510. Similar entrance score disparities occur in other subjects, such as dentistry and nursing. The second point regarding means, geography, and ethnicity is a point that is compounded for a student who is from a poor, rural, ethnic background. Since inclusion and equity in Myanmar traditionally focus on the poor demographic rather than ethnicity and language, it is then little surprise that rural ethnic youth are 'least likely to achieve similar education outcomes than their Bamar urban counterparts' (Kandiko-Howson & Lall, 2019, p. 118). As alluded to previously, language figures prominently in conversations about equity, since language of schooling is an issue woven into domestic identity politics, decades of civil war, and intermittent peace talks. Education, peace, and conflict are interrelated in Myanmar, though are not always factored into policy resolutions where the presence or absence of conflict can determine the availability of, and access to, education (South & Lall, 2016, p. 150). As such, these gender-based and ethnogeographic inequities double as access issues, and are rooted in cultural and structural violence that is, in many respects, normalised to such a depth that they are not often questioned. Indeed, the kammatic tenet that informs and guides the daily cultural practices of Bamar Buddhism can result in inequalities not being perceived as iniquitous (Koenig, 1990, p. 45), which means that such inequalities can 'look, even feel, right' in the Myanmar worldview (Galtung, 1996, p. 196).

As part of the NESP, a quality assurance committee (NAQAC) was established to address the fact that 'universities in Myanmar have little-to-no experience with QA' (Niedermeier & Pohlenz, 2019, p. 39). In 2018, NAQAC released a draft policy regarding standards and guidelines for institutional quality assurance. The current political uncertainty in Myanmar, however, leaves that draft policy and its implementation in serious question. In general, several issues surrounding quality include public expenditure, teacher training, and the transfer-rotation system. Public expenditure on education, as noted above, remains the lowest in the southeast Asia region in terms of GDP. From this, HE was allocated 17% of the national budget in the 2017–2018 financial year. The compounding effect of COVID-19, the coup, the war in Ukraine, and the increase in both global and local resources, has facilitated inflation, prompting the World Bank to project an 18% downturn in Myanmar's GDP for the 2021 financial year, with modest incremental improvements in subsequent years (World Bank, 2021, 2022, 2023). From this, it is reasonable to conclude that public expenditure on HE in the short-term will shrink rather than grow. This can only have a negative impact on the quality of HE facilities and delivery, regardless of the military coup, which, according to long-established precedent will only cause further deterioration in a multitude of ways.

On the other hand, teacher training during the previous civilian government period experienced important changes for the better. Namely, the decentralisation of access to education colleges for people of ethnic minority languages in rural areas promised to improve rural-ethnic student performance in the long-run (Salem-Gervais & Raynaud, 2020, p. 108). Education colleges also underwent reforms to change from two-year programs to become four-year education degree colleges, with a presence in each State and Region around the country (Khaing Phyu Htut et al., 2022, p. 5; UNESCO, 2016). Though issues still lingering include the very low remuneration of teaching staff, the high number of female teachers yet disproportionate number of females in senior roles, and logistical problems associated with family movements and the MOE's rotation system of education staff as civil servants (Lall, 2020). Indeed, the transfer rotation system involving teachers being rotated every few years to a new location will continue to have a negative impact on HE quality. A continuation of the centralised command and control practices of consecutive junta periods, this system basically disempowers teachers and researchers due to their inability to establish and grow local teaching or research profiles. Without continuity and consistency in terms of HE programme design, delivery, and research projects, this piecemeal and typically arbitrary movement of HE staff ensures that individual institutions cannot strengthen their delivery of education nor grow their research profile, thus ensuring that institutions and the system as a whole remain in a fragile state.

CONCLUSION

In 2011, Myanmar transitioned from a military dictatorship to quasi-democratic governance under military tutelage. This political shift ushered in multilateral reviews of, and investments in, the education sector, which resulted in strategic overhauls of the sector, including HE. Changes in the HE sector were slow to start in 2016 but were gaining some momentum by 2020. The military coup in 2021 then caused substantial damage to Myanmar's HE sector. Such damage includes, for example: mass suspensions of university staff, unsurprisingly low student turnouts, a question mark hanging over the previous 10 years of progress (e.g. the NESP, the NEPC, institutional autonomy, education colleges), not to mention over 6,000 non-combatant civilians killed since February 2021 (Min Zaw Oo & Tønneson, 2023), 24,000 anti-coup protesters arrested (HRW, 2024), the presence of martial law in 61 of 330 townships (18.5%) across the country (Irrawaddy, 2024a), mass internal displacement, and a continuing civil war that has now scaled-up from Myanmar's 'traditional' ethnic conflicts to a nationwide conflict. HE will survive, but its remaining form cannot in reality be anticipated. The extent of the damage is yet to be seen as the coup and civic resistance continue.

In Myanmar, the tradition of university student resistance runs deep. The highly centralised, bureaucratic, and hierarchical structure of HE is designed to control dissent. Yet, spaces for communicative action continue to resist the junta's hubris, to buckle the verticality of the junta's structural violence, and to reinterpret the junta's fiction of the military as guardians of the country. Immediately after the coup, the emergence of the public voice on the streets was clear, loud, and reverberated throughout the country. The conflict that cripples the country, also cripples HE. For the university student today, the set of choices before them has diminished compared to the choices available to them before the coup. Indeed, the choice is stark. Attend university and risk the ignominy associated with complicity. Or continue with civil disobedience and risk the precarity associated with a lack of formal education. In either case, the future for university students and of HE is fragile. Students in Myanmar have the capacity to excel in HE, but what is lacking is a set of real opportunities for them to choose from, and from which both student and sector could flourish.

REFERENCES

Allot, A. J. (1985). Language policy and language planning in Burma. In D. Bradley (Ed.), *Papers in South-East Asian Linguistics: Language policy, language planning and sociolinguistics in South-East Asia* (pp. 131–154). ANU Research School of Pacific Studies.

ASEAN University Network (AUN). (2020). ASEAN University Network Annual *Report, 2019–2020*. Office of the AUN Secretariat. http://www.aunsec.org/annualreport2019-2020.php

Aung Kin. (1983). Burma in 1982: On the road to recovery. *Southeast Asian Affairs*, 87–101.

Boshier, C. A. (2018). *Mapping cultural nationalism. The scholars of the Burma Research Society, 1910–1935*. NIAS Press.

Brown, M. (2022). Myanmar's higher education in 2021: Reforms deformed by Covid-Coup Conundrum. *Higher Education in Southeast Asia and Beyond (HESB)*, *11*, 16–20.

Brown, M., & Hung, N. (2022). Higher education in Myanmar. In L. P. Symaco & M. Hayden (Eds.), *International handbook on education in South East Asia*. Springer International Handbooks of Education. Springer. https://doi.org/10.1007/978-981-16-8136-3_33-2

Chao, R. Y., Jr. (2020). Intra-ASEAN student mobility: Overview, challenges and opportunities. *Journal of Applied Research in Higher Education*. https://doi.org/10.1108/JARHE-07-2019-0178

Cheesman, N. (2003). School, state and Sangha in Burma. *Comparative Education*, *39*(1), 45–63.

CHINLONE [Connecting Higher Education Institutions for a New Leadership on National Education] Project. (2018). Myanmar's higher education reform: Which way forward? University di Bologna. site.unibo.it/chinlone/it/report

Cho, V., & Gilbert, D. (2021). Ethnicity, culture, and religion: Centralisation, Burmanisation and social transformation. In A. Simpson & N. Farrelly (Eds.), *Myanmar. Politics, economy, and society* (pp. 219–233). Routledge.

Department of Population (DOP). (2017). *Thematic report on disability. Census Report Volume 4-K*. Ministry of Labour, Immigration and Population.

Eaint Thet Su. (2019, July 22). University admission: Deciding in the dark. Frontier Myanmar. https://www.frontiermyanmar.net/en/university-admission-deciding-in-the-dark/

Eden Centre for Disabled Children (ECDC). (2015). *A space to learn for all children? Inclusive education and children with disabilities in Yangon, Myanmar*. ECDC/VSO.

Egreteau, R. (2016). *Caretaking democratization. The military and political change in Myanmar*. Hurst and Company.

Ford, M., Gillan, M., & Thein, H. H. (2016). From cronyism to oligarchy? Privatisation and business elites in Myanmar. *Journal of Contemporary Asia*, *46*(1), 18–41. http://dx.doi.org/10.1080/00472336.2015.1072731

Frontier. (2021a, March 30). 'The Shooting was Relentless': Terror Grips a Yangon Ward. Frontier Myanmar. https://www.frontiermyanmar.net/en/the-shooting-was-relentless-terror-grips-a-yangon-ward/

Frontier. (2021b, May 6). Parents, teachers and students boycott 'slave education system'. Frontier Myanmar. https://www.frontiermyanmar.net/en/parents-teachers-and-students-boycott-slave-education-system/

Frontier. (2021c, June 2). Misery at Mindat: Displaced Chin Communities Desperate for Aid. Frontier *Myanmar*. https://www.frontiermyanmar.net/en/misery-at-mindat/

Frontier. (2021d, June 8). Junta Plan to Replace Striking Staff Will Wreck Education, Say Teachers. Frontier Myanmar. https://www.frontiermyanmar.net/en/junta-plan-to-replace-striking-staff-will-wreck-education-say-teachers/

Frontier. (2021e, August 23). Disputing Junta Narrative, Magway Villagers Blame Security Forces for Massive Fire. Frontier Myanmar. https://www.frontiermyanmar.net/en/disputing-junta-narrative-magway-villagers-blame-security-forces-for-massive-fire/

Frontier. (2022, January 17). Education vs. Revolution: School Reopenings Bring Hard Choices. Frontier Myanmar. https://www.frontiermyanmar.net/en/education-vs-revolution-school-reopenings-bring-hard-choices

Frontier. (2023, May 22). The Fading Hopes of Myanmar's University Students. Frontier Myanmar. https://www.frontiermyanmar.net/en/the-fading-hopes-of-myanmars-university-students/

Frontier. (2024, February 16). Thousands Seek to Quit Myanmar After Military Service Announcement. Frontier Myanmar. https://www.frontiermyanmar.net/en/thousands-seek-to-quit-myanmar-after-military-service-announcement/

Galtung, J. (1969). 'Violence, peace, and peace research.' *Journal of Peace Research*, *6*(3), 167–191.

Galtung, J. (1996). *Peace by peaceful means. Peace and conflict, development and civilization*. Sage.

Habermas, J. (1987). *The theory of communicative action. Volume 2. Lifeworld and system: A critique of functionalist reason*. [Trans. T. McCarthy]. Beacon Press.

Hayden, M., & Martin, R. (2013). 'Recovery of the education system in Myanmar'. *Journal of International and Comparative Education*, *2*(2), 47–57.

Heslop, L. (2019). *Encountering internationalisation: Higher education and social justice in Myanmar.* [PhD Thesis. University of Sussex]. Sussex Research Online (sro.sussex.ac.uk/).

Hong, M. S., & Kim, H. (2019). 'Forgotten' democracy, student activism, and higher education in Myanmar: Past, present, and future. *Asia Pacific Education Review, 20*, 207–222.

Hotta, T. (2020). The development of 'Asian Academic Credits' as an aligned credit transfer system in Asian higher education. *Journal of Studies in International Education, 24*(2), 167–189. https://doi.org/10.1177/1028315318822797

HRW (Human Rights Watch). (2024). *World Report 2024. Events of 2023.* Human Rights Watch. https://www.hrw.org/world-report/2024

Ikeya, C. (2011). *Reconfiguring women, colonialism, and modernity in Burma.* University of Hawaii Press.

Irrawaddy. (2021, February 18). Myanmar Military's New Education Minister Faced Finance Probes. *The Irrawaddy.* https://www.irrawaddy.com/news/burma/myanmar-militarys-new-education-minister-faced-finance-probes.html

Irrawaddy. (2022, June 27). Almost 100 Civilians Tortured to Death by Myanmar Regime Since Coup. The Irrawaddy. https://www.irrawaddy.com/news/burma/almost-100-civilians-tortured-to-death-by-myanmar-regime-since-coup.html

Irrawaddy. (2024a, March 5). Number of Townships Placed Under Martial Law by Myanmar Junta Rises to 61. *The Irrawaddy.* https://www.irrawaddy.com/news/burma/number-of-townships-placed-under-martial-law-by-myanmar-junta-rises-to-61.html

Irrawaddy. (2024b, March 6). Myanmar's Junta is Racing Ahead with Military Conscription. *The Irrawaddy.* https://www.irrawaddy.com/news/burma/myanmars-junta-is-racing-ahead-with-military-conscription.html

James, H. (2005). *Governance and civil society in Myanmar: Education, health, and environment.* Routledge.

Joliffe, K., & Speers Mears, E. (2016). *Strength in diversity: Towards universal education in Myanmar's ethnic areas.* The Asia Foundation.

Kandiko-Howson, C., & Lall, M. (2019). Higher education reform in Myanmar: Neoliberalism versus an inclusive development agenda. *Globalisation, Societies and Education, 18*(2), 109–124. https://doi.org/10.1080/14767724.2019.1689488

Kaung. (1963). A survey of the history of education in Burma before the British Conquest and After. *Journal of the Burma Research Society, 46*(2), 1–124.

Khaing Phyu Htut, Lall, M., & Kandiko Howson, C. (2022). Caught between COVID-19, coup and conflict – What future for Myanmar higher education reforms? *Education Sciences, 12*(2), 67–87.

Khammai Dhammasami. (2018). *Buddhism, education and politics in Burma and Thailand: From the seventeenth century to the present.* Bloomsbury.

Ko Hyat Aung. (2020). Barriers for the rights of CWDs to education. *Parami Journal of Education, 1*(1), 32–38.

Koenig, W. J. (1990). *The Burmese Polity, 1752-1819. Politics, Administration, and Social Organization in the Early Kon-baung Period.* Center for South and Southeast Asian Studies, The University of Michigan.

Kyaw Yin Hlaing. (2007). Associational life in Myanmar: Past and present. In N. Ganesan & Kyaw Yin Hlaing (Eds.), *Myanmar. State, society, and ethnicity* (pp. 143–171). ISEAS.

Lall, M. (2016). *Understanding reform in Myanmar.* Hurst and Company.

Lall, M. (2020). *Myanmar's education reforms. A pathway to social justice?* UCL Press.

Metro, R. (2017). Whose democracy? The university student protests in Burma/Myanmar, 2014-2016. In J. Millican (Ed.), *Universities and conflict. The role of higher education in peacebuilding and resistance* (pp. 205–218). Routledge.

Metro, R. (2021, June 24). The emerging alternatives to 'military slave education'. Frontier Myanmar. https://www.frontiermyanmar.net/en/the-emerging-alternatives-to-military-slave-education/

Min Zaw Oo, & Tønneson, S. (2023). Counting Myanmar's dead: Reported civilian casualties since the 2021 Military Coup. *Peace Research Institute Oslo (PRIO) Paper.* PRIO. https://www.prio.org/publications/13516

Ministry of Education (MOE). (2016). *National education strategic plan 2016-2021.* Ministry of Education. https://www.britishcouncil.org/sites/default/files/myanmar_national_education_strategic_plan_2016-21.pdf

Ministry of Planning and Finance (MPF). (2018). *Myanmar statistical yearbook*. Central Statistical Organization.

Mizzima. (2022, January 28). *Living in a dark era one year after Myanmar's coup*. https://www.mizzima.com/article/living-dark-era-one-year-after-myanmars-coup

Myanmar Now. (2021, May 10). National Unity Government fights junta's 'slave education' with plan to build parallel system. *Myanmar Now*. https://www.myanmar-now.org/en/news/national-unity-government-fights-juntas-slave-education-with-plan-to-build-parallel-system

Myat Mon. (2000). The economic position of women in Burma. *Asian Studies Review, 24*(2), 243–255.

Myo Kywe. (2020). CEPR Education Newsletter. Special Issue, July 2020. Interview with Dr. Myo Kywe by Thiri Nyo and Tint Sabei Soe Win. Center for Education Policy Research. https://www.parami.edu.mm/newletter

Naw Say Phaw Waa. (2021, May 14). Junta Suspends Thousands of Academics, University Staff. *University World News*. https://www.universityworldnews.com/post.php?story=20210514110259910

Naw Say Phaw Waa. (2022, January 28). Universities, professors and students still under attack. *University World News*. https://www.universityworldnews.com/post.php?story=2022012812432689

Niedermeier, F., & Pohlenz, P. (2019). *State of play report. Higher education quality assurance in the ASEAN Region* (2nd ed.). ASEAN Secretariat, SHARE Project Management Office. https://share-asean/eu/publications/reports

Nu Nu Lusan & Fishbein, E. (2021, September 22). Amid education boycotts, ethnic schools help to fill the gap. Frontier Myanmar. https://www.frontiermyanmar.net/en/amid-education-boycots-ethnic-schools-help-fill-the-gap

OPHI (Oxford Poverty and Human Development Initiative). (2019). *Global MPI Country Briefing 2019: Myanmar (East Asia and the Pacific)*. https://ophi.org.uk/country-briefings-2019/

Padone. (2023, April 26). Enrolment in State-run Universities down '70%' since Coup. *University World News*. https://www.universityworldnews.com/post.php?story=20230426140655766

Padone. (2024, February 21). Compulsory Army Conscription Law Shatters Education Hopes. *University World News*. https://www.universityworldnews.com/post.php?story=20240221102634648

Reuters. (2021, May 23). *More than 125,000 Myanmar teachers suspended for opposing coup*. https://www.reuters.com/world/asia-pacific/more-than-125000-myanmar-teachers-suspended-opposing-coup-2021-05-23/

RFA (Radio Free Asia). (2024a, January 8). University Student Population has Plunged 90% since Coup. Radio Free Asia. https://www.rfa.org/english/news/myanmar/universities-01082024154241.html

RFA (Radio Free Asia). (2024b, February 28). Battle Erupts on Northern Myanmar University Campus. Radio Free Asia. https://www.rfa.org/english/news/myanmar/campus-battle-02282024194951.html

Salem-Gervais, N., & Raynaud, M. (2020). *Teaching ethnic minority languages in government schools and developing the local curriculum: Elements of decentralization in language-in-education policy*. Konrad-Adenauer Stiftung.

Schober, J. (2011). *Modern Buddhist Conjunctures in Myanmar. Cultural narratives, colonial legacies, and civil society*. University of Hawaii Press.

Selth, A. (2021). *Myanmar's military mindset: An exploratory survey*. Griffith University.

Shah, R., & Lopes Cardozo, M. T. A. (2019). Myanmar's education system: Historical roots, the current context, and new opportunities. In M. T. A. Lopes Cardozo & E. J. T. Maber (Eds.), *Sustainable peacebuilding and social justice in times of transition* (pp. 65–86). Springer.

Smith, M. (1999). *Burma. insurgency and the politics of ethnicity*. Zed Books.

Smith, M. (2018). Ethnic politics and citizenship in history. In A. South & M. Lall (Eds.), *Citizenship in Myanmar. Ways of being in and from Burma* (pp. 26–54). ISEAS Publishing.

South, A., & Lall, M. (2016). Language, education and the peace process in Myanmar. *Contemporary Southeast Asia: A Journal of International and Strategic Affairs, 38*(1), 128–153.

Steinberg, D. (1981). Burma under the military: Towards a chronology. *Contemporary Southeast Asia, 3*(3), 244–285.

Thet Zin Soe. (2020, September 4). Myanmar gov't grants autonomy to 16 universities. Myanmar Times. https://www.mmtimes.com/news/myanmar-govt-grants-autonomy-16-universities.html

Turnell, S. (2009). *Fierty dragons: Banks, moneylenders and microfinance in Burma*. NIAS Press.

UNESCO. (2016). *Education college curriculum framework for 4-year degree.* https://edc.moe.edu.mm/my-MM/resource/education-college-curriculum-framework-for-4-year-degree

UNESCO. (2020). UNESCO Institute for Statistics. Retrieved December 30, 2020, from www.data.uis.unesco.org.

UNICEF. (2018). *Myanmar 2018 education brief.* Retrieved January 06, 2021, from https://www.unicef.org/myanmar/reports/myanmar-2018-education-budget-brief

Wa Lone and Sandar Lwin. (2014, May 26). Back in Session. *Myanmar Times.* https://www.mmtimes.com/special-features/182-education-2014/10494-back-in-session.html

Waite, M. (2015). A space to learn for all children? Inclusive education and children with disabilities in Yangon, Myanmar. *Global Studies of Childhood, 5*(4), 381–394.

Walton, M. J. (2013). The 'Wages of Burman-ness': Ethnicity and Burman privilege in contemporary Myanmar. *Journal of Contemporary Asia, 43*(1), 1–27.

Walton, M. J. (2017). *Buddhism, politics, and political thought in Myanmar.* Cambridge University Press.

Welch, A., & Hayden, M. (2013). Myanmar Comprehensive Education Sector Review (CESR). Phase 1: Rapid Assessment. Technical Annex on the Higher Education Subsector. ADB and UNESCO.

Win Min. (2012). Burma: A historic force, forcefully met. In M. L. Weiss & E. Aspinall (Eds.), *Student activism in Asia: Between protest and powerlessness* (pp. 181–204). University of Minnesota Press.

World Bank. (2021, July). *Myanmar economic monitor. Progress threatened; resilience tested.* World Bank. https://www.worldbank.org/en/country/myanmar/publication/myanmar-economic-monitor-reports

World Bank. (2022, July). *Myanmar economic monitor.* Reforms reversed. https://www.worldbank.org/en/country/myanmar/publication/myanmar-economic-monitor-reports

World Bank. (2023, January). *Myanmar economic monitor.* Navigating uncertainty. https://www.worldbank.org/en/country/myanmar/publication/myanmar-economic-monitor-reports

World Health Organization (WHO). (2011). *World report on disability.* World Health Organization. https://www.who.int/publications/i/item/9789241564182

Ye Myo Hein. (2022, July 12). Myanmar Military's Culture of Atrocities. The Irrawaddy. https://www.irrawaddy.com/opinion/guest-column/myanmar-militarys-culture-of-atrocities.html

APPENDIX: COMPILATION AND EXTRAPOLATION OF DATA FROM MPF (2018)

Table A1. Enrolments in Basic Education.

	Primary	Middle	High	Matriculation Pass Rate*	Students Eligible for University
2013–2014	5,166,317	2,542,830	730,866	31.67%	231,465
2014–2015	5,121,203	2,687,801	792,670	37.60%	298,044
2015–2016	5,071,458	2,730,879	840,706	29.92%	251,539
2016–2017	5,143,230	2,846,812	926,536	33.89%	314,003
2017–2018	5,038,627	2,935,984	1,009,770	32.89%	332,113
Average	5,108,167	2,748,861	860,110	33.19%	285,505
Retention 1		53.8%	31.3%		
Retention 2			16.8%		
Retention 3					5.6%

Data source: MPF (2018, pp. 159–181).
Retention 1: Primary school to middle school and middle school to high school. Retention 2: Primary school to high school. Retention 3: Primary school to university as a percentage of the age-relevant population.
*The matriculation exam is the final high school exam. A student's matriculation score forms the basis of what they will study at university.

Table A2. Enrolments and Growth in HE.

Institutes	2013–2014	2014–2015	2015–2016	2016–2017	2017–2018
Professional Universities	140,754	134,273	131,925	121,369	131,074
Arts and Science ('Non-Professional') Universities	430,853	516,321	601,614	765,594	800,106
Total	571,607	650,594	733,539	886,963	931,180
Growth per year		13.8%	12.7%	20.8%	5.0%
Growth from 2013 to 2014			28.3%	55.2%	62.9%

Data source: MPF (2018, pp. 159–181).

Higher Education in Myanmar: Coup, Conflict, and Educational Crisis

Table A3. Teaching and Research Staff in HE.

Institutes	2013–2014	2014–2015	2015–2016	2016–2017	2017–2018
Professional Universities	6,332	10,211	10,883	10,980	11,840
Arts and Science ('Non-Professional') Universities	11,434	12,378	12,455	12,221	12,785
Total	17,766	22,589	23,338	23,201	24,625
Growth per year		27.1%	3.3%	–0.6%	6.1%
Growth from 2013–2014			31.4%	30.6%	38.6%

Source: MPF (2018, pp. 159–181).

Table A4. Teacher/Student Ratios in HE.

	2013–2014	2014–2015	2015–2016	2016–2017	2017–2018
Students at Professional Universities	140,754	134,273	131,925	121,369	131,074
Teachers at Professional Universities	6,332	10,211	10,883	10,980	11,840
Number of students per teacher	**22.2**	**13.1**	**12.1**	**11.1**	**11.1**
Students at Arts and Science ('Non-Professional') Universities	430,853	516,321	601,614	765,594	800,106
Teachers at Arts and Science ('Non-Professional') Universities	11,434	12,378	12,455	12,221	12,785
Number of students per teacher	**37.7**	**41.7**	**48.3**	**62.6**	**62.6**
Total students	571,607	650,594	733,539	886,963	931,180
Total teachers	17,766	22,589	23,338	23,201	24,625
Overall number of students per teacher	**32.2**	**28.8**	**31.4**	**38.2**	**37.8**

Source: MPF (2018, pp. 159–181).

CHAPTER 7

HIGHER EDUCATION IN THE PHILIPPINES: ISSUES AND CHALLENGES

Maria Alicia Bustos-Orosa[a] and
Lorraine Pe Symaco[b]

[a]De La Salle University, Philippines
[b]Zhejiang University, China

ABSTRACT

Philippine higher education is fraught with challenges in access, relevance, and quality. Initiatives at addressing these issues have often been adopted as government-mandated regulations. Academic program offerings are likewise highly regulated. Private institutions make up most of the higher education providers but differentiation in regulatory policies for private and public institutions are often imbalanced and partial to the latter. Higher education institutions are also tasked to contribute to the goals of achieving social equality and ensuring employability, with the push for internationalization being linked to quality concerns. This chapter will discuss issues of access, quality, and internationalization in Philippine higher education.

Keywords: Access; quality; internationalization; employability; universities; SDG; ASEAN

Higher Education in Southeast Asia
International Perspectives on Education and Society, Volume 49, 91–102
Copyright © 2025 by Maria Alicia Bustos-Orosa and Lorraine Pe Symaco
Published under exclusive licence by Emerald Publishing Limited
ISSN: 1479-3679/doi:10.1108/S1479-367920240000049007

INTRODUCTION

The earliest account of formal higher education in the Philippines can be traced back to Spanish colonial rule in 1611 with the founding of the Royal Pontifical University of Santo Tomas (UST) by a Dominican friar led by Fray Miguel de Benavides. From 1565 until 1863, universities were instituted primarily for the propagation of the Catholic faith and religious life with the Spanish language as the medium of instruction. Other religious orders followed in establishing universities from which only many well-off, elite, and Spanish-speaking Filipinos could attend. The Spanish rulers perceived these universities as harbors of rebellion and free thinking. Paradoxically, among these graduates, several prominent historical figures led the rebellion against the Spanish rulers in the end.

In 1899, the rebellion against Spanish colonial rule saw American rulers prevail. The Americans established the first teacher-training institution, the Philippine Normal University in 1901 and the first national university, the University of the Philippines in 1908. Nonetheless, the Americans likewise established the *pensionado* system of scholarship where qualified students from mostly elite families were sent to the US mainland to pursue higher education. The goal of the *pensionado* system was to immerse Filipinos in the American government system, culture, language, and democratic values. Upon their return to the country, the pensionado scholars would become leaders in the public and private sectors. When the country declared its independence from American rule in 1946, the country's basic and higher educational ecosystem was already developed with the strong presence of both private and public schools and universities. To this day, Philippine higher education is essentially modeled after the US educational system.

The Commission on Higher Education (CHED) in the Philippines was formed in 1994 through the *Higher Education (HE) Act* of 1994. Before this, the Educational Commission in Education (EDCOM) in 1992 pushed forward the three-way focus of the education system in the country, thus creating the CHED for higher education, the Department of Education for Basic Education and TESDA for technical and vocational education. The CHED is mandated through the HE Act of 1994 to (i) promote relevant and quality HE; (ii) ensure that HE is accessible to all; (iii) guarantee academic freedom and develop effective leadership in HE; (iv) commit to moral ascendancy and institutionalize transparency in the system (CHED, n.d.-e, para 6). Consisting of a Chairman and four Commissioners each with a term of four years, the Commission En Banc of the CHED is responsible for formulating related policies and strategies involving HE (CHED, n.d.-c).

The push for further development of HE in the country also saw the creation of the *Higher Education Modernisation Act* (1997) which promoted a coordinated and integrated system through a uniform governing body of State University Colleges (SUCs). HE in the Philippines is mainly provided for by SUCs which are funded by the national government, Local University Colleges (LUCs), which are financed and supported by local governments and private universities and colleges. Other government schools (e.g., CHED supervised institutions, or special higher education institutions (HEIs) that focus on military science and national

Table 1. Higher Education Enrolment (Academic Year 2019–2020).

Program level	Enrolment AY (2019–2020)		
	Private	Public	Total
Doctorate	17,960	14,373	32,333
Master's	125,636	106,223	231,859
Post Baccalaureate	2,343	11,082	13,425
Baccalaureate	1,660,628	1,387,690	3,048,318
Pre-Baccalaureate	26,213	56,277	82,490
Grand Total	1,832,780	1,575,645	3,408,425

Source: CHED (2020).

defense) account for a minimal count in the sector (i.e., 13 out of the more than 2,000 HEIs) (CHED, n.d.-d).

The Philippines has one of the largest higher education systems in South East Asia (second only to Indonesia) with 3.4 million students, 2,396 HEIs (including SUC satellite campuses) consisting mainly of private HEIs (1,729), followed by SUCs (533) and LUCs (121) (CHED, 2020). The country's young median age of 25, also one of the youngest in the region, further propels the demand for HE in the country, which shows a heightened enrolment (Table 1) in government institutions (1.5 million, mostly in SUCs) versus private ones (1.8 million), despite a more pronounced number of private HEIs.

In terms of enrolment, the latest statistics show more females (1.87 million) compared to males (1.53 million) are enrolled in HE (CHED, 2020), though there is little information on the stride toward Sustainable Development Goal (SDG) 4.3 in the HE sector. Figures in basic education show however a decreasing net enrolment rate (for the year 2020) from elementary education (89% for males and females) to senior high school (57.4% for females, 42.1% for males). The drop-out rate is also higher for males in the senior high school level at 8% versus 5.3% for females (NEDA, n.d.).

RELATED ISSUES IN PHILIPPINE HE

Issues concerning quality and access are at the forefront of HE provisions in the Philippines. Enrolment and quality concerns have been raised for SUCs and LUCs (Felipe, 2023; Villegas, 2022), while access concerns are supposed to be addressed by the law established in 2017, i.e., *the Universal Access to Quality Tertiary Education Act*, which institutionalizes free tuition (and other) fees in SUCs and LUCs, notwithstanding criticisms to the said Law of not being genuinely pro-poor, when rich students outnumber the poorest in public HEIs (Orbeta & Paqueo, 2017). This Law is also reported by the Philippine government as one of the initiatives brought forward to attain SDG 4 (Quality Education). The country's aim to improve quality in HE is also echoed in the drive to promote internationalization, wherein the *Transnational Higher Education Act* (2019) gives weight to this goal.

Given the broad scope of the HE sector challenges in terms of achieving SDG 4.3 through greater quality and access/equity remain. The following sections will discuss the issues of quality, access, and internationalization in Philippine HE.

Access

The United Nations Population Fund Philippines (2023 a, b) reports that the Philippines has the largest generation of young people in its history, 30 million young people between the ages of 10 and 24 account for 28% of the Philippine population. Given this significant potential of college-bound population, HEIs must remain responsive and relevant to the needs of these age groups. The attendance rates in Philippine HEIs are high, given the country's income level, but still lag behind other Association of Southeast Asian Nations (ASEAN) member-states. In 2021, it was reported by the Second Congressional Commission in Education (EDCOM, 2024) that the country had a gross enrolment ratio in tertiary education of 34.89%, trailing behind its ASEAN neighbors. Despite gains in increasing enrolment, the predicament in access is further exacerbated by increases in attrition rates for tertiary education (EDCOM, 2024). Additionally, a source of disparity in access to HE is evident in the disproportionate number of HEIs in urban versus rural areas. The most number of college degree programs are offered in the National Capital Region (Metro Manila) with 7,393 programs, followed by CALABARZON with 5,674 program offerings (CHED, 2020). CALABARZON (Cavite, Laguna, Batangas, Rizal, and Quezon) represent the nearest provinces South of the capital of Metro Manila. This scenario highlights the disparities in the options offered for those students who live in urban versus rural areas, which may have implications for implications for achieving SDG 4.3 with the goal of equal access to affordable technical, vocational and higher education.

As mentioned earlier, Philippine HE providers include both public institutions, funded by local or national government, and private institutions which rely on revenues from tuition fees. The country's higher education system depends largely on the private sector to meet the growing demands (Tan, 2017). Nonetheless, such private sector dominance in the higher education landscape has been faced with increasing expansion of state-funded institutions in the country. Yee (2022, p. 1) reports that between 2000 and 2015 alone, private enrollment share declined steeply from 68% to just 48%. The Philippines is a forerunner in private higher education in the region, enacting laws such as *The Corporation Law* (1906) and *The Private School Law* (1917), and related regulatory CHED memorandums (e.g., Manual Regulations for Private HEIs). However, the recent aggressive expansion of state and local HEIs that serve as political fodder in many cities and provinces has imperiled private HEIs.

Significant gaps in enrolment among socioeconomic groups have also persisted despite programs that seek to ensure access to higher education for poor families. Although college attendance among the poorest has improved from 1.7% in 1999 to 6.1% in 2019, the share of the economically-advantaged students is twice as much (Bayudan-Dacuycuy et al., 2023). Scholarship programs in the sector include grants-in-aid, student loans and the *Universal Access to Quality*

Tertiary Education Act of 2017 (UAQTEA). The UAQTEA has four components, namely: (1) free higher education; (2) tertiary education subsidy (TES); (3) student loans; and (4) free technical and vocational education and training. It was reported that in AY 2021–2022, recipients of free education reached 2 million students, while the TES reached about 364,000 students (Commission on Higher Education, 2023a, 2023b). However, EDCOM (2024) reported that there is evident inequitable distribution and utilization of the financial resources of the UAQTEA which poor student grantees often missed out. Recent scholarship programs also include the Scholarship Program for Coconut Farmers and their Families (CoScho), and the Scholarship Grant Program for Children and Dependents of Sugarcane Industry Workers and Small Sugarcane Farmers.

Earlier, the Enhanced Education Act (Law) of 2013 sought to improve the education system by lengthening the number of years of basic education from 10 to 12 years (i.e., K-12). The Law also attempts to address inequities prior to college admission at the basic education levels by preparing poor students to compete for entry into prestigious state universities. Tan (2017) noted however that given this assumption on the benefits of K-12, it has 'misdirected reform that spreads budgets even more thinly over the basic education system and gives some up to the tertiary system as well in the form of free college tuition' (p. 135). The benefits of the K-12 reform have also been questioned where the supposed easier entry to the labor market has yet to be realized, this bears consequence to poorer families that have to spend the extra two years in basic education (Symaco & Bustos, 2021). Proposals to rationalize the funding schemes around free education toward that which is more equitable and sustainable are suggested, with equitable support for both public and private HE. Such a scheme will allow for critical improvements and investments in among others, academics, technology, faculty development, and infrastructure, which would then yield long-term and broader social and economic outcomes as a whole.

Quality

In 2012, as part of the country's mid-term development plans, CHED introduced *"Policy Standard to Enhance Quality Assurance in Philippine Higher Education through Outcomes-based and Typology-based QA"* which determined the path of both public and private HEIs. Under this policy, quality is defined "as the alignment and consistency of the learning environment with the institution's vision, mission, and goals demonstrated by exceptional learning and service outcomes" (p. 3). Quality assurance in the country demands both internal and external QA agencies, primarily through accreditation. Moreover, the shift to OBE (outcome-based education) was mandated by the policy for all colleges and universities, citing the need to provide a direct assessment of educational outcomes and degree programs, as well as the integration of an audit system within institutions.

A significant development in the policy was the introduction of a horizontal and vertical typology for all private HEIs as a means of differentiation and rationalization. The horizontal typology classifies HEIs into three types: professional institutions, colleges, or universities. HEIs are assessed under this typology through faculty qualifications, type of degree programs offered, learning resources and support services, linkages, and outreach activities (CHED, 2014, pp. 13–14). Meanwhile, on a vertical typology, HEIs would be assessed based on the elements of quality, with a strong emphasis on program excellence and institutional capacities. There are again three types of HEIs on the vertical typology: Autonomous, Deregulated, or Regulated HEIs. Each status is intended to accrue benefits for HEIs which gain worth as an autonomous institution, thus receiving less oversight and regulation from CHED. For the years 2019–2020, of the 1,729 private HEIs, 68 were granted Autonomous status and 16 were granted Deregulated status (CHED, 2019). Nonetheless, criticisms were hurled against the typologies, citing its impingement on institutional academic freedom and questioning its rationale. Notwithstanding debates around the policy's basis, CHED pushed forward with its implementation. In 2023, in addition to the typologies, the CHED included international QA mechanisms and graduate employability as key criteria in awarding Autonomous/Deregulated status.

Philippine HEIs have also adopted internal mechanisms to ensure quality in instruction, one of which is the Total Quality Management (TQM) approach. TQM in Philippine HEIs is an approach which adheres to among others, leadership commitment and stakeholder satisfaction (Rodriguez et al., 2018). Additionally, aside from the local accrediting bodies (discussed below), some HEIs obtain accreditation and certification for the Quality Management System (QMS) through the ISO. External quality assurance on the one hand primarily comes in the form of voluntary accreditation. HEIs that have complied with CHED regulatory requirements are encouraged to undergo voluntary accreditation with recognized non-governmental accreditation agencies. Accreditation is deemed as an internal quality and improvement mechanism at either the program or institutional level. Level IV is the highest level of accreditation awarded to institutions/programs that meet the standards in quality, operations, and services.

Voluntary accreditation has a long history in the Philippines with distinctions for public and private HE accreditation. Notwithstanding, each accrediting agency adopts its own set of established performance criteria that HEIs need to meet to qualify for recognition. Depending on the nature of the HEI, private HEIs may opt to apply for accreditation among three agencies: the Philippine Association of Colleges and Universities Commission on Accreditation (PACUCOA) established in 1973 for non-sectarian HEIs; the Philippine Accrediting Association of Schools, Colleges and Universities (PAASCU), established in 1957 for private Catholic HEIs, and the Association of Christian Schools, Colleges and Universities Accrediting Association Inc. (ACSCU-AAI) established in 1976 for Protestant HEIs. All these private accrediting agencies are under the remit of the Federation of Accrediting Agencies of the Philippines (FAAP). However, it is reported that few private HEIs undergo institutional accreditation. Based on the 2022 data from the PAASCU, only 12 HEIs have institutional accreditation, 5 of which are in the National Capital Region (NCR) (Bayudan-Dacuycuy et al., 2023).

Meanwhile, two agencies serve public HEIs, specifically: the Chartered Colleges and Universities in the Philippines (AACCUP), established in 1987, and the Association of Local Colleges and Universities Commission on Accreditation

(ALCUCOA), established in 2003 that fall under the remit of the National Network of Quality Assurance Agencies (NNQAA). But despite the availability of QA mechanisms through voluntary accreditation, the uptake to this remains low in HEIs due to costs, diminishing enrolment and the perceived lack of industry and program accreditation connections (Conchada & Tiongco, 2015).

An institution's commitment to excellence is further manifested in the awarding of Centers of Development (COD) and Centers of Excellence (COE) for degree programs within the university. For a degree program to become a COD or COE, HEIs must demonstrate consistent excellent performance in instruction, research and publication, extension and linkages, and faculty qualifications. Additionally, for an HEI to be conferred a COD or COE, it must have successfully hurdled external quality assurance and accreditation. CHED data show only 182 HEIs have COEs and CODs (7.61% of the total HEIs) with observed regional disparities since COEs and CODs are located within the developed urban centers of the NCR and CALABARZON (CHED, n.d.-a). The below-average quality of Philippine HEIs is also evident in the passing percentages of its graduates in professional board exams across different disciplines. For years 2014–2018, the average passing percentage in pre-board examinations was less than 40% (CHED, n.d.-e). Such dismal performance may be an outcome of the lack of qualified faculty who teach these professional programs. Regarding faculty qualifications, barely half of the faculty/academic members in the country have graduate degrees, and only 15% have a doctorate (PhD). In addition, only 29% of HEIs have accredited programs and more academic staff with master's and PhD degrees work in private HEIs (CHED, n.d.-b).

In recent years, the mandate for quality assurance among Philippine HEIs has extended beyond local accreditation to international QA initiatives. Among the international standards that Philippine HEIs have participated in include the Times Higher Education (THE) World University Ranking and the Quacquarelli Symonds (QS) ranking systems. In a study by Florida and Quinto (2015), comparisons were made on the criteria adopted by local versus international accrediting agencies which revealed differences. Local accrediting agencies focused more on instruction, community involvement, faculty profile, library collections, laboratory facilities and administration, while international rankings focused on the citations of published articles, among others (p. 58). In 2023, only four HEIs in the Philippines are included in the Times Higher Education World Asia university rankings. It should be noted that the bulk of government support for R&D is biased toward state-run HEIs. However, using productivity metrics based on Scopus entries, it was revealed that among state-run HEIs, only 9%, or 10 out of 112 state universities, produced cited scholarly work in 2013–2014. In contrast, 6 private HEIs contributed to 19% of Scopus entries in 2013 and 24% in 2014 (Regadio & Tullao, 2015). Notwithstanding, projects that aim to improve quality, research and development, and faculty performance include CHED's Philippine-California Advanced Research Institute (PCARI) project initiated in 2013, and the *Philippine Qualifications Framework Act* (2017), with the latter aiming to "align domestic qualification standards with the international framework" (GoP, 2017, section 4a).

Related to quality concerns is the relevance of programs in the HE sector. Orbeta et al. (2016) evaluated the effectiveness of Philippine HEIs in responding to labor market changes. Wage premium analysis at the discipline level indicate that there is an imbalance in the graduates provided by HEIs with an oversupply in agriculture, humanities, and theology, while lacking graduates in other disciplines such as allied medical sciences, social sciences, business, and law (p. 18). An oversupply deflates wages, whereas graduates in underrepresented disciplines tend to receive higher wages. Recognizing the role of higher education in driving economic and social progress, the issue of whether Philippine HEIs succeed in their purpose warrants a complicated response. The issue of job-education mismatch has prompted strong criticisms against HEIs, where training and skills obtained are seen as inadequate (Tutor et al., 2021). Quality in HE is also measured against the successful performance of graduates in professional board licensure examinations. However, the lack of a database on specific HEI categories relative to the graduates' performance on board examinations hinders the development of interventions or clear policies in this regard (EDCOM, 2024).

Internationalization

In the Philippines, the initiatives for both home-based internationalization and cross-border education are neither absent nor new. One example would be the presence of student mobility programs in Philippine HEIs, although relatively lower in comparison to its Southeast Asian neighbors like Thailand and Malaysia (Killingley & Illieva, 2015). Recognizing the move toward internationalization, Valdez and Steel (2014) narrate how Philippine universities have engaged toward this goal through the hiring of foreign academic staff, undergoing accreditation, and conducting extensive partnerships with international universities. The CHED also presupposes that internationalization as a strategy would serve to enhance the quality of Philippine HE, uphold its reputation in niche programs, and serve as the mechanism for partnerships with global academic and economic communities. In 2016, the Commission issued the *"Policy Framework and Strategies on the Internationalization of Philippine Higher Education"* defining internationalization in HE as:

> the integration of international/intercultural dimensions to HEIs' purpose, functions, and/or delivery; it involves a process of interchange of higher education between nations, between national systems of higher education, and between institutions of higher education. It is the expansion of higher learning within and beyond national borders and centers of scholarly studies. Internationalization of higher education is a much broader concept than cross-border education. (CMO 55, s. 2016, Section 1, p. 2)

Pushing for greater internationalization in the country, in 2022, a technical working group for Transnational Education (TNE) was formed for CHED as a result of the *Transnational Education Law* being established in 2019. But as early as 2003, CHED has already set out policies and guidelines on international partnerships and TNE. One aspect of the Philippine education system that has boosted the drive toward TNE is the country's use of English as a medium of instruction in HEIs. Low living costs and tuition fees in the country have seen some increase in international students (Symaco, 2017). Despite this, the country has one of the lowest numbers of international students among the ASEAN. Although the Philippines has become a popular destination for learners of English as a second language and is sometimes characterized as the home of the world's "budget" English teacher, the data suggest that this competitive advantage has not yet been realized (McGeown, 2012, p. 13).

The shift toward establishing collaboration among HEIs in ASEAN may be construed as the foreseeable result of regional cooperation in trade, culture and education through the ASEAN 2020 *"One Vision, One Identity, One Community."* Zhang (2020) in a documentary analysis of published ASEAN strategic plans and policies covering the period of 2011–2018 inferred that ASEAN regional cooperation serves social, cultural and economic dimensions. Foremost in the agenda is the development of an ASEAN identity and awareness among the youth. Secondly, the ASEAN agenda reflects a common commitment to democracy, human rights, and peace-oriented curriculum. Moreover, the constructivist role of higher education is deemed as means to develop regional solidarity, and to develop human resources and highly skilled labor in response to the demands of the knowledge economy. Within ASEAN, stakeholders in the study recognize the openness of HE instructional systems and support for the international mobility of students, researchers, academic programs, and university research among ASEAN HEIs (Jamaludin et al., 2020). In the Philippines, Albia and Chan (2017) maintain that the country has undertaken specific initiatives in response to the ASEAN HE regionalism vision. Such response would include: the adoption of OBE at the program level, establishment of linkages with other ASEAN universities, pursuit of international QA, investments in resource-building, and changes in leadership within HEIs.

With the emphasis on globalization in higher education, Philippine universities are likewise confronted with both opportunities and challenges in engaging within the region. Greater HE standardization in the ASEAN is evidenced through the formation of the ASEAN University Network (AUN). Established in 1995, AUN provides a systematic mechanism to support collaboration, integration, and government investment in universities in Southeast Asia. There are currently 3 (out of the 30) Philippine HEI members in the AUN. Also, the ASEAN Mutual Recognition Arrangements (MRA) are set to align credentials and competencies across select professions for greater labor mobility within the region. However, this goal of labor mobility has not been fully achieved. Ofreneo (2017) attributes this to the lack of articulation among ASEAN nations on a common framework, given that ASEAN countries have differing practices for the recognition of competencies and credentials of HEI graduates.

CLOSING REMARKS

This chapter has discussed issues of access, quality, and internationalization in Philippine HE. The role of Philippine HEIs in producing the needed labor force for economic growth and social integration, alongside its contribution to achieving SDG4 is emphasized. The country's HE has also evolved throughout its long colonial history up to its current environment that focuses on regional integration and internationalization. At present, the HE landscape is composed of private and public HEIs with overlapping thrusts and programs. The complementarity between private and public HEIs remains disputed with government policy support and governance largely skewed toward public HEIs. Despite its best efforts, HEIs in the country also struggle to meet standards and reforms needed to compete globally.

Regionalization has indeed created both opportunities and challenges for Philippine universities to thrive in a competitive academic landscape in Asia, through the prevalence of quality assurance and rankings. Nonetheless, issues of access and quality to HE are highlighted through existing variations in per capita income and in-country regional development. Struggles in HE were also exacerbated by the COVID-19 emergency which highlighted among others, the lack of educational resources, digital infrastructure, and relevant teacher training. The pandemic and other possible disruptions to HE delivery in the future reveal the vulnerabilities and unevenness among the capacities of HEIs across the country. The country's HE sector would need to strike a balance in resolving issues of access, relevance and quality within and beyond its borders, where strategic government support and a favorable policy environment are needed.

REFERENCES

Albia, J. E., & Chan, S. J. (2017). Understanding regionalisation in Philippine higher education. *Higher Education Evaluation and Development, 11*(2), 95–110. https://doi.org/10.1108/heed-07-2017-0003

Bayudan-Dacuycuy, C., Orbeta, A., & Ortiz, K. (2023, May). The quest for quality and equity in the Philippine higher education: Where to from here? *PIDS Policy Notes.* Philippine Institute for Development Studies.

Commission on Higher Education (CHED). (2003). *CHED Memorandum Order No. 6, s. 2003. Policies and guidelines on transnational education.*

Commission on Higher Education (CHED). (2012). *CHED Memorandum Order No. 46, s. 2012. Policy standard to enhance quality assurance in Philippine higher education through an outcomes-based and typology based QA.*

Commission on Higher Education (CHED). (2014). *Handbook on typology, outcomes-based education, and institutional sustainability assessment.*

Commission on Higher Education (CHED). (2016). *CHED Memorandum Order No. 55, s. 2016. Policy framework and strategies on the internationalization of Philippine higher education.*

Commission on Higher Education (CHED). (2019). *Grant of autonomous and deregulated status by evaluation to private higher education institutions.*

Commission on Higher Education (CHED). (2020). *Facts and figures.* Retrieved January 11, 2024, from https://ched.gov.ph/2020-higher-education-facts-and-figures/

Commission on Higher Education (CHED). (2023a). *CHED Memorandum Order No. 2, s. 2023. Standardized guidelines on the implementation of the Tulong Dunong program for state univerisities and colleges for the first semester of academic year 2023-24.*

Commission on Higher Education (CHED). (2023b). *CHED Memorandum Order No. 5, s. 2023. Tertiary education subsidy (TES) slots for fiscal year 2023.*

Commission on Higher Education (CHED). (n.d.-a). *Extension on the validity period of designated COEs and CODs.* Retrieved March 2, 2024, from https://ched.gov.ph/wp-content/uploads/Extension-of-validity-2019-List-of-COE-and-CODs_compressed.pdf

Higher Education in the Philippines: Issues and Challenges
101

Commission on Higher Education (CHED). (n.d.-b). *Higher education data and indicators*. Retrieved March 2, 2024, from https://ched.gov.ph/wp-content/uploads/Higher-Education-Data-and-Indicators-AY-2009-10-to-AY-2019-20.pdf

Commission on Higher Education (CHED). (n.d.-c). *About the commission*. Retrieved January 11, 2024, from https://ched.gov.ph/about-us/

Commission on Higher Education (CHED). (n.d.-d). *Distribution of HEIs*. Retrieved January 11, 2024, from https://ched.gov.ph/distribution-of-higher-education-institutions-by-institution-type-ay-2018-19/

Commission on Higher Education (CHED). (n.d.-e). *PRC national passing percentage*. Retrieved March 2, 2024, from https://ched.gov.ph/wp-content/uploads/2004_2018-PRC-natl-pass-rate-from-2393-heis-as-of-18June2019.pdf

Conchada, M., & Tiongco, M. (2015). *A review of the accreditation system for Philippine higher education institutions*. Retrieved January 11, 2024, from https://ideas.repec.org/p/phd/dpaper/dp_2015-30.html

EDCOM. (2024). Complete citation second congressional commission on education (EDCOM). *Miseducation: The failed system of Philippine education, EDCOM II year one report*. Second Congressional Commission on Education.

Felipe, C. (2023). *Universities, colleges seeking tuition hike (Philippine Star)*. Retrieved January 11, 2024, from https://www.philstar.com/headlines/2023/05/12/2265686/universities-colleges-seeking-tuition-hike

Florida, J., & Quinto, M. (2015, October). Quality indicators in higher education institutions: Implications to global competitiveness. *The Online Journal of Quality in Higher Education, 2*.

Government of the Philippines (GoP). (2017). PQF Act (Republic Act 10968).

Jamaludin, R., McKay, E., & Ledger, S. (2020). Are we ready for Education 4.0 within ASEAN higher education institutions? Thriving for knowledge, industry and humanity in a dynamic higher education ecosystem? *Journal of Applied Research in Higher Education, 12*(5), 1161–1173. https://doi.org/10.1108/JARHE-06-2019-0144

Killingley, P., & Illieva, J. (2015). *Opportunities and challenges in the internationalization of the Philippine higher education sector*. British Council.

McGeown, K. (2012). The Philippines: The World's Budget English Teacher. *BBC News Service*. https://www.bbc.com/news/business-20066890

National Economic Development Authority (NEDA). (n.d.). *Goal 4 in numbers*. Retrieved January 11, 2024, from https://sdg.neda.gov.ph/goal-4/

Ofreneo, R. (2017). *Mobility of skilled labor in the ASEAN: Free or unfree?* Paper delivered at the Policy Forum on "Legal Framework on ASEAN Mutual Recognition Arrangements (MRAs): The Need for National Regulatory Change," sponsored by the King Prajadhipok's Institute (KPI) with the cooperation of the National Assembly of Thailand, June 22, 2017, Royal Princess Hotel, Bangkok, Thailand.

Orbeta, A., Gonzales, K., & Cortes, S. (2016). Are higher education institutions responsive to changes in the labor market? *Discussion Paper Series 2016-08*. Philippine Institute for Development Studies.

Orbeta, A., & Paqueo, V. (2017). *Who benefits and loses from an untargeted tuition subsidy for students in SUCs?* Retrieved January 11, 2024, from https://serp-p.pids.gov.ph/publication/public/view?slug=who-benefits-and-loses-from-an-untargeted-tuition-subsidy-for-students-in-sucs

Quality Assurance Agency for Higher Education and the British Council. (2018). *Country report: The Republic of the Philippines*.

Quitoras, M. C. L., & Abuso, J. E. (2021). best practices of higher education institutions (HEIs) for the development of research culture in the Philippines. *Pedagogical Research, 6*(1), em0087. https://doi.org/10.29333/pr/9355

Regadio, C., & Tullao, T. (2015). The role of the government in enhancing research productivity of SUCs and private HEIs in the Philippines. *Conference proceedings presented at the DLSU Research Congress 2015*, De La Salle University, Manila, Philippines, March 2-4, 2015.

Rodriguez, J., Valenzuela, M., & Ayuyao, N. (2018). TQM paradigm for higher education in the Philippines. *Quality Assurance in Education, 26*(1), 101–114. https://doi.org/10.1108/QAE-12-2015-004

Santiago, A., Largoza, G., & Conchada, M. (2007). What does it cost a university to educate one student? *International Journal of Education Policy and Leadership*, *2*(2), 1–11.

Symaco, L. P. (2017). Education, language policy and language use in the Philippines. *Language Problems and Language Planning*, *41*(1), 87–102. https://doi.org/10.1075/lplp.41.1.05sym

Symaco, L. P., & Bustos, M. T. (2021). Overview of education in the Philippines. In L. P. Symaco & M. Hayden (Eds.), *International handbook on education in South East Asia*. Springer. https://doi.org/10.1007/978-981-16-8136-3_1-3

Tan, E. (2017). Quality, inequality, and recent education reform. *The Philippine Review of Economics*, *LIV*(2), 110–136.

Tutor, M., Orbeta, A., & Miraflor, J. (2021). *The 4th Philippine Graduate Tracer Study: Examining higher education as a pathway to employment, citizenship, and life satisfaction from the learner's perspective*. Philippine Institute for Development Studies.

United Nations Population Fund Philippines (UNFPA). (2023a). *The Philippines today has the largest proportion of young people in its history*. Retrieved June 10, 2023, from https://philippines.unfpa.org/en/node/15309#:~:text=The%20Philippines%20today%20has%20the,percent%20of%20the%20Philippine%20population

United Nations Population Fund Philippines (UNFPA). (2023b). *The Philippines today has the highest teenage pregnancy rate in Southeast Asia, with 10 percent of the Philippine population*. Retrieved from UNFPA Philippines website on June 10, 2023.

Valdez, P., & Steel, K. (2014). The representation of internationalization in higher education in the Philippines: The case of the university newsletter. *Asia-Pacific Education Researcher*, *23*(1), 125–133. https://doi.org/10.1007/s40299-013-0086-9

Villegas, B. (2022). *More appropriate role of SUCs (Manila Bulletin)*. Retrieved January 11, 2024, from https://mb.com.ph/2022/10/11/more-appropriate-role-of-sucs/

Yee, K. (2022). The changing landscape of Philippine higher education: Going beyond the public and private debate. In F. Paragas (Ed.), *Contemporary issues in Philippine higher education: Public policy monograph series*. University of the Philippines Center for Integrative and Development Studies Higher Education Research and Policy Reform Program.

Zhang, Y. (2020). Higher education regionalism in Southeast Asia: Integrating multiple roles for regional development. In H. De Wit & T. DeLaquil (Eds.), *Innovative and inclusive internationalization: Proceedings of the WES-CIHE Summer Institute*. Boston College Center for Higher Education. https://doi.org/10.3102/1584059

CHAPTER 8

HIGHER EDUCATION IN SINGAPORE: CHALLENGES FOR INSTITUTIONS OF CONTINUOUS LEARNING

Shien Chue

Centre for Research and Development in Learning (CRADLE), Nanyang Technological University, Singapore

ABSTRACT

This chapter explores the landscape of higher education in Singapore as the nation positions itself to emerge stronger after the pandemic. A focus on three major issues facing higher education – digital transformation, job readiness of graduates, and access to quality education, describes education-based initiatives for addressing these challenges in Singapore. Local autonomous universities are woven into the tapestry of sustainable growth and development within Singapore's economy. Connections between the development of education-based initiatives are made to illustrate how these institutions of continuous learning are positioning for relevance considering current developments and to suggest some areas for enhancement for promoting lifelong learning opportunities for all.

Keywords: Higher education; continuing education; lifelong learning; digital transformation; job-readiness; applied learning pathways; curriculum and pedagogy

Higher Education in Southeast Asia
International Perspectives on Education and Society, Volume 49, 103–118
Copyright © 2025 by Shien Chue
Published under exclusive licence by Emerald Publishing Limited
ISSN: 1479-3679/doi:10.1108/S1479-367920240000049008

INTRODUCTION

Developing higher education in Singapore is a key strategy for engineering sustainable growth and development in Singapore's economy (Gopinathan & Lee, 2011). Since the independence of Singapore in 1965, the state has placed a strong emphasis on education, both in terms of achieving the goal of universal primary and secondary education and the continual expansion of higher education. With an increasingly competitive global marketplace and the advancement of today's knowledge-based economy, the Singapore Government has conducted comprehensive public policy reviews and implemented a variety of education system reforms to promote quality education (Natarajan et al., 2020).

Central to Singapore's vision for Higher Education Institutions (HEIs) is to create a culture of lifelong learning for learners to engage in continuing learning at different junctures of their life journeys (Chan, 2022a). As a result, HEIs need to engage with different modes of pedagogy and andragogy to create multiple learning pathways for working adults. Notably, digital transformation disrupts longstanding practices of learning (James, 2020), and enabling learning to become a ubiquitous activity for anyone will certainly require a concerted effort from key stakeholders.

However, strong headwinds from challenges in digital transformation, preparing graduates to be job-ready and access to quality education are also disrupting how HEIs can inoculate a culture of lifelong learning. Local universities are tightly woven into the growth and development of our country's economy. Within the education system of Singapore, how are these institutions facing up to the above challenges for ingraining a culture of lifelong learning for the nation? This chapter will trace the key essence of digital transformation, graduate job-readiness, and access to quality education to highlight the organisational landscape within HEIs for tackling these issues for achieving the goal of inclusive quality education and promoting lifelong learning opportunities for all.

BACKGROUND OF HIGHER EDUCATION IN SINGAPORE

Singapore is a small country with human resources as its only natural resource (Ng, 2013) and thus, human resource development is a key strategy to meet the challenges of industrialisation for economic growth. This was realised early with a strong emphasis placed on education and technical training (Osman-Gani & Tan, 1998) within a three-tier public higher education system consisting of universities, polytechnics and the Institute of Technical Education (Natarajan et al., 2020). Since the early 1980s, through governance and funding systems put in place to assure the quality of university education, the Singapore Government has expanded the capacity of the universities to meet the challenges of industrialisation.

The roots of the National University of Singapore (NUS) can be traced back to 1905 as a modest medical school and had evolved to form the University of Malaya in 1949 to serve the education needs of the people of Singapore and the Federation of Malaya. The Singapore campus of the University of Malaya became an autonomous institution known as the University of Singapore in 1962. Following the break of Singapore from Malaysia in 1965, it became the NUS when the University of Singapore and Nanyang University, a privately funded Chinese university, merged in 1980 (NUS, n.d.).

With the establishment of the NUS in 1980 and the Nanyang Technological University (NTU) in 1991, was an increased cohort participation in the sector from 5% in 1980 to 21% in 2001 (Singapore Department of Statistics, 2002, p. 62). To meet the rising number of graduates required to service the economy, the third university, Singapore Management University (SMU) was established in 2000. As both NUS and NTU were developed largely based on the British university model, an alternative model from the United States underpinned the tertiary education system in SMU to add a new dimension to tertiary education in Singapore. To encourage competition and avoid wasteful duplication, the three universities developed their unique characteristics and niches. While NUS performs its role as a comprehensive university and NTU is a specialist institution in engineering and business disciplines, SMU would focus on management, business and economics to service the business and service sectors of the local economy (Mok & Lee, 2003). While there is no published data to date regarding caps on enrolment in specific degree programmes, access to higher education is critically supported through the automatic provision of tuition grants for every Singaporean undergraduate by the Ministry of Education to cover a substantial portion of the fees of the degree programmes (Tan, 2022).

With the emergence of the knowledge-based economy in the 21st century, the Singapore government identified globalisation as one of the driving forces behind rapid changes in knowledge and information (Singapore-Government, 1999). This was a phenomenon impacting the country's economic competitiveness as well as the flow of knowledge and people amidst uncertainty and disorientation. In June 1997, Prime Minister Goh Chok Tong announced a blueprint for reforming the education system through curriculum restructuring and digitalisation for developing citizens capable of making good decisions as the nation transforms into a knowledge economy. This was an education reform that required a mindset change among Singaporeans to bring about a spirit of innovative learning by doing, and self-improvement for achieving the ambition of national excellence (Goh, 1997). Critically, this education reform reiterated the important role of education in managing the impact of globalisation by preparing workers and the next generation for lifelong learning and employability (Goh, 1999).

In response to the above changing social and economic context, universities have a strategic role by strengthening their capacities in the dissemination, creation, and application of knowledge. There are currently six local universities in Singapore, namely the NUS, NTU, SMU, Singapore University of Technology and Design (SUTD), Singapore University of Social Sciences (SUSS), and the Singapore Institute of Technology (SIT). Of interest are the younger universities established as part of the nation's strategy to become a global education hub. The SUTD based on a strategic partnership with the Massachusetts Institute of Technology and Zhejiang University in China is but one example of how local universities form partnerships with quality foreign universities to expand and diversify the local higher education landscape (Chan & Ng, 2008). Similarly, the SIT established in 2009 provides polytechnic diploma graduates with higher education opportunities with strong applied pathways. Its model of applied university education focuses on integrating work and study, as well as building deep links to industry particularly useful for professionals in areas such as nursing, allied health, and early childhood education. With applied degree pathways focusing on practice-oriented learning, opportunities are widened for learners to pursue their degree-level qualification in Singapore.

Over the past three decades, Singapore's university system has expanded and transformed from an elite system into a mass system, in which over 40% of the age cohort is enrolled in one of the six publicly funded autonomous universities (Tan, 2022). Notably the sixth university, the SUSS granted autonomous status under the ambit of the Ministry of Education in 2017 which previously was known as SIM University, a privately-funded, not-for-profit institution. The SUSS embraced the mission to develop lifelong learners who are professionally competent, and socially conscious through experiential and applied learning for fresh school leavers, working adults, and senior learners (SUSS, n.d.). Table 1 presents the enrolment data from 2018 to 2022 for the various HEIs in Singapore described above. Interestingly, the increase in enrolment in newer institutions such as SIT and SUSS could suggest their growing reputation and the establishment of new programmes appealing to current student interest and industry needs.

More recently in 2022, the Ministry of Education announced the establishment of the University of the Arts Singapore (UAS) for 2024 for nurturing learners at the intersection of technology and art (Chan, 2022c). Within the structure of this young university is the alliance of the Nanyang Academy of Fine Arts (NAFA) and the LASALLE College of the Arts, both institutions with decades of experience in arts education in Singapore to offer a range of publicly funded

Table 1. Enrolment Figures 2018–2022.

Name of Institution (Year of Establishment)	Enrolment Figures (2018–2022)					
	Sex	2018	2019	2020	2021	2022
NUS (1980)	Total (MF)	29,037	30,033	30,420	31,191	30,842
	F	14,981	15,440	15,262	15,693	15,405
NTU (1991)	Total (MF)	22,813	23,063	23,758	24,074	23,876
	F	10,896	11,120	11,499	11,352	11,085
SMU (2000)	Total (MF)	8,182	8,656	9,144	9,580	9,883
	F	4,486	4,855	5,276	5,512	5,512
SIT (2009)	Total (MF)	6,951	7,714	8,201	9,015	9,688
	F	2,905	3,128	3,423	3,725	4,062
SUTD (2009)	Total (MF)	1,658	1,730	1,406	1,429	1,409
	F	626	624	518	534	502
SUSS (2005)	Total (MF)	2,049	2,601	3,153	3,656	3,910
	F	1,399	1,683	2,014	2,312	2,394

Source: Ministry of Education (MOE, 2023), p. 44.

degree programmes from visual to performing arts for growing the diverse talent pool towards making Singapore a creative, innovation-driven city and a thought leader in the creative arts in Southeast Asia (Ng, 2022).

The importance placed on education by the government is also reflected through education spending where publicly funded autonomous universities received an estimated Singapore (S) \$2.65 billion, a substantial sum of the total Ministry of Education budget of S\$14.75 billion in 2024 (Singapore-Government, 2024). Recognising these universities as engines of knowledge creation alongside plenty of job opportunities offered due to the government's policy of rapid industrialisation, unemployment has been kept low (Gopinathan & Lee, 2011). This is further supported by an annual Joint Autonomous Universities Graduate Employment Survey reporting in each of the three years from 2018 to 2020 where more than 90% of first-degree graduates from four publicly funded autonomous universities managed to find full-time employment within six months of graduation (Ang, 2021, as cited by Tan, 2022), thus pointing towards the important role of publicly funded universities in preparing their students for the workforce.

SUSTAINABLE DEVELOPMENT GOAL 4.0 AND HIGHER EDUCATION IN SINGAPORE

Adopted in 2015, the 2030 Agenda for Sustainable Development aims to contribute to sustainable social development for all and to ensure the survival of the planet for generations to come. Within this agenda are 17 goals (SDGs) to (i) eliminate extreme poverty; (ii) reduce inequalities and injustices; (iii) promote peace and justice; and (iv) solve the climate crisis (United Nations & Department of Economic & Social Affairs, 2015). SDG4 is specifically aimed at education, calling on countries to 'ensure inclusive and equitable quality education and promote lifelong learning opportunities for all'. This requires higher education to act as pivotal change agents for making this goal an integral part of research, teaching and study at HEIs. However, accomplishing this goal can be complex. While the Ministry of Education has achieved its undergraduate enrolment target of 40% of each age cohort in publicly funded autonomous universities (Tan, 2022), the constant challenge of responding to global trends like the shift towards knowledge-based societies, and digital transformation affecting the way people live and work remain.

Singapore supports the 2030 Agenda and keenly understands the challenges of sustainable development as a small country with limited land and a void of natural resources. Specific to SDG4.3 which targets equal access for all women and men to affordable and quality technical, vocational and tertiary education, including university, data reveals a high participant rate of 92.7% for youths aged 16–24 in education and training with lower participation of 56.6% for adults aged 25–65, the working age population of which 52.9% are females (Department of Statistics Singapore, 2022).

Also, Singapore participated in the Support to Higher Education in the ASEAN Region (SHARE) Programme which organised the 14th Policy Dialogue in 2022 online to explore how partnerships amongst higher education stakeholders can increase impacts on the 17 SDGs, in particular SDG 4.0 to ensure inclusive and equitable quality education and to promote lifelong learning opportunities for all. The state's commitment to keeping education affordable for all Singaporeans was also reiterated by the Minister of Education (Chan, 2022b) through the provision of generous support for universities to build up endowments to achieve self-sustainability and to ensure no Singaporean is denied a place in university for financial reasons.

However, the pandemic has with great force and speed magnified the fault lines of higher education where public spending for higher education is expected to decrease. This is not helped by the massification of higher education as a means to boost the quality of human resources is also demanding policy initiatives from HEIs to balance and coordinate between research and teaching (Shin, 2015). Closer to home, Singapore believes SDGs should focus on being concrete and making substantive improvements. Challenges remain for higher education in Singapore, primarily, digital transformation, job-readiness of graduates, and access to quality education are shifting the goalpost for universities to examine how they can engage working adults to learn by tapping on individual motivations and with different modes of teaching and learning underpinned by digital technologies.

DIGITAL TRANSFORMATION
AND HIGHER EDUCATION

In a rapidly evolving digital era, Singapore is dedicated to transforming the nation through technology. Established in 2017, the Smart Nation and Digital Government Office (SNDGO), under the Prime Minister's Office, strategizes Smart Nation projects to develop digital capabilities for public and industry adoption. Taking a collective approach to building a Smart Nation with the Government Technology Agency (GovTech), both entities are collectively known as the Smart Nation and Digital Government Group (SNDGG). This adaptive and innovative nature of Singapore is also evident in the digital transformation of higher education.

Digital transformation presents HEIs with opportunities to design, develop, and retain competitive advantages (Hashim et al., 2022). As a pioneer in Southeast Asia in the acceleration of life-long learning for its citizens (Guan et al., 2015), online learning was introduced in Singapore in 2011 when the government found the potential of online platforms to facilitate learners' self-directed learning (Tay et al., 2021). Critically, HEIs in Singapore have actively adapted to the challenges of digitalisation for learning innovations with support from the government's enforcement and universities' support (Tay et al., 2021; Watermeyer et al., 2021).

In the *Report of the Committee on the Future Economy: Pioneers of the Next Generation* (Ministry of Trade & Industry, 2017), seven interconnected strategies mapped out ways for preparing the nation for the technological challenges ahead.

Three strategies explicitly mentioned are higher education and adult learning (i) deepen and diversify our international connections, (ii) acquire and utilise deep skills, and (iii) build strong digital capabilities. The first education strategy for deepening and diversifying international connections can be pursued in education through the Global Innovation Alliance (GIA) initiative intended to build new networks through which youth can facilitate innovation. The alliances formed between Singapore's institutes of higher learning and major innovation hubs around the world also facilitate collaborations with overseas partners (Gleason, 2018). The second education strategy relevant to higher education relates to the acquisition and utilisation of deep skills. Where deep skills include analytical and evaluative capacities combined with complex problem-solving and effective team collaboration capabilities, this policy required two significant shifts in social understandings of education: the acquisition of deeper skills that create value and lifelong learning of such skills (Gleason, 2018). Concretely, research centres and laboratories were jointly established between universities and industry partners to foster entrepreneurial activity, along with launchpads that aimed to encourage technology commercialisation and start-up development (Lim, 2014). Within the higher education curriculum for imbuing students with the necessary entrepreneurial skills are programmes such as NTU's Renaissance Engineering Programme, SMU's Master of Innovation and NUS Faculty Engineering's Innovation and Design-Centric Programme (Woo, 2018).

At the Asia-Pacific Association for International Education (APAIE) 2018 Conference hosted by local universities to discuss the transformations and disruptions brought about by Industry 4.0 on higher education in the Asia Pacific, Education Minister Ong Ye Kung called for Singapore to "examine more carefully the pathways that are most suitable for different groups of students, to help them achieve these good outcomes" (Ong, 2018, para 13). This required universities to look beyond measures of academic achievements, employment outcomes and rankings to also focus on learners' resilience, risk-taking, and creativity. To do so, Minister Ong stressed the importance of an education system that supports lifelong learning (Lung, 2018). As such, university programmes such as the NUS Lifelong Learners Programme encourage alumni to continue to invest in their personal and professional growth to remain relevant to the evolving demands of the workforce (NUS, n.d.). As part of the programme, student enrolment is valid for 20 years and beyond from the point of undergraduate/postgraduate admission. Nanyang Technical University (NTU), SUSS, and several of Singapore's polytechnic tertiary schools have also launched more than 500 skills-based modular courses between 2015 and 2017 (Gleason, 2018), further bolstering resources to provide Singaporeans with deep skill learning.

The third strategy for building strong digital capabilities was a response to the new industries emerging from digitisation and the resulting big data production. This requires strong human capacity in data analytics and cybersecurity for supporting "high-potential growth industries" as well as bolstering core capabilities to support digitalisation in other industries. This requires joint laboratories between industry stakeholders and the government to train data scientists (Gleason, 2018) and collaboration with tertiary education institutions has been consistent throughout the development of Smart Nation Singapore. Specifically, within the SkillsFuture for Digital Workplace (SFDW), a national initiative that gears Singaporeans with foundational digital skills and a mindset for digital transformation, HEIs combine efforts with Smart Nation and SkillsFuture to upskill and educate a workforce for digital transformation through bite-size professional learning modules on digital transformation. Critically with the pandemic upending learning in traditional classroom settings into virtual spaces, the importance of digital transformation has hastened the timeline for digital transformation in education with online home-based learning and acceleration of blended learning for the school system in Singapore (Hung et al., 2020; Tan et al., 2022).

JOB-READINESS OF GRADUATES

While employment prospects of graduates remain high for most (NUS, 2022b; Teng, 2019), studies conducted within the Asia Pacific region have raised at least three challenges that HEIs encounter while preparing graduates to be job-ready. The first challenge lies in the discrepancy between the HE curriculum and workplace requirements. For example in Malaysia, graduates were reported to lack critical dispositions, technological competency, and attributes such as multitasking capacity (Mohd Salleh et al., 2019). This has led to a mismatch in skills between employers' expectations and graduate attributes. Similarly, a quarter of Vietnamese university graduates are either struggling to secure a job that is related to their degrees or meet employer's expectations of employable skills that include soft skills (creative thinking, information technology, leadership, and problem-solving) and good work attitude (Nguyen et al., 2018). This is not helped when employers from the six Asia-Pacific Economic Cooperation (APEC) nations – Australia, Singapore, Vietnam, Malaysia, Taiwan, and Indonesia – shared also their difficulties in securing graduate employees due to their deficient technical skills and undeveloped workplace competencies (Cameron et al., 2015). Industry reports from Myanmar and Indonesia have also reported insufficient focus on preparing students to be work-ready in terms of their administrative abilities, project management, and ability to apply their theory into practice (Myint et al., 2021; Nurjanah & Ana, 2022).

The gap between higher education curriculum provision and workplace organisation requirements is further complicated by rapidly changing needs in education and practices of workers at the workplace. Universities are under growing pressure to develop a 'smart curriculum' that prepares their students for the new Industry 4.0 which is characterised by technological advancements such as data analytics, artificial intelligence, and digitalisation (Borg et al., 2019). Institutes of higher learning in Malaysia have responded by shifting towards a 'smart curriculum' that incorporates concepts such as creative design thinking, information and communications technology (ICT), problem-solving, digital data management, and user experience (UX) to reflect the changing demands in the employment market (Teng et al., 2019). HEIs in Singapore have also responded to the incoming Fourth Industrial Revolution in their unique ways. At the NUS, initiatives to introduce new courses in the field of artificial intelligence, technology, and data science have been rolled out. In 2022, all NTU students will have a compulsory interdisciplinary module on science technology, and sustainability. Similarly, to prepare students for the technological transformation in business and entrepreneurship, the SUSS has also introduced digitalisation electives on cybersecurity and the Internet of Things (IoT) (Lim, 2022).

Apart from developing a 'smart curriculum' that empowers graduates to harness technological skills, HEIs are also pressed by other changing needs in the workplace. Workplace organisation seeks higher-order contemporary skills such as critical thinking, collaboration, and creativity that better enhance job performance (Sarrico et al., 2017). This raises the need for universities to incorporate personal competencies into the current curriculum, which poses a challenge for HEIs to forecast and anticipate future needs while rethinking existing approaches and curricula.

The absence of a uniform model or definition to accurately assess graduate work readiness for the changing workplace (Prikshat et al., 2019) can be problematic and this is not helped by the different graduate attributes that local universities aim to nurture (Waring et al., 2019). For instance, NTU focuses on harnessing their graduates with the 5 C's of character, creativity, competence, communication, and civic-mindedness while NUS have identified attributes such as resilience, curiosity, adaptability, insight, emotional sensing, entrepreneurial thinking, pursuing convictions, and vision as key attributes in future-ready graduates. However, Jackson et al. (2013) argue that 'work-readiness' is distinct from employability attributes. Tomlinson (2008) similarly asserts work-readiness as an 'X Factor' that is difficult to describe but distinct from university-led employability. Work readiness is generally described as a concept associated with various labels such as job readiness, key competencies, and graduate employability. Which, work-readiness is defined as "a concept that encompasses individual students' ability to possess a range of skills and attributes that enable them to successfully transition into professional work. It encompasses both the perceived needs and competencies desired by employers and graduates themselves" (Borg et al., 2019, p. 53). Hence, work-readiness is not merely a set of graduate attributes pre-conceptualised but should also include a strategic focus on competencies preferred by the individual and the workplace.

In responding to these challenges, universities in Singapore have implemented a myriad of actions and programmes to equip students with the requisite professional and technical skills to be job-ready. This includes the provision of a fixed period of industry attachment that exposes undergraduates to the professional work culture and environment that aims to enhance job readiness (Mohd Salleh et al., 2019). For instance, some HEIs have taken on a dual Technical Vocational Education and Training (TVET) system that encourages learning to take place in two spaces school and the workplace (Nurjanah & Ana, 2022).

In August 2012, the Committee on University Education Pathways Beyond 2015 (CUEP), made a recommendation to create a new applied degree pathway. The applied pathway was to focus on the practical application of specialised knowledge and to prepare learners for specific professions with a strong connection with the industry and economy. As a result, the SIT and the SUSS were identified as the two applied universities for this mission. Alongside, all six autonomous universities in Singapore offer and encourage students to independently source for internships or have the option for universities to place them in internship programs both locally and overseas to create a talent pipeline for the work industries (Chue et al., 2022). The impact of these efforts is corroborated by high employment rates reported with a significant number of graduates offered jobs through their internships during the recent joint graduate employment survey conducted by the six universities (Teng, 2019).

Universities are also revamping their curriculum and revising their learning pedagogy to enhance the work readiness of graduates. For example, NUS officially launched two digital platforms in 2022, the Internship-As-A-Service (IAAS) and conNectUS to prepare undergraduates for the working world (NUS, 2022a). Building on the tight-knit support from the NUS Centre for Future-ready Graduates (NUS CGF) and NUS Enterprise, IAAS provides NUS students with opportunities to gain work experience from short-term work gigs and internships from a broad spectrum of projects and companies. Complementing the IAAS is the conNectUS portal that connects NUS students and alumni in a professional and gated networking space. In this way, undergraduates' learning experiences are enriched through gaining career insights and development opportunities from their alumni and experienced professionals within their fields.

Critically, intertwining universities and workplace organisations allows for institutions to become more attuned and responsive to industry labour demands. This has prompted universities to provide education and training programmes that match the changing work context through a more balanced approach between theory and practice (Cameron et al., 2015). This is observed through the emergence of an evidence-based graduate program developed through collaborative open dialogue and feedback loops between stakeholders on industry trends and relevant graduate skills (Verma et al., 2018). For Singapore, in 2017, the Government Technology Agency of Singapore (GovTech) announced the signing of six Memorandums of Understanding (MOU) and two Memorandums of Intent (MOI) with eight HEIs to develop deep technical capabilities that correspond with their development plans towards a Smart Nation. Through this partnership, GovTech aims to provide hands-on training opportunities for over 300 learners through internships, attachments, final-year projects, and tech-related competitions (GovTech, 2017). Local universities have also launched Work-Study Degree programmes since 2017 to increase employer participation with academic institutions through co-design, co-assess and multi-modal means of delivering curricula closely tied to theory and practice.

ACCESS TO QUALITY EDUCATION

Quality education is emphasised in Singapore. Recognised worldwide as a robust system that produces results, the current emphasis is to transform learning from a focus on quantity to a focus on quality. Through a policy called "Teach Less Learn More" (Ng, 2008), these improvements in quality are innovative teaching practices and curricula responsive to schooling needs. However, current knowledge and skills are fast becoming obsolete requiring learners to acquire knowledge and skills even after graduation and adapting themselves to be productive and up-to-date (Li, 2022). Hence, even as quality education is emphasised within an education system that strives to give bring out the best in every child (Heng, 2014), the current pace of technological change in the rapidly changing knowledge economy is challenging Singapore to tweak its education system so that it may provide learners with a platform for lifelong learning, holistic education and creativity over the lifespan of the learner (Chan, 2022b).

In relation to higher education, accessibility has been increased by reducing heavy dependence on academic grades for admission decisions. The Ministry of Education announced in 2020 that the NUS, NTU, and SMU would begin giving more weightage to aptitude-based admission as part of the Ministry's plans to encourage greater flexibility in terms of education pathways. To equip students with lifelong learning skills through interdisciplinary education, Interdisciplinary Collaborative Core (ICC) courses at NTU allow learners to address issues such as ethics, sustainability, and entrepreneurship (NTU, n.d.). Similarly recognising the benefits of interdisciplinary learning, NUS has set up the College of Humanities and Sciences (CHS) that incorporates a new Common Curriculum consisting of integrated modules with problem-based pedagogy and the modules have also been adopted by the Faculty of Engineering and School of Design and Environment (NUS, 2021). Similarly, SMU has also adopted a multidisciplinary approach to develop a Core Curriculum that tailors a broad scope of topics, including pandemic-related issues to reflect global trends and dynamics (SMU, 2021).

Accessing quality education is also encapsulated in the promotion of lifelong learning for all. The Singapore Government launched the SkillsFuture initiative in 2014 where fostering a culture of lifelong learning was a key thrust out of the other three namely helping individuals make well-informed choices in education, training, and careers; developing an integrated responsive high-quality system of education and training; and promoting career development based on skills and mastery. The enactment of this movement was in the creation of the SkillsFuture Division within the Ministry of Education which currently plans and formulates policies to support continual learning through close collaboration with institutions of higher learning for developing multiple pathways for skills acquisition and mastery. In addition, the Continuing Education and Training (CET) Masterplan, launched by the Ministry of Education in 2008, was refreshed in 2014 to align formative education and adult learning as one seamless lifelong journey for adult workers.

Critically, strengthening the applied pathway is a critical route to social mobility and one that has increasingly been on the agenda of the government (Tharman, 2015). As the SkillsFuture movement is a long-term national movement to shift the societal mindset of mere academic achievement through a university degree to one where knowledge and skills are emphasised, whether, through formal education or work experience, it is now the order of the day for universities to pay attention to CET with an applied focus (Cheong, 2018). With study and work seen as interspersing with each other rather than cophasal, learning thus is envisioned as lifelong, skills-based, and passion-driven (Ong, 2019). This will require learners and organisations alike to weave across and between, sites of learning and work (Bound & Lee, 2014).

CODA

The 2030 Agenda for Sustainable Development has reinvigorated the concept of lifelong learning and reconnected it with its humanistic origins, with SDG4 promoting lifelong learning opportunities for all. Increasingly, universities are redefining themselves as centres of lifelong learning by diversifying their provision, tailoring it to the knowledge and skills needed for the economy and the diversity of learners (Milic, 2013). The irony of digital transformation is that it can disrupt longstanding relationships and practices making it difficult to conceive of new provisions that will serve the emerging needs of either the industry or the individuals (James, 2020). While HEIs in Singapore are responding through at least three interrelated dimensions: digitalisation of learning, wider participation through flexible learning pathways and preparing learners for the world of work, Singapore's education policies will need to continue to work towards balancing sociocultural expectations of formal certification with vocational training that encourages one to be able to adapt and handle workplace diversity (Tan, 2017). From the science of lifelong learning, evidence confirms that individual learners, lifestyle, psycho-socio-emotional and environmental factors interact with cognitive processes and learning across the lifespan (Goodwill & Chen, 2021), it may also be timely to pay attention to research emerging from this field for informing SDG4.

ACKNOWLEDGMENT

The author would like to acknowledge Cheryl Ong for her research assistance for this chapter.

REFERENCES

Borg, J., Scott-Young, C. M., & Turner, M. (2019). Smarter education: Leveraging stakeholder inputs to develop work ready curricula. In *Smart education and e-learning* (pp. 51–61). Springer. https://doi.org/10.1007/978-981-13-8260-4_5

Bound, H., & Lee, W. C. (2014). Teaching and learning across boundaries: Work, classroom and in between. *Advances in Scholarship of Teaching and Learning, 1*(1). https://tlc.suss.edu.sg/research/AdvSoTL/pdf/helen_bound.pdf

Cameron, R., Nankervis, A., Burgess, J., Brown, K., Connell, J., & Dhakal, S. P. (2015). *Enhancing work-readiness of vocational and higher education graduates: Asia Pacific Region.* 9th International Conference for Researching Work and Learning, 9–11 December, Singapore.

Chan, C. S. (2022a). *Speech by Minister Chan Chun Sing at the Launch of Prof Arnoud De Meyer's Book, "Building Excellence in Higher Education: Singapore's Experience", at the Singapore Management University.* MOE. Ministry of Education. https://www.moe.gov.sg/news/speeches/20220221-speech-by-minister-chan-chun-sing-at-the-launch-of-prof-arnoud-de-meyers-book-building-excellence-in-higher-education-singapores-experience-at-the-singapore-management-university?msclkid=86567a87c1d511ecaa08d9b87f944a1a

Chan, C. S. (2022b). *Speech by Minister Chan Chun Sing for the Global Lifelong Learning Summit, at the Pan Pacific Singapore.* MOE, Ministry of Education. https://www.moe.gov.sg/news/speeches/20221102-speech-by-minister-chan-chun-sing-for-the-global-lifelong-learning-summit-2022-at-pan-pacific-singapore

Chan, H. C. (2022c, August 31). Why a university of the arts now? *The Straits Times.* https://www.straitstimes.com/opinion/why-a-university-of-the-arts-now

Chan, D., & Ng, P. T. (2008). Similar agendas, diverse strategies: The quest for a regional hub of higher education in Hong Kong and Singapore. *Higher Education Policy, 21*(4), 487–503.

Cheong, H. K. (2018). A Singapore University catering to the needs of a population amidst a volatile and changing economy. In T. Chye & A. Soon (Eds.), *Univer-cities: Strategic dilemmas of medical origins and selected modalities: Water, quantum leap & new models* (Vol. 3, pp. 205–229). https://doi.org/10.1142/9789813238732_0012

Chue, S., Pang, E., Pang, P., & Lee, Y.-J. (2022). Post-secondary education institutions internships – The Singapore experience. In Y. J. Lee (Ed.), *Education in Singapore* (pp. 117–129). Springer.

Department of Statistics Singapore. (2022). Retrieved November 23, 2022, from https://www.singstat.gov.sg/find-data/sdg/goal-4

Gleason, N. W. (2018). Singapore's higher education systems in the era of the fourth industrial revolution: Preparing lifelong learners. In *Higher education in the era of the Fourth Industrial Revolution* (pp. 145–169). Palgrave Macmillan. https://doi.org/10.1007/978-981-13-0194-0_7

Goh, C. T. (1997, June 2). *Shaping our future: Thinking schools, learning nation.* https://www.nas.gov.sg/archivesonline/data/pdfdoc/19970602_0001.pdf

Goh, C. T. (1999, November 11). *Making globalisation work with social accountability.* https://www.nas.gov.sg/archivesonline/data/pdfdoc/1999111101.htm

Goodwill, A., & Chen, S. A. (2021). *The science of lifelong learning.* UNESCO. https://doi.org/10.31234/osf.io/juefx

Gopinathan, S., & Lee, M. H. (2011). Challenging and co-opting globalisation: Singapore's strategies in higher education. *Journal of Higher Education Policy and Management, 33*(3), 287–299. https://doi.org/10.1080/1360080x.2011.565001

GovTech. (2017, February 13). *GovTech partners with eight institutes of higher learning to develop deep technical capabilities in students to help build a smart nation.* https://www.tech.gov.sg/media/media-releases/govtech-partners-with-eight-institutes-of-higher-learning-to-develop-deep-technical-capabilities

Guan, C., Ding, D., & Ho, K. W. (2015). E-Learning in higher education for adult learners in Singapore. *International Journal of Information and Education Technology, 5*(5), 348–353. https://doi.org/10.7763/ijiet.2015.V5.528

Hashim, M. A. M., Tlemsani, I., & Matthews, R. (2022). Higher education strategy in digital transformation. *Education and Information Technologies, 27*(3), 3171–3195. https://doi.org/10.1007/s10639-021-10739-1

Heng, S. K. (2014). *Opening address by Mr Heng Swee Keat, Minister for Education, at the international conference of teaching and learning with technology (iCTLT) at the Suntec International Convention and Exhibition Centre,* April 2014. Retrieved from https://www.aps.sg/files/in-the-news/opening-address-by-mr-heng-swee-keat-at-the-international-conference-of-teaching-and-learning-with-technology.pdf

Hung, D., Huang, J. S., & Tan, C. (2020). Leadership in times of pandemics: Reflections from Singapore. *International Studies in Educational Administration, 48*(2), 56–63.

Jackson, D., Sibson, R., & Riebe, L. (2013). Delivering work-ready business graduates-keeping our promises and evaluating our performance. *Journal of Teaching and Learning for Graduate Employability, 4*(1), 2–22. https://doi.org/10.21153/jtlge2013vol4no1art558

James, D. (2020). Is lifelong learning still useful? Disappointments and prospects for rediscovery. *Journal of Education and Work, 33*(78), 522–532.

Li, L. (2022). Reskilling and upskilling the future-ready workforce for industry 4.0 and beyond. *Information Systems Frontiers*, 1–16.

Lim, K. M. (2014). *Linkage and collaboration between universities and industries in Singapore*. Presentation at SEAMEO RIHED Regional Seminar on Linkage and Collaboration between the Higher Education Institutions and Industries. Da Nang, Vietnam, September 2014.

Lim, K. (2022, March 12). The Big Read in short: Are S'pore's universities nimble enough to stay relevant. *TODAY*. https://www.todayonline.com/big-read/big-read-short-are-spores-universities-nimble-enough-stay-relevant-1844401

Lung, N. (2018, March 27). *Singapore Minister of Education on the importance of higher education reform for Industry 4.0*. Open Gov Asia. https://opengovasia.com/singapore-minister-of-education-on-the-importance-of-higher-education-reform-for-industry-4-0/

Milic, S. (2013). The twenty-first century university and the concept of lifelong learning. *Australian Journal of Adult Learning*, *53*(1), 151–170.

Ministry of Education (MOE). (2023). *Education statistics digest 2023*. Ministry of Education. https://www.moe.gov.sg/-/media/files/about-us/education-statistics-digest-2023.pdf

Ministry of Trade and Industry. (2017). *Report of the committee on the future economy*. https://www.mti.gov.sg/Resources/publications/Report-of-the-Committee-on-the-Future-Economy

Mohd Salleh, N., Mapjabil, J., & Legino, R. (2019). Graduate work-readiness in Malaysia: Challenges, skills and opportunities. In *The transition from graduation to work* (pp. 125–142). https://doi.org/10.1007/978-981-13-0974-8_8

Mok, J. K., & Lee, M. H. (2003). Globalization or glocalization? Higher education reforms in Singapore. *Asia Pacific Journal of Education*, *23*(1), 15–42.

Myint, M. M., Kyaw, T., & Zaw, Z. M. (2021, March 7–11). An explorative study to build the work readiness for engineering students. *11th Annual International Conference on Industrial Engineering and Operations Management*, Singapore.

Natarajan, U., Loke, H. Y., & Gopinathan, S. (2020). Globalization and higher education: The changing context and landscape in Singapore. In N. V. Varghese, & S. Mandal, (Eds.), *Teaching learning and new technologies in higher education* (pp. 29–39). Springer.

National University of Singapore (NUS). (n.d.). https://www.nlb.gov.sg/main/article-detail?cmsuuid=a733f1d4-f0e8-47d6-8f1e-dadaaea396d4#:~:text=Background,a%20medical%20school%20in%201905

National University of Singapore (NUS). (2021). *Strong interest in interdisciplinary learning with high acceptance rates*. NUS Web. https://news.nus.edu.sg/strong-interest-in-interdisciplinary-learning-with-high-acceptance-rates/

National University of Singapore (NUS). (2022a, January 29). *New platforms to help students land internships and build professional networks*. NUS Web. https://news.nus.edu.sg/new-platforms-to-help-students-land-internships-and-build-professional-networks/

National University of Singapore (NUS). (2022b, February 17). *NUS graduates achieve better employment outcomes, higher starting salaries*. NUS Faculty of Arts & Social Sciences. https://fass.nus.edu.sg/news/2022/02/17/nus-graduates-achieve-better-employment-outcomes-higher-starting-salaries/

National University of Singapore (NUS). (n.d.). *NUS lifelong learners programme (NUS L3)*. National University of Singapore. https://www.nus.edu.sg/alumnet/lifelong-learning

Ng, P. T. (2008). Educational reform in Singapore: From quantity to quality. *Educational Research for Policy and Practice*, *7*(2), 5–15.

Ng, P. T. (2013). The global war for talent: Responses and challenges in the Singapore higher education system. *Journal of Higher Education Policy and Management*, *35*(3), 280–292.

Ng, W. K. (2022). *Singapore's first arts university to open in August 2024, applications accepted from 2023*. https://www.straitstimes.com/singapore/parenting-education/university-of-the-arts-singapore-to-open-in-august-2024-applications-accepted-from-2023

Nguyen, N. D., Ngoc, N. B., & Montague, A. (2018). Enhancing graduate work-readiness in Vietnam. In *The transition from graduation to work* (pp. 221–237). Springer Singapore. https://doi.org/10.1007/978-981-13-0974-8_13

NTU. (n.d.). *Interdisciplinary collaborative core (ICC)*. Nanyang Technological University. https://www.ntu.edu.sg/education/inspire/interdisciplinary-collaborative-core-(icc)

Nurjanah, I., & Ana, A. (2022, March). Work readiness of TVET graduates in the context of Industry 4.0. In *4th International conference on innovation in engineering and vocational education (ICIEVE 2021)* (pp. 34–38). Atlantis Press.

Ong, Y. K. (2018). *Speech by Mr Ong Ye Kung, Minister for Education at APAIE Conference and Exhibition.* https://www.moe.gov.sg/news/speeches/20180326-speech-by-mr-ong-ye-kung-minister-for-education-higher-education-and-skills-at-apaie-2018-conference-and-exhibition

Ong, Y. K. (2019). *Speech by Mr Ong Ye Kung, Minister for Education at the growth net summit 2019, New Delhi, India.* Ministry of Education. https://www.moe.gov.sg/news/speeches/20190607-speech-by-mr-ong-ye-kung-minister-for-education-at-the-growth-net-summit-2019-new-delhi-india

Osman-Gani, A. M., & Tan, W.-L. (1998). Human resource development: The key to sustainable growth and competitiveness of Singapore. *Human Resource Development International, 1*(4), 417–432.

Prikshat, V., Kumar, S., & Nankervis, A. (2019). Work-readiness integrated competence model. *Education + Training, 61*(5), 568–589. https://doi.org/10.1108/et-05-2018-0114

Sarrico, C., McQueen, A., & Samuelson, S. (2017). *The state of higher education 2015–16* (OECD Higher Education Programme (IMHE), Issue). https://www.oecd.org/education/imhe/The%20State%20of%20Higher%20Education%202015-16.pdf

Shin, J. C. (2015). Mass higher education and its challenges for rapidly growing East Asian higher education. In J. C. Shin, G. A. Postiglione, & F. Huang (Eds.), *Mass higher education development in East Asia* (pp. 1–23). Springer.

Singapore Department of Statistics. (2002). *Singapore 2002 statistical highlights.* Singapore Department of Statistics.

Singapore-Government. (1999). *Singapore 21: Together, we make the difference.* Singapore 21 Committee.

Singapore-Government. (2024). *Ministry of Education.* The Revenue and Expenditure Estimates for the Financial Year 2024: Head K, Ministry of Finance. https://www.mof.gov.sg/docs/librariesprovider3/budget2024/download/pdf/27-moe-2024.pdf

SMU. (2021). *SMU core curriculum: Readying a new generation for the future.* The SMU Blog. https://blog.smu.edu.sg/departments/core-curriculum/smu-core-curriculum-readying-a-new-generation-for-the-future/

SUSS. (n.d.). *The SUSS difference.* Singapore University of Social Sciences. https://www.suss.edu.sg/about-suss/why-choose-suss/the-suss-difference

Tan, C. (2017). Lifelong learning through the SkillsFuture movement in Singapore: Challenges and prospects. *International Journal of Lifelong Education, 36*(3), 278–291.

Tan, J. (2022). Higher education in Singapore. In *International handbook on education in South East Asia* (pp. 1–17). https://doi.org/10.1007/978-981-16-8136-3_8-1

Tan, S., Rudolph, J., Crawford, J., & Butler-Henderson, K. (2022). Emergency remote teaching or andragogical innovation? Higher education in Singapore during the COVID-19 pandemic. *Journal of Applied Learning and Teaching, 5*(Sp. Iss. 1), 64–80.

Tay, L. Y., Lee, S.-S., & Ramachandran, K. (2021). Implementation of online home-based learning and students' engagement during the COVID-19 pandemic: A case study of Singapore Mathematics Teachers. *The Asia-Pacific Education Researcher, 30*(3), 299–310. https://doi.org/10.1007/s40299-021-00572-y

Teng, A. (2019). Pay for fresh university graduates rose last year; strong job prospects for those in IT. *The Straits Times.* https://www.straitstimes.com/singapore/education/pay-for-fresh-university-graduates-rose-last-year-strong-job-prospects-for-those

Teng, W., Ma, C., Pahlevansharif, S., & Turner, J. J. (2019). Graduate readiness for the employment market of the 4th industrial revolution. *Education + Training, 61*(5), 590–604. https://doi.org/10.1108/et-07-2018-0154

Tharman, S. (2015). *Budget 2015 Building our future, strengthening social security.* https://www.mof.gov.sg/docs/default-source/default-document-library/singapore-budget/budget-archives/2015/fy2015_budget_statement.pdf?sfvrsn=a5e8446e_2

Tomlinson, M. (2008). 'The degree is not enough' students' perceptions of the role of higher education credentials for graduate work and employability. *British Journal of Sociology of Education, 29*(1), 49–61. https://doi.org/10.1080/01425690701737457

United Nations, Department of Economic and Social Affairs. (2015). *Transforming our world: The 2030 Agenda for sustainable development.* United Nations. https://sdgs.un.org/2030agenda

Verma, P., Nankervis, A., Priyono, S., Mohd Salleh, N., Connell, J., & Burgess, J. (2018). Graduate work-readiness challenges in the Asia-Pacific region and the role of HRM. *Equality, Diversity and Inclusion: An International Journal, 37*(2), 121–137. https://doi.org/10.1108/edi-01-2017-0015

Waring, P., Vas, C., & Bali, A. S. (2019). The transition from graduation to work: Challenges and strategies in Singapore. In *The transition from graduation to work* (pp. 161–178). https://doi.org/10.1007/978-981-13-0974-8_10

Watermeyer, R., Chen, Z., & Ang, B. J. (2021). 'Education without limits': The digital resettlement of post-secondary education and training in Singapore in the COVID-19 era. *Journal of Education Policy*, 145–169. https://doi.org/10.1080/02680939.2021.1933198

Woo, J. J. (2018). Educating the developmental state: Policy integration and mechanism redesign in Singapore's SkillsFuture scheme. *Journal of Asian Public Policy, 11*(3), 267–284.

CHAPTER 9

HIGHER EDUCATION IN THAILAND

Oliver S. Crocco[a] and Sukanya Chaemchoy[b]

[a]Louisiana State University, USA
[b]Chulalongkorn University, Thailand

ABSTRACT

From its beginnings in the late 19th century, higher education in Thailand has evolved from primarily preparing the nation's wealthy elite men in the capital of Bangkok to enrolling over half of the men and women throughout the Kingdom. This chapter overviews this historical development and examines the contemporary issues of policy and governance, quality, and workforce preparation in Thai higher education. It also reflects Thailand's efforts to meet the United Nations Sustainable Development Goal of ensuring equal access for all to affordable and high-quality higher education. It concludes by discussing these issues within the Southeast Asian context, particularly highlighting Thailand's focus on internationalization and the role of the ASEAN University Network, headquartered in Thailand. While Thai higher education faces many challenges, such as declining enrollment due to demographic changes and an urban–rural divide in access, this chapter argues that continued efforts to promote equity and quality, relying partially on technological advances, will bring Thai higher education into a new era.

Keywords: Thailand; higher education; ASEAN; quality; policy; governance; workforce preparation

---

Higher Education in Southeast Asia
International Perspectives on Education and Society, Volume 49, 119–137
Copyright © 2025 by Oliver S. Crocco and Sukanya Chaemchoy
Published under exclusive licence by Emerald Publishing Limited
ISSN: 1479-3679/doi:10.1108/S1479-367920240000049009

INTRODUCTION

At the end of the 19th century, King Chulalongkorn of Thailand (King Rama V, 1853–1910) began a transformative reformation of the Thai administrative structure (Engel, 2020; Wyatt, 1969), which required establishing centers to train civil servants, mostly young men from elite families, beyond basic education. Given the primacy of Buddhism in Thai culture, the first of these colleges was the sangha college Mahadhatu College (1887), which would eventually become Mahachulalongkornrajavidyalaya University (MCU, n.d.). This was followed by the Bhatayakorn medical school of Siriraj Hospital (1889), which later became the University of Medical Sciences (1943) and then Mahidol University (1969). King Chulalongkorn's brother, Prince Damrong Rajanupab, established the Civil Service Training School (1899) – later the Royal Pages School (1902) – which his son and successor, King Vajiravudh (King Rama VI, 1881–1925), worked to elevate the college to Chulalongkorn University in 1917 as Thailand's first university (Chulalongkorn University, n.d.).

Until the 1960s, higher education in Thailand was centralized mainly in Bangkok. Guided by King Bhumibol Adulyadej (King Rama IX, 1927–2016), who was passionate about education and economic development throughout all of Thailand's provinces as well as Thailand's first Economic and Development Plan (1961), higher education spread through the establishment of Chiang Mai University (1964) in the north, Khon Kaen University (1964) in the northeast, and Prince of Songkla University (1967) in the south. Additionally, the National Institute of Development Administration (1969) was founded in Bangkok to facilitate national development through targeted graduate degree programs. Another central point of historical development included the Royal Proclamation of the Private College Act of 1969, which finally opened Thailand up to private higher education. Payap College (1974) was the first private higher education institution (HEI) to receive accreditation, which became Payap University (1984), followed by Assumption Business Administrative College (1975), which later became Assumption University (1990). Given the desire to expand access, Thailand established two open admission and distance universities: Ramkhamhang University (1971) and Sukhothai Thammathirat Open University (1978). Today, there are 83 public universities and 72 private universities (155 total). Thailand's landmark National Education Act 1999 specified the mission of HEIs in four parts – produce quality graduates, research, provide academic service to the community, and conserve Thai arts and culture. The National Education Act (1999) also empowered autonomous universities, which are HEIs guided by their own royal decrees, such as the Chulalongkorn University Act B.E. 2551 (2008), which provides them more internal autonomy regarding operations, budget, and staffing (Chulalongkorn University, 2008). Suranaree University of Technology was the first autonomous university, founded in 1990 (Lao, 2018).

The monarchy has always played an essential role in Thai higher education. Beginning a practice begun by King Prajadhipok (Rama VII, 1893–1941), King Bhumibol personally conferred each diploma at Thai universities and military academies. It was only until the 1990s when gross enrollment reached 15% that

Higher Education in Thailand 121

the King delegated this duty to other members of the Royal family, and this practice continues today. Given the centrality of Buddhism to Thai culture, there are two universities dedicated to providing higher education to monks and laypeople, both Thai and non-Thai (Mahamakut Buddhist University and Mahachulalongkornrajavidyalaya University). Buddhism is also a core component of co-curricular activities of many universities, such as Chiang Mai University's annual journey up the mountain to Wat Doi Suthep. Thai university students are still required to wear uniforms in public and private universities and even in international colleges with students from other countries. Meant originally to represent politeness and convey respect to teachers and the institution, uniforms have also shed light on the stark social hierarchy in Thailand and gender roles (Bunyawanich et al., 2018). Only recently have some transgender students been allowed to wear uniforms aligned with their gender identity (Sabpaitoon, 2019).

The latest data show that in 2021, there were 1.9 million students enrolled in HEIs across all levels, representing a steady decline from 2.2 million in 2017 (see Table 1). This 15% decrease in total enrollment is largely due to the demographic changes plaguing Thailand. In the year 2021, just over 544,000 babies were born at a rate of 1.2% compared with the 1960s–1980s when as many as 1 million children were born each year at rates as high as 5.1% (Charoesuthipan & Wipatayotin, 2022). (National Statistics Office, n.d.-a). Not only is total enrollment drooping, but the gross enrollment ratio in tertiary education has also decreased in recent years. After a dramatic increase over the last 50 years from 3% in the early 1970s to a peak of 55% in 2007, the gross enrollment ratio in tertiary education has dropped to 49% in 2022 (World Bank, n.d.).

The current population (ages 15+) is 58.6 million (54% male; 46% female) of whom 12.0 million (20.1%) have attained higher education (Ministry of Labor, 2023). This marks a steady increase since 2016 when the population (ages 15+) was 55.6 million but only 9.5 million (17.2%) had attained higher education (Ministry of Labor, 2023). Higher education graduates make up the largest group of employed persons (24.6%) when compared to other levels of educational attainment, e.g., upper secondary (19.4%), lower secondary (17.1%), elementary (21.2), less than elementary (13.7), and no schooling (2.9%) (Ministry of Labor, 2023).

Table 1. Higher Education Enrollment by Level and Year (2017–2021).

Educational Level	Academic Year				
	2017	2018	2019	2020	2021
Undergraduate	2,086,005	2,025,251	1,947,219	1,919,260	1,762,617
Graduate Diploma	9,984	9,707	8,771	9,150	10,363
Master's Degree	127,999	109,268	95,461	101,955	100,458
Higher Graduate Diploma	1,760	1,792	1,544	1,228	1,299
Doctoral Degree	23,013	25,645	23,929	26,656	27,955
Total	2,248,761	2,171,663	2,076,924	2,058,249	1,902,692

Source: Adapted from the National Statistics Office (n.d.-a).

Despite being the only Southeast Asian country not officially colonized – due mainly to the presence and leadership of the monarchy and the fact that it served as a buffer state between French and British colonies – higher education in Thailand still reflects a high degree of Western influence (Lao, 2015; Rungfamai, 2018). The early universities in Thailand each reflected a certain international orientation that informed their policy and practice. For example, Chulalongkorn University was oriented more toward the British system, Thammasat University toward the French, and Kasetsart University and Mahidol University toward the United States (Chaemchoy et al., 2021). These influences were not forced upon Thai policymakers but reflected a habit of borrowing (Lao, 2015), which is evident in the subsequent sections of this chapter on policy and governance, quality, and workforce preparation.

POLICY AND GOVERNANCE

Governance in higher education has emerged in several stages, beginning with the founding of the Ministry of University Affairs in 1972, which was replaced by the Office of Higher Education Commission (OHEC) in 2003 under the supervision of the Ministry of Education (MOE). Then, in 2019, OHEC merged with the Ministry of Science and Technology to become the Ministry of Higher Education, Science, Research, and Innovation (MHESI), which currently oversees and administers both public and private HEIs throughout the country, except for select institutions under specific ministries and agencies (see Chaemchoy et al., 2021). On the one hand, the creation of MHESI represented a shift away from bureaucratic challenges under the jurisdiction of the MOE from 2003 to 2019 (Chaemchoy et al., 2021), but it also represented a series of new challenges.

MHESI is guided by Thailand's National Strategy (2018–2037), which includes six core national development strategies, two of which are directly related to HE and are outlined in MHESI's (2021b) Action Plan for 2022: "Competitiveness Enhancement" and "Developing and Strengthening Human Capital" (Government Gazette, 2018, pp. 7–8). The bipartite mission of MHESI (n.d.) is to prepare Thai people for the 21st century and to cultivate knowledge and innovation to develop the country. The eight principles guiding the ministry include transformation, the foundation of the future, leading through strategic funding, empowerment, autonomy with accountability, modern management agencies, flow and collaborative networks, and policy and process innovations. The three key reform areas of MHESI are administration, regulation, and budget (Chaemchoy, 2019). The roles of MHESI are to (1) promote, support, and supervise higher education in response to a rapidly changing world and meet national development; (2) promote, support, and supervise research and innovation of HEIs and other agencies under MHESI; and (3) build an ecosystem and infrastructure that develop higher education, science, and research and innovation.

The core governance issues plaguing Thai higher education are bureaucracy, limited autonomy, and administrative fragmentation (Chaemchoy et al., 2021).

Ask virtually any faculty member of any academic rank, at any institution, Thai citizen or non-Thai, in engineering or fine arts, about their workload and they will likely tell you about the onerous paperwork and administrative duties required. One Thai academic recounts her experience as a junior faculty member at Chulalongkorn University: "… new academics at my faculty will be assigned the administrative workload like the secretary of the faculty. You know, I spent half of my entire working hours on the administrative work" (Rungfamai, 2017, p. 11). As a result, even promising junior faculty members with doctorates from elite institutions abroad and a passion for research can be pushed to burnout while working at Thai HEIs. This occurs partly because of hierarchical governance structures in Thai institutions with time-consuming approval processes for proposed research, programs, or activities (Amornpipat & McLean, 2014).

Administrative fragmentation emerges amidst the plethora of stakeholders that make coordinating the higher education sector difficult. While the establishment of MHESI appears to be quelling some concerns about the bureaucracy of MOE, the fact that there are still 12 ministries that offer higher education services (e.g., the National Defense College of Thailand and the Ministry of Public Health) almost entirely detached from the rest of the higher education system contributes to this administrative fragmentation (Chaemchoy et al., 2021). There are no signs yet that these issues are being resolved. Still, many are optimistic that establishing MHESI will help lessen these issues. An increasing number of public universities have become autonomous, which has given them the flexibility to enhance their research and innovation capacity. For instance, King Mongkut's University of Technology Thonburi (KMUTT) has been so effective in attracting outside research grants that state subsidies account for only 34% of its budget (Lao, 2018). Still, regardless of institutions having autonomous status, this does not mean they are free from burdensome administrative bureaucracy. In the case of Chulalongkorn University, a "bureaucratic mindset" permeates the university even long after becoming autonomous (Rungfamai, 2017, p. 8). This is deeply embedded as university faculty and staff of public universities have long been regarded as "government officials" and subject to "bureaucratic red tape" (Prangpatanpon, 1996, p. 16).

The minister of MHESI also sits as chairman of the Office of National Higher Education, Science, Research, and Innovation Policy Council (NXPO), which was founded in 2008 by the Ministry of Science and Technology long before the merger and has refocused its attention toward the integration of higher education and science, research, and innovation (NXPO, 2020). According to the 2022 Action Plan, NXPO (2021) plans to continue promoting higher education reforms that will lead to an "innovation-driven economy" by boosting research expenditure and promoting lifelong learning through its "upskill/reskill/new skill" framework in line with the National Strategy (paras 3–5). The policy work of NXPO is impressive. Its ability to integrate with OHEC in 2019 under MHESI and expand its purview has led to more comprehensive policy initiatives that intertwine higher education, research, and innovation toward achieving the ministry-level and national-level strategic directions. Given that this merger is still relatively new, the impact in terms of increased quality has yet to be measured.

QUALITY

Quality in higher education comprises quality graduates (i.e., learning outcomes) and quality assurance (QA). According to OHEC (2006), learning outcomes consist of five domains: (1) Knowledge, (2) Cognitive Skills, (3) Interpersonal Skills and Responsibility, (4) Analytical and Communication Skills, and (5) Ethical and Moral Development, as specified in the Thai Qualification Framework (TQF) which is comparable to that of other countries in the Association of Southeast Asian Nations (ASEAN). In addition to these five domains, other fields of study that use movement, such as art and music, include psychomotor skills as a learning outcome domain. Internal QA (IQA) is the establishment of systems and mechanisms for the development, monitoring, and evaluation of HEI operations following the policy (Chaiya & Ahmad, 2021). IQA is one of the responsibilities of higher education management which requires HEIs to submit annual reports to the parent agency. IQA can be viewed at three levels: curriculum, faculty, and university. IQA embodies nine areas, including (1) objectives, philosophies, and commitment, (2) research, (3) academic services, (4) culture and art preservation, (5) management and administration, (6) budgeting and finance, (7) systems and mechanisms of IQA, (8) teaching and learning, and (9) student development activities. These indicators cover the four mentioned missions of the HEIs. Assessing higher education graduates' quality is a responsibility of the National Institute of Educational Testing Service (NIETS), established in 2005, which is developing a University National Educational Test (U-NET) for quality graduate assessment. Thai graduates should be highly equipped in all aspects, including body, heart, wisdom, 21st-century skills, high ethical integrity, respect for the law, leadership talents, awareness of the global context, comprehension of and passion for the nature of being Thai, and lifelong learning (Chaemchoy et al., 2021). This shows a clear connection between higher education quality and Thai identity.

Whereas the assessment of quality graduates is conducted internally via MHESI, the vast majority of external QA is facilitated by the Office for National Education Standards and Quality Assessment (ONESQA) in higher education (Crocco & Pitiyanuwat, 2022). ONESQA conducts the external quality assessment on educational institutions, including HEIs, every five years through a process called Kalayanamit (amicable assessment) in the spirit of formative assessment to help HEIs improve their quality and to be the best they can be (Pitiyanuwat et al., 2018). However, beginning in 2019 with the Higher Education Act (Section 64), universities may choose other international or foreign agencies to conduct external quality assurance according to the Higher Education Standards Committee. Pitiyanuwat et al. (2018) showed that an external quality assessment institution needs to be a public organization that is neither a government office nor a public enterprise to accomplish the most efficiency because of the need for complete autonomy and power in decision-making to overcome bureaucracy. Despite specific criteria and assessment guidelines, each university has the freedom to create its own quality frameworks and systems. Some universities adopt the ASEAN University Network Quality Assurance (AUN-QA) framework, while others initiate their own frameworks. For instance, Chulalongkorn University calls its quality assurance framework Chulalongkorn University Quality Assurance 100 (CUQA100).

Quality in higher education is also about excellence. The Baldrige Performance Excellence Framework (Education) has been translated, compiled, and adapted to the Thai context by MHESI so that Thai HEIs can conduct self-assessments and increase performance excellence. MHESI began using this framework to respond to national development and international competitiveness (MHESI, 2021a). Mahidol University adopted this framework and its self-assessment in 2017 reported it was in the early stages (Jarupoom & Sirisunhiran, 2020). Their preliminary findings reveal that the effectiveness of the administration for performance excellence at Mahidol University was at a moderate level, and three priorities included (1) knowledge management and information technology, (2) listening to customers to improve results, and (3) strategic management and implementation and human resources management. While the framework does appear to help increase performance toward strategic objectives, it clearly represents an example of the "culture of borrowing" described by Lao (2015), and the long-term effectiveness of yet another quality framework is still to be seen (p. 7).

As competent graduates are a criterion of quality, quality is inevitably associated with teaching, which is also now linked to research and innovation as a means of contributing to societal development. Some strategies can be considered as building the research and innovation capacity of HEIs. The Royal Thai Navy provides a compelling case of this interconnection. According to Sorapan and Kulophas (2019), HEIs under the Royal Thai Navy improved management through advances in curriculum and instruction. They also built a research culture among students and faculty by expanding research budgets and incentives as well as cultivating partnerships in research and innovation with external stakeholders (Sorapan & Kulophas, 2019). Research and innovation are top agenda items for higher education, manifested in examples like Chulalongkorn University's motto, "Innovation for Society."

While international rankings systems of higher education or competitiveness are not perfect measures of higher education quality, they are explicitly mentioned in NXPO documents as key performance indicators (NXPO, n.d.) of the higher education system. Of the 64 countries ranked by the World Competitiveness Rankings (IMD, 2023), Thailand ranks 30th overall with the university education index one of the biggest improvements from 2020 to 2021; however, higher education achievement ranked 46th, and education was its single lowest-ranking indicator at 54th. International higher education rankings signal little improvement. According to four top international university rankings systems in 2023, 27 Thai universities made at least one of these lists, with Chulalongkorn University ranking first (or tied for first) on three of the four lists (see Table 2).

Key reasons for this poor showing internationally include burdensome administrative workloads for faculty, limited incentives and resources for publishing research, and low English-language proficiency, all three of which negatively affect research output in international journals, which is a top contributor to university rankings (Chaemchoy et al., 2021).

OLIVER S. CROCCO AND SUKANYA CHAEMCHOY

Table 2. International Rankings of Thai Universities.

QS	US	THE	ARWU	University
211	547	601–800	501–600	Chulalongkorn University
382	512	601–800	601–700	Mahidol University
571	739	801–1,000	601–700	Chiang Mai University
901–950	1,190	1,201–1,500	801–900	Prince of Songkla University
951–1000	1,222	1,201–1,500	901–1,000	Khon Kaen University
600	1,350	1,201–1,500	–	Thammasat University
951–1,000	1,008	801–1,000	–	King Mongkut's University of Technology Thonburi

Sources: QS Top Universities (2024); U.S. News & World Report (2023); Times Higher Education (2024); ShanghaiRanking Consultancy (2023).

Another issue is the low quality of graduates, as claimed by employers (Chaemchoy et al., 2021). According to a report from Thailand's Office of the Auditor General, around 20% of courses given by Thai public and private HEIs do not fulfill needed requirements (Lamubol, 2017). In addition, the MOE discovered that 20 academic programs offered by 10 private universities did not meet its requirements. With rapid technological and societal change occurring all around the world, HEIs are finding it difficult to adapt and modify their courses to meet the needs of an era marked by disruption (Gleason, 2018).

One option for universities to enhance overall quality assessment has been for them to link and align with various regional and worldwide quality assurance networks (Crocco & Pitiyanuwat, 2022). This implies a vision for Thai HEIs to become world-class universities.

TQF was one mechanism that attempted to begin shifting the Thai higher education system from being more input-driven to outcome-based; however, the dramatic top-down changes required cumbersome documentation (Tanprasert, 2018). While the TQF came under criticism for increases in paperwork (Panyalimpnant, 2018) and excessive borrowing from Western countries (Lao, 2015), in an analysis of public administration programs, the TQF has had a positive influence on program quality (Tamronglak, 2020).

WORKFORCE PREPARATION

King Bhumibol (Rama IX) saw learning as a lifelong process that continued even after graduation and spoke at a graduation ceremony that "Those who wish to advance in their work must constantly seek more knowledge" (Grossman et al., 2011, p. 221). The King was incredibly practice-oriented, reminding graduates, "You should not get stuck with textbook or theoretical knowledge" (Grossman et al., 2011, p. 221). Higher education in Thailand plays a vital role in the larger ecosystem of human resource development (HRD) at the individual and organizational levels, as well as workforce development at the national level (Crocco, 2021). Higher education is also related to the work of the Office of National

Higher Education, Science, Research, and Innovation Policy Council (NXPO) mentioned above, which works on various areas related to workforce preparation, such as talent mobility, skill mapping, and sustainable development. What is most relevant is the connection and alignment between higher education curricula and industry needs, also called work readiness. There are several different conceptualizations and ways of measuring work readiness; however, most include a combination of competencies such as job-specific skills along with intellectual and problem-solving skills, self-management skills, and communication skills (Prikshat et al., 2019). There are key challenges facing graduate work-readiness in Thailand, namely the low quality of the education system broadly, the lack of career counseling and knowledge of career development, and skill mismatches based on content and language proficiency (Promsit, 2019). In fact, Promsit (2019) reports that the top three desired skills of graduates by startups and SMEs were English language, technology, and information analysis.

Given that English language skills are a high priority for employers in Thailand and across Southeast Asia, the Thai government instituted a new policy that required all graduates to take an English exit examination aligned with the Common European Framework of Reference for Languages (Wudthayagorn, 2021). In a study of 81 public universities implementing the policy, Wudthayagorn (2021) found that universities designed a variety of different tests in alignment with the framework, which sends a message to students that English is vital for their success and serves as a tool to check progress. Part of the problem lies in the fact that according to Thailand's 2021 Skill Development Survey, only 9.3% of the population expressed a desire to develop their skills, most of whom came from Thailand's northern and northeastern regions (National Statistics Office, 2021).

One way that Thai higher education has sought to promote workforce preparation is through cooperative and work-integrated education (CWIE) programs (Srisa-An & Pramoolsook, 2019). Beginning in Thailand at Suranaree University of Technology in 1993, these programs require students to work in professional placements during their undergraduate studies to promote practical skill development and align their education with industry needs (Srisa-An & Pramoolsook, 2019). In 2020, a Memorandum of Understanding (MOU) was signed regarding the promotion and support of CWIE programs by (a) government bodies, i.e., MHESI, the Department of Skill Development of the Ministry of Labor, and the Community Development Department of the Ministry of Interior; (b) higher education bodies, i.e., the Council of University Presidents of Thailand, the Meeting of Rajabhat University Presidents, the Council of Rajamangala University of Technology Presidents, and the Association of Private Higher Education Institutions of Thailand; and, (c) industry partners, i.e., the Federation of Thai Industries, the Thai Chamber of Commerce and Board of Trade of Thailand, the Board of Investment of Thailand, the Eastern Economic Corridor Office of Thailand, and the Association for Cooperative Education (MOU, 2020). The fruits of this collaborative endeavor are yet to be seen but hold great promise.

In a mixed-methods exploratory study of desired digital workforce competencies in Thailand, "lifelong learning, personal attitude, teamwork, dependability, and IT foundations" were the top desired competencies for the IT industry and non-IT industries (Siddoo et al., 2019, p. 1). Higher education administrators should consider robust studies such as this to inform curricular decisions. Given that many of these competencies are not directly related to curricula but also co-curricula, there may be opportunities to elevate existing co-curricula on Thai campuses to cultivate these competencies (Crocco & Wakeman, 2014).

Digital skills and infrastructure are a crucial part of workforce preparation. In a Delphi study of Thai university administrators, digital resources and curricula aligned with industry needs were the top-ranked characteristics for Thai HEIs (Komoldit et al., 2018). To achieve its strategic goals, Thailand must "overhaul education and improve the capabilities and talent of its workforce," which requires government buy-in and improvements in infrastructure such as the internet (Baxter, 2017, p. 3). This must include provisions for its migrant population. There is a push by policymakers to utilize open and distance education for skill development and knowledge acquisition among migrant workers in Thailand, particularly in acquiring language abilities, legal knowledge related to rights and laws, and skill development (Toyama & Suvanvihok, 2020).

SDG 4.3

Thailand has made efforts to meet the United Nations Sustainable Development Goal (SDG) of ensuring equal access for all to affordable and high-quality higher education. MHESI (n.d.) explicitly mentions its purpose in human capital development [การพัฒนาทุนมนุษย์] as in line with the SDGs, but much work is yet to be done. One international ranking organization, Times Higher Education (2023), has come out with Impact Rankings that assess universities against the SDGs. Of the 1,705 universities from 115 countries ranked, Thailand has four universities in the top 100: Chulalongkorn University (17), Mahidol University (38), Chiang Mai University (78), and Khon Kaen University (97). Of the 65 Thai universities assessed, 19 are in the top 600.

Enrollment in higher education reached 50% of the gross corresponding age group for the first time in 2005 and has remained around that number since (World Bank, n.d.). Despite only 3% of women enrolled in higher education in 1976, women surpassed 50% in the gross enrollment ratio in 2005 and have remained between 56 and 60% since (World Bank, n.d.). Still, stagnating enrollment percentages over the last 15 years represent a challenge to Thailand, not only as an issue of sustainable development but also related to the country's ability to "produce innovators and innovations that can enhance competitiveness in global markets" (Ruchiwit et al., 2019, p. 7). Thus, a significant need for Thailand in this area is to promote access and increase its overall enrollment to reach beyond the stage of massification (i.e., 15–50% enrollment of relevant age group) to universal access (beyond 50%) (Trow, 2006).

The most expansive reform to promote access to higher education has been the Rajabhat University Act (2004), which elevated the many teacher colleges around rural areas in Thailand to university status (Crocco, 2018). Similarly,

Rajamangala Institutes of Technology were converted into universities in 2003. Together, these comprise nearly a third (48) of Thailand's 155 HEIs. Since the greater Bangkok area has over 30 of Thailand's non-Rajabhat or Rajamangala universities, these universities represent a powerful commitment to educational access in Thailand's other regions. In a study of the official mottos of 82 Thai universities, Laosrirattanachai and Wongthai (2018) found that many universities – in particular Rajabhat universities, given their embeddedness in community development – had mottos that conveyed messages of access and inclusivity such as "A leading quality university for all" (Suan Sunadha Rajabhat University), "Institution of higher education serving local communities" (Nakhon Sawan Rajabhat University), and "University for all" (Sukhothai Thammathirat Open University) (pp. 1152–1153).

Private higher education represents another way access to higher education has proliferated since the Private College Act of 1969 and now includes providers such as religious organizations, such as Fatoni University (Yala Province), families as is in the case of Shinawatra University (Pathum Thani Province), and international branch universities, which includes Webster University Thailand (Phet Buri Province). Corporations and corporate-university partnerships also play a role in private higher education, as in the case of the Panyapiwat Institute of Management in Nonthaburi Province, founded by CP Group (Crocco et al., 2017). In 2022, enrollment in private higher education made up 25.9% of total enrollments, up from 13.6% of total enrollments in 2017 but still far short of the government's target rate of 35% (National Statistics Office, n.d.-b). This occurs for a variety of reasons. First, public universities overshadow private universities in reputation, prestige, and funding due to the low tuition fees public institutions can offer because of government subsidies (Punyasavatsut, 2013). Other reasons include overly burdensome quality assurance paperwork for private universities and obstacles to innovation. For example, there are anecdotes of private universities trying innovative educational initiatives that the government shut down, only to pop up later in public universities after the private universities lost their competitive edge. In many ways, private universities are often seen as competitors to public universities instead of partners (Crocco, 2018).

To improve access, there must be care taken to address issues related to students with disabilities and mental health issues. Despite gains in the enrollment of women, gender parity has swung in the other direction regarding the stress of Thai students on campus. In a study of 478 Thai university students using random cluster sampling, Calderon et al. (2019) found that male students had lower happiness and psychological well-being than women students, and both had higher perceived stress when compared to comparable studies in the United States and the United Kingdom. Regarding people with disabilities, according to OEC (2021), there were 1.6 million people with disabilities in the education system nationally but only 23,000 (1.46%) in higher education. That said, one emergent path forward that can partially address disparities in access is the use of technology.

The Office of Higher Education Council (now under MHESI) established the Thailand Cyber University (TCU) Project in 2005, which delivers Massive Open

Online Courses (MOOCs) on over 700 topics. According to TCU (n.d.), as of March 13, 2024, over 1,869,000 students have participated in a TCU MOOC, up from 800,000 in March 2021. Through coordination by MHESI, TCU allows all Thai universities to host MOOCs on their site, track completion, and create an e-portfolio that can be used to track credits earned (Association of Southeast Asian Nations Cyber University Secretariat, 2021). According to the 2021 Trend Report of Higher Education e-Learning of ASEAN – Thailand, the most popular Thai MOOC courses were English for Communication, Applied Psychology to Work through Success, Happiness, and Wealth, Creation of Good Feeling for Oneself, Psychology and Daily Life, and Graphic Design Crash Course (Association of Southeast Asian Nations Cyber University Secretariat, 2021). Online technology is promising for improving access. Earlier studies have already shown that Facebook has the potential to enhance peer-to-peer feedback and develop writing ability in the Thai context (Wichadee, 2013). Online technology is promising as research shows unique technological interventions such as movie-based mobile learning have the potential to increase English speaking skills and intercultural communication abilities (Chaya & Inpin, 2020).

Internet infrastructure is vital for technological advances to increase higher education access, especially in rural areas. In a mixed-methods study of students at Walailak University in the south of Thailand, Ulla and Perales (2021) found that students easily transitioned to using Facebook as a quasi-Learning Management System (LMS) for their courses because of the COVID-19 pandemic; however, 75% of those surveyed either agreed or strongly agreed that their internet connection at home was weak. According to the Speedtest Global Index in February 2022, Thailand's mobile internet speed ranked 55th in the world with a median download speed of 32 Mbps (only behind Brunei, Singapore, and Vietnam in Southeast Asia) (Ookla, n.d.). That said, these data come primarily from major cities and does not capture the urban–rural digital divide.

THAI HIGHER EDUCATION IN THE SOUTHEAST ASIAN CONTEXT

There are many ways that Thai higher education has embedded itself within the international context, particularly in Southeast Asia. For one, Thailand's geographic centrality in the region has made it the home of the ASEAN University Network (AUN) and the Southeast Asia Ministers of Education Organization (SEAMEO) Regional Centre for Higher Education and Development (RIHED), both founded in the 1990s. The AUN was founded to support the regional development and coordination of higher education among Member States of the Association of Southeast Asian Nations (ASEAN) (AUN, n.d.). Since 2009, the AUN has been run by Thai scholar Choltis Dhirathiti who has led the expansion of the organization's strategic focus to include curriculum development, quality assurance, cross-border student experiences, academic research collaboration, and networking (AUN, n.d.). Instead of following its original vision to establish an ASEAN University, the AUN has facilitated membership into a body of

ASEAN universities called the AUN30, which has five Thai member institutions: Burapha University, Chiang Mai University, Chulalongkorn University, Mahidol University, and Prince of Songkla University (AUN, n.d.). Thailand also has an additional 11 associate member universities.

There are 37 Thai universities in the Association of Southeast Asian Institutions of Higher Learning (ASAIHL), which is part of the SEAMEO (ASAIHL, n.d.). Among other things, ASAIHL hosted its 43rd conference at Sripatum University in Thailand in 2019 under the theme "Revitalizing Higher Education for Sustainable Development" (ASAIHL, 2019). Also, part of SEAMEO is the RIHED, established in 1993. The center is based in Bangkok and informs higher education policy in the region.

Thai universities have expanded their international programs to host students from countries around the world. Thailand has 315 international degree programs (138 bachelor's, 84 master's, 92 doctoral, and one other) offered nationwide at public and private universities (OEC, 2021). In 2019, Thailand had 26,635 international students, with the highest sending countries being China (14,017), Myanmar (2,266), Cambodia (1,599), Vietnam (821), and Lao PDR (781) (OEC, 2021). China is one of the ASEAN+3 University Network countries, which also strengthens the connection between Chinese and Thai higher education. Chinese students, while not members of ASEAN, make up an increasing percentage of higher education students in the Thai context in both international and even Thai programs. In one Thai university with roughly 3,000 Chinese nationals, a survey of 900 found that the majority (81%) were undergraduate students, and 45% studied finance and accounting (Chen et al., 2018). Thailand may be able to recruit more international students through new programs such as Payap University's PhD in Cannabis and Medicinal Plants for Local Development, which was announced after Thailand became the first Asian country to legalize marijuana for medicinal use (Payap University, n.d.).

Recruiting international students to Thailand relies on a variety of factors, including the availability of scholarships, personal connections to a Thai university, and geographical considerations such as ease of travel (e.g., a student from Lao PDR may choose a Thai university in Northern Thailand) (Snodin, 2019). In a study of international student satisfaction in Thai public universities, responsiveness was the strongest dimension affecting service quality (Darawong & Sandmaung, 2019). Strengthening international collaborations could also support the development of global competencies among graduates. In a study of desired global competencies for engineering graduates, 63 Thai companies reported preferring global competencies such as a global mindset and the "ability to work in international teams" over a high grade-point average or even work experience (Rawboon et al., 2019). One of the key barriers, however, has been attracting non-Thai talent to Thai universities. Non-Thai academics who have migrated to Thailand struggled primarily with language barriers and burdensome visa procedures (Snodin et al., 2021).

The demographic changes that pose a severe challenge to Thai higher education are shared by other Southeast Asian countries. Thailand's fertility rate – as defined by total births per woman living to the end of childbearing years – has plummeted from over 6.0 in the 1960s to 1.51 in 2019, which is the lowest of its Southeast Asian neighbors Brunei (1.82), Cambodia (2.48), Indonesia (2.29), Lao PDR (2.63) the Philippines (2.53), Malaysia (1.98), Myanmar (2.14), Timor-Leste (3.94), and Vietnam (2.05) with the exception of Singapore (1.14) (World Bank, n.d.). There are many possible explanations for this, but one report by the Economist Intelligence Unit (2019) noted the lack of affordable housing, income inequality, and the cultural expectation that the youngest daughter of a family is responsible for caring for aging parents.

There are other issues related to Thai culture that influence Thai higher education. For example, Thai students continually struggle with critical analysis. In a comparative study of information literacy for the Industrial Revolution 4.0, Chusniyah et al. (2020) found that Thai university students had the least advanced skills in information literacy (i.e., critically evaluating text) compared to their Indonesian and Malaysian counterparts. This is likely the result of notions of social hierarchy and the inappropriateness of critically challenging ideas of those of higher social status. Relatedly, plagiarism remains a problem in Thai higher education. Khathayut and Walker-Gleaves (2020) revealed that Thai academics had "both limited understanding and low awareness of plagiarism" (p. 558). Despite burdensome administrative and teaching duties, Thai academics are under enormous pressure to publish in top-tier international outlets.

Given emergent global disruptions in higher education, hastened by the COVID-19 pandemic (Garcia-Morales et al., 2021), there are several possible ways Thai higher education can meet these challenges by linking with innovation and digital technology. The recent move of moving higher education out of the MOE and forming MHESI in combination with NXPO may be the beginning of the "revolution" needed in Thai higher education (Chaemchoy et al., 2021, p. 19). This union has the chance to link NXPO's aggressive goals in research and development with higher education's efforts and talent. And given the interconnectivity of Southeast Asia via ASEAN, there is increasing opportunity for higher education to integrate into regional workforce development (Crocco, 2021). There are risks involved with such a market-focused higher education system; however, changing demographics and globalization are pushing universities to prove their worth to Thai society and the world now more than ever.

CONCLUSION

There is no doubt that Thai higher education, along with the rest of the world, is going through a tumultuous time of change. As Deputy Education Minister Udom Kachinton cautioned, Thai HEIs need to adapt or risk further irrelevance (Dumrongkiat, 2019). While skeptics may argue that Thailand's efforts have not risen to these challenges, the recent efforts of MHESI and others are earnest attempts to meet the moment. In many ways, Thai higher education's greatest asset is its connection to Thai culture and identity, which have created and sustained robust institutions over the last century and have served the Kingdom of Thailand. Like many higher education systems worldwide, higher education in

Higher Education in Thailand 133

Thailand began as centralized, insular, male-dominated, and embedded in social hierarchy. Evolving beyond these roots will allow for the emergence of a Thai cosmopolitanism and ethic of trust that values all learners, trusts institutions, and empowers faculty with the most precious of all resources: time.

REFERENCES

Amornpipat, I., & McLean, G. N. (2014). *Faculty development in a Thai private university: HRD in higher education*. The 15th International Conference on Human Resource Development across Europe.

ASEAN University Network (AUN). (n.d.). *Discover AUN*. https://www.aunsec.org/discover-aun

Association of Southeast Asian Institutions of Higher Learning (ASAIHL). (n.d.). *Who is ASAIHL?* https://www.seameo.org/asaihl/

Association of Southeast Asian Institutions of Higher Learning (ASAIHL). (2019). *The proceedings of the 43rd ASAIHL Thailand Conference: The Association of Southeast Asian Institutions of Higher Learning*. http://asaihl.spu.ac.th

Association of Southeast Asian Nations Cyber University Secretariat. (2021). *2021 Trend Report of Higher Education e-Learning of ASEAN – Thailand*. http://www.aseanoer.net/main.acu

Baxter, W. (2017, March 29). Thailand 4.0 and the future of work in the kingdom. *International Labour Organization*. https://www.ilo.org/wcmsp5/groups/public/--dgreports/--dcomm/documents/meetingdocument/wcms_549062.pdf

Bunyawanich, S., Järvelä, M., & Ghaffar, A. (2018). The influence of uniform in establishing unity, hierarchy, and conformity at Thai universities. *Journal of Education and Training Studies*, *6*(7), 28–37. https://doi.org/10.11114/jets.v6i7.3151

Calderon, R., Pupanaed, S., Prachakul, W., & Kim, G. (2019). Happiness, perceived stress, psychological well-being, and health behaviors of Thai university students: Preliminary results from a multinational study on well-being. *Journal of American College Health*, *69*(2), 176–184. https://doi.org/10.1080/07448481.2019.1657871

Chaemchoy, S. (2019). Thai education system and educational management system [Thai]. In P. Petpon (Ed.), *Leadership in educational management and quality assurance* (pp. 5–65). Chulalongkorn University Press.

Chaemchoy, S., Puthpongsiriporn, T. S., & Fry, G. W. (2021). Higher education in Thailand. In *Oxford Research Encyclopedia of Education* (pp. 1–28). Oxford University Press. https://doi.org/10.1093/acrefore/9780190264093.013.1510

Chaiya, C., & Ahmad, M. M. (2021). Success or failure of the Thai higher education development – – critical factors in the policy process of quality assurance [Article]. *Sustainability (Switzerland)*, *13*(17), Article 9486. https://doi.org/10.3390/su13179486

Charoesuthipan, P., & Wipatayotin, A. (2022, February 6). When the baby well runs dry. *The Bangkok Post*. https://www.bangkokpost.com/thailand/special-reports/2259507/when-baby-well-runs-dry

Chaya, P., & Inpin, B. (2020). Effects of integrating movie-based mobile learning instruction for enhancing Thai university students' speaking skills and intercultural communicative competence. *English Language Teaching*, *13*(7), 27–45. https://doi.org/10.5539/elt.v13n7p27

Chen, P., You, X., & Chen, D. (2018). Mental health and cross-cultural adaptation of Chinese international college students in a Thai university. *International Journal of Higher Education*, *7*(4), 133–142. https://doi.org/10.5430/ijhe.v7n4p133

Chulalongkorn University. (2008). *Chulalongkorn University Act B.E. 2551 (2008)*. https://www.chula.ac.th/wp-content/uploads/2020/06/Chulalongkorn-University-Royal-Decree-2008-.pdf

Chulalongkorn University. (n.d.). *History: Thailand's first institution of higher learning*. https://www.chula.ac.th/en/about/overview/history/

Chusniyah, T., Firmanto, A., Kuswandi, D., Binti Jaafar, J. L. S., Chaiwutikornwanich, A., & Mustapa, A. (2020). The importance of information literacy to face the challenges of the industrial revolution 4.0: Study of Indonesian, Malaysia, and Thai students. *Advances in Social Science, Education and Humanities Research*, *395*, 57–60.

Crocco, O. S. (2018). Thai higher education: Privatization and massification. In G. Fry (Ed.), *Education in Thailand: An old elephant in search of a new mahout* (pp. 223–255). Springer Nature. https://doi.org/10.1007/978-981-10-7857-6_9

Crocco, O. S. (2021). *Developing human resources in Southeast Asia: A holistic framework for the ASEAN Community*. Palgrave Macmillan. https://doi.org/10.1007/978-3-030-79697-6

Crocco, O. S., Cseh, M., & Hemmapattawe, D. (2017). Corporate universities and corporation-university partnerships in Thailand: Complementing education in learning, leadership, and change. *Journal of International and Comparative Education, 6*(1), 17–31. https://doi.org/10.14425/JICE.2017.6.1.1732

Crocco, O. S., & Pitiyanuwat, S. (2022). Higher education in Thailand. In L. P. Symaco & M. Hayden (Eds.), *International handbook on education in South East Asia*. Springer Nature. https://link.springer.com/chapter/10.1007/978-981-16-8136-3_23-2

Crocco, O. S., & Wakeman, E. (2014). Learning and living together in higher education: How co-curricular efforts enhance curricular education and foster thriving communities. In J. Teng, Y. Fang, B. Muniady, & P. D'Souza (Eds.), *The heart of education: Learning to live together*. UNESCO Bangkok.

Darawong, C., & Sandmaung, M. (2019). Service quality enhancing student satisfaction in international programs of higher education institutions: A local student perspective. *Journal of Marketing for Higher Education, 29*(2), 268–283. https://doi.org/10.1080/08841241.2019.1647483

Dumrongkiat, M. (2019, January 4). Thai universities struggle to keep up. *The Bangkok Post*. https://www.bangkokpost.com/thailand/general/1604990/thai-unis-struggle-to-keep-up

Economist Intelligence Unit. (2019). *The disappearing workforce? Why countries in Southeast Asia need to think about fertility rates before it's too late*. https://www.eiu.com/graphics/marketing/pdf/fertility-in-south-east-asia-final.pdf

Engel, D. M. (2020). *Law and kingship in Thailand during the reign of King Chulalongkorn*. University of Michigan Center for South and Southeast Asian Studies.

Garcia-Morales, V. J., Garrido-Moreno, A., & Martin-Rojas, R. (2021). The transformation of higher education after the COVID disruption: Emerging challenges in an online learning scenario. *Frontiers in Psychology, 21*, Article 616059. https://doi.org/10.3389/fpsyg.2021.616059

Gleason, N. W. (2018). *Higher education in the era of the fourth industrial revolution*. Springer Nature.

Government Gazette. (2018). ยุทธศาสตร์ชาติ (พ.ศ. ๒๕๖๑ – ๒๕๘๐) [National Strategy (2018 2037)]. http://www.ratchakitcha.soc.go.th/DATA/PDF/2561/A/082/T_0001.PDF

Grossman, N., Baker, C. J., & Faulder, D. (Eds.). (2011). *King Bhumibol Adulyadej: A life's work*. Editions Didier Millet.

Institute for Management Development. (2023). *Country profile: Thailand (2023)*. https://worldcompetitiveness.imd.org/countryprofile/overview/TH

Jarupoom, R., & Sirisunhiran, S. (2020). The effectiveness of the administration of educational quality assurance system for performance excellence in Mahidol university. *Kasetsart Journal of Social Sciences, 41*(3), 604–613. https://doi.org/10.34044/j.kjss.2020.41.3.24

Khathayut, P. & Walker-Gleaves, C. (2020). Academic faculty conceptualisation and understanding of plagiarism – A Thai university exploratory study. *Journal of Further and Higher Education, 45*(4), 558–572. https://doi.org/10.1080/0309877X.2020.1795093

Komoldit, K., Tawisook, M., & Pilanthananond, N. (2018). Graduate school management characteristics to ensure production of quality graduates for sustainable competitiveness. *Mediterranean Journal of Social Sciences, 9*(4), 121–129. https://doi.org/10.2478/mjss-2018-0121

Lamubol, S. (2017, September 21). *Drastic population drop to hit higher education funding*. Retrieved November 2, from https://www.universityworldnews.com/post.php?story=20170921174413542

Lao, R. (2015). *A critical study of Thailand's higher education reforms: The culture of borrowing*. Routledge.

Lao, R. (2018). Quality and autonomous universities: Policy promises and the paradox of leadership. In G. W. Fry (Ed.), *Education in the Asia-Pacific Region* (Vol. 42, pp. 257–270). https://doi.org/10.1007/978-981-10-7857-6_10

Laosrirattanachai, P., & Wongthai, N. (2018). An investigation of the focus of Thai university mottos. *Veridian E-Journal, Silapakorn University, 11*(4), 1140–1156.

Mahachulalongkornrajavidyalaya University (MCU). (n.d.). *A brief history of MCU*. https://www. mcu.ac.th/pages/history

Ministry of Higher Education, Science, Research, and Innovation (MHESI). (n.d.). ความเป็นมา [History]. https://www.mhesi.go.th/index.php/en/aboutus/history.html

Ministry of Higher Education, Science, Research, and Innovation (MHESI). (2021a). เกณฑ์คุณภาพการศึกษา เพื่อการดำเนินการที่เป็นเลิศ ฉบับปี 2563 – 2566 [Education Criteria for Excellence Performance 2020-2023]. http://www.edpex.org/2020/11/edpex-2563-2566.html

Ministry of Higher Education, Science, Research, and Innovation (MHESI). (2021b). แผนปฏิบัติราชการ อว. ปีงบประมาณ พ.ศ. ๒๕๖๕ [Annual Government Action Plan 2022]. https://www.go.th/images/2565/docs/mhesiActionPlan2022.pdf

Ministry of Labor. (2023). หนังสือสถิติแรงงานประจำปี 2565 [Labor Statistics Yearbook 2022]. https://www.mol.go.th/wp-content/uploads/sites/2/2023/06/-2565-.pdf

National Statistics Office. (2021). *The skill development survey 2021*. http://www.nso.go.th/sites/2014en/Survey/social/labour/skill/2021/full_report.pdf

National Statistics Office. (n.d.-a). จำนวนนักเรียน นิสิต นักศึกษาในระบบโรงเรียน จำแนกตามระดับการศึกษา และชั้น ปีการศึกษา 2560 – 2564 [Number of Students in The Formal School System by Level of Education and Grade: Academic Year 2017 – 2021]. http://statbbi.nso.go.th/staticreport/page/sector/th/03.aspx

National Statistics Office. (n.d.-b). จำนวนนักเรียน นิสิต นักศึกษาในระบบโรงเรียน ในสถานศึกษาของรัฐบาลและเอกชน จำแนก ตามระดับการศึกษา และชั้น ปีการศึกษา 2560 – 2564 [Number of Students in the Formal School System in Public and Private Institutions by Level of Education and Grade: Academic Year 2017 – 2021]. http://statbbi.nso.go.th/staticreport/page/sector/th/03.aspx

NXPO. (2020). *NXPO annual report 2020*. https://www.nxpo.or.th/th/wp-content/uploads/2021/04/AnnualReport-2563.pdf

NXPO. (2021, August 3). *NXPO outlines its 2022 action plan*. https://www.nxpo.or.th/th/en/8419/

NXPO. (n.d.). *Thailand's performances in the world competitiveness rankings*. https://www.nxpo.or.th/th/en/thailands-performances-in-the-world-competitiveness-rankings/

Office of the National Education Commission. (1999). *National education act: B.E. 2542 (1999)*. https://www.onesqa.or.th/upload/download/file_697c80087cce7f0f83ce0e2a98205aa3.pdf

Office of Education Council. (2021). *Education in Thailand 2019–2021*. http://www.onec.go.th/th.php/book/BookView/1926

OHEC. (2006). *National qualifications framework for higher education in Thailand implementation handbook*. http://www.mua.go.th/users/tqf-hed/news/FilesNews/FilesNews8/NQF-HEd.pdf

Ookla. (n.d.). *Speedtest global index: Global median speeds February 2022*. https://www.speedtest.net/global-index

Panyalimpnant, T. (2018, February 5). Thai education quality assurance: Helper or obstruction to academics? (in Thai). *BBC News*. https://www.bbc.com/thai/thailand-42916401

Payap University. (n.d.). ปรัชญาดุษฎีบัณฑิต (กัญชาศาสตร์และพืชสมุนไพรเพื่อการพัฒนาท้องถิ่น) [Doctor of Philosophy (Cannabis and Medicinal Plants for Local Development)]. https://www.payap.ac.th/_public/Cannabis_Doctor.html

Pitiyanuwat, S., Phanphruk, S., & Pitiyanuwat, T. (2018). Educational testing, assessment, and quality assurance. In G. W. Fry (Ed.), *Education in Thailand: An old elephant in search of a new mahout* (pp. 597–623). Springer Singapore. https://doi.org/10.1007/978-981-10-7857-6_24

Prangpatanpon, S. (1996). Higher education in Thailand: Traditions and bureaucracy. *International Higher Education*, 6, 14–16.

Prikshat, V., Nankervis, A., Burgess, J., & Dhakal, S. (2019). Conceptualising graduate work-readiness: Theories, concepts and implications for practice and research. In S. Dhakal, V. Prikshat, A. Nankervis, & J. Burgess (Eds.), *The transition from graduation to work: Challenges and strategies in the twenty-first century Asia Pacific and beyond* (pp. 15–30). Springer.

Promsit, S. (2019). Graduate work-readiness in Thailand. In S. Dhakal, V. Prikshat, A. Nankervis, & J. Burgess (Eds.), *The transition from graduation to work: Challenges and strategies in the twenty-first century Asia Pacific and beyond* (pp. 203–220). Springer.

Punyasavatsut, C. (2013). Thailand: Issues in education. In L. P. Symaco (Ed.), *Education in South-East Asia* (pp. 275–298). Bloomsbury.

QS Top Universities. (2024). *QS world university rankings 2024*. https://www.topuniversities.com/world-university-rankings

Rawboon, K., Yamazaki, A. K., Oda, S., & Wongsatanawarid, A. (2019). Assessment of global competencies for the development of global engineering education. *Proceedings of the 2019 International Conference on Digital Technology in Education, Japan, 3*, 190–194. https://doi.org/10.1145/3369199.3369244

Ruchiwit, M., Patchotasingh, M., & Phanphairoj, K. (2019). Strategies for creating innovators in Thailand's higher education. *Journal of Medical Education and Curricular Development, 6*, Article PMC6628523. https://doi.org/10.1177/2382120519863078

Rungfamai, K. (2017). Research-university governance in Thailand: The case of Chulalongkorn University. *Higher Education 74*, 1–16. https://doi.org/10.1007/s10734-016-0024-x

Rungfamai, K. (2018). State, university, and society: Higher educational development and university functions in shaping modern Thailand. *Higher Education, 78*, 149–164. https://doi.org/10.1007/s10734-018-0335-1

Sabpaitoon, P. (2019, November 13). Chula's transgender students can now wear uniform of choice. *The Bangkok Post*. https://www.bangkokpost.com/thailand/general/1793354/chulas-transgender-students-can-now-wear-uniform-of-choice

ShanghaiRanking Consultancy. (2023). 2023 Academic ranking of world universities. https://www.shanghairanking.com/rankings/arwu/2023

Siddoo, V., Sawattawee, J., Janchai, W., & Thinnukool, O. (2019). An exploratory study of digital workforce competency in Thailand. *Heliyon, 5*, Article e01723. https://doi.org/10.1016/j.heliyon.2019.e01723

Snodin, N. (2019). Mobility experiences of international students in Thai higher education. *International Journal of Educational Management, 33*(7), 1653–1669. https://doi/org/10.1108/IJEM-07-2018-0206

Snodin, N., Young, T., Thongnuan, T., Bumrungsalee, I., & Nattheeraphong, A. (2021). The migration of international academics to Thailand and their experiences of Thai higher education. *SOJOURN: Journal of Social Issues in Southeast Asia, 36*(2), 225–257. https://www.jstor.org/stable/10.2307/27035256

Sorapan, C., & Kulophas, D. (2019). Management strategies for higher education institutions under the Royal Thai Navy according to the concept of capacity building for innovation research and development [in Thai]. *Journal of Education Studies, 47*(1), 95–117.

Srisa-An, W., & Pramoolsook, I. (2019). Development of cooperative and work-integrated education in Thailand: Looking back, looking now, and looking forward. In Y. Tanaka & K. E. Zegwaard (Eds.), *Cooperative and work-integrated education in Asia: History, present, and future issues* (pp. 105–127). Routledge.

Tamronglak, A. (2020). Impacts of Thailand qualification framework–Public administration on public administration education in Thailand. *Journal of Public Affairs Education, 26*(3), 276–290. https://doi.org/10.1080/15236803.2020.1771991

Tanprasert, K. (2018). Innovative teaching, learning and technologies for transformation of Thai higher education towards outcome-based education. In E. Jean-Francois (Ed.), *Transnational perspectives on innovation in teaching and learning technologies* (pp. 118–137). Brill. https://brill.com/flyer/title/37942?print=pdf&pdfGenerator=headless_chrome

Thailand Cyber University (TCU). (n.d.) หน้าหลัก [Home Page]. https://thaicyberu.go.th

Times Higher Education. (2024). *World university rankings 2024*. https://www.timeshighereducation.com/world-university-rankings/2024/world-ranking

Toyama, M., & Suvanvihok, V. (2020). The opportunities for open and distance education in the enhancement of migrant labour skills and competencies in ASEAN: The case of Thailand. *ASEAN Journal of Open and Distance Learning, 12*(2), 42–54.

Trow, M. (2006). Reflections on the transition from elite to mass to universal access: Forms and phases of higher education in modern societies since WWII. In J. J. F. Forest & P. G. Altbach (Eds.), *International handbook of higher education* (pp. 243–280). Springer.

U.S. News & World Report. (2023). *2022-2023 Best global universities rankings*. https://www.usnews.com/education/best-global-universities/rankings

Ulla, M. B., & Perales, W. F. (2021). Facebook as an integrated online learning support application during the COVID19 pandemic: Thai university students' experiences and perspectives. *Heliyon, 7*, Article e08317. https://doi.org/10.1016/j.heliyon.2021.e08317

Wichadee, S. (2013). Peer feedback on Facebook: The use of social networking websites to develop writing ability of undergraduate students. *Turkish Online Journal of Distance Education, 14*(4), 260–270.

World Bank. (n.d.). *World Bank open data.* https://data.worldbank.org

Wudthayagorn, J. (2021). An exploration of the English exit examination policy in Thai public universities. *Language Assessment Quarterly.* https://doi.org/10.1080/15434303.2021.1937174

Wyatt, D. K. (1969). *The politics of reform in Thailand: Education in the reign of King Chulalongkorn.* Yale University Press.

CHAPTER 10

DEVELOPING HIGHER EDUCATION IN TIMOR-LESTE: A WORK IN PROGRESS

Margie Beck

ICFP Baucau, Timor-Leste

ABSTRACT

Since Timor-Leste achieved its independence in 2002, the higher education sector has grown from 1 public university to 18 accredited and 3 pending accreditation tertiary institutions. This chapter discusses several key issues, particularly concerning the young people who make up more than half the 1.2 million population. As each year passes, more students complete secondary school, and the majority of these young people want to continue their studies in a tertiary institute. Other issues confronting the higher education sector, including how the government of Timor-Leste responds to achieving Sustainable Development Goal 4, how to increase quality education in the tertiary sector and the capacity for further academic progression for faculty and staff are addressed in light of the lack of qualified and appropriate staffing in institutions. The needs of the labor market and the mismatch between these needs and the degrees that tertiary institutions offer, are briefly discussed. Finally, the difficulties faced by higher education institutions in meeting the requirements for accreditation in the drive for membership of ASEAN are reviewed.

Keywords: Higher Education; development of emerging states; Sustainability Development Goals (SDG); ASEAN and Timor-Leste; Quality Assurance (QA); National Education Strategic Plan (NESP); labor market and unemployment

---

Higher Education in Southeast Asia
International Perspectives on Education and Society, Volume 49, 139–150
Copyright © 2025 by Margie Beck
Published under exclusive licence by Emerald Publishing Limited
ISSN: 1479-3679/doi:10.1108/S1479-367920240000049010

INTRODUCTION

Timor-Leste is still in the early stages of development, striving to build an economically viable nation from a largely basic subsistence lifestyle, to take on a strong voice and place on the world stage. With its main resources being fuel and gas and a smaller coffee export business, Timor-Leste has relied heavily on its fuel resources to build the country's development, while being strongly supported on other development projects by governments and non-government organizations from the United Nations, the European Union as well as countries such as China, Australia, Portugal, and Brazil. After more than 500 years of Portuguese colonialism and 25 years of Indonesian rule, Timor-Leste finally achieved independence in 2002, following a 24-year bloody resistance and culminating in extreme post referendum violence in 1999, to become a free nation. The vote for independence led to the exit of all Indonesian government structures, including teachers in schools and post school institutions, as well as the destruction of most of the infrastructure and utilities throughout the country including the only university, the University of Timor (UNTIM) which had opened in 1986.

Since 2002, the higher education sector in Timor-Leste has grown exponentially, at a faster pace and intensity than the regulating and supervising capacity of the state and the labor market's employment capacity to absorb the number of people seeking work. New tertiary institutions continue to open and apply for accreditation, despite the small number of students applying in the private sector when compared to the only government-funded university. The first university in Timor-Leste opened in 1986 during the Indonesian period of rule. The National UNTIM, now called UNTL (National University of Timor-Leste), was the first public university and continues today as the only state-financed institution. Other early post-independence included the University of Dili (UNDIL) which had commenced as a higher institution for Economics (*Tinggi Tinggi Ilni Economy* (STIE) before the referendum for independence in 1999. The rectors and lecturers who worked with colleagues in Indonesia were involved in reopening the Institution, aimed to transform this institution into a university called the UNDIL and to offer different courses to UNTL. In 2001, the *Institute Superior Cristal* (ISC) was quickly followed by *Universidade de Paz* (UNPAZ), with other private universities and institutions opening during the early years of independence. Indeed, in less than 10 years, the number of private universities and higher education institutions (HEIs) had grown to more than 30. *La'o Hamutuk*, (Walking Together), a journal that publishes research into issues affecting the country, had already reported that "of the fourteen tertiary institutions operating in the country, most were in a 'worrisome' situation, with few resources, uncertain funding and lack of qualified staff" (cited in La'o Hamutuk (2003), Higher Education in East Timor, 2003).

The number of students studying in higher education in 1999, before the referendum vote for independence in August, was about 5,000 (MESCC, 2021), but in the following year, because of the destruction of the infrastructure by departing Indonesian military and local militia, the education system, as with all government departments, had collapsed. As a result, no new students enrolled until

2000/2001, when approximately 5,000 students continued or began their tertiary studies. In 2017, more than 65,000 students were enrolled in the various universities and institutions throughout the country. Of the current 1.37 million people of Timor-Leste, there is a concentration in the age group between 18 and 35, so the need for the availability of higher education will continue for many years to come. The median age of Timorese is 20.9 (World Population Review, 2024).

The number of graduates has followed the same pattern with 5,000 students graduating in 2003, none in 2004 and 2006 (this was because of internal civil disturbances), 1,200 in 2007 and increasing annually to 4,700 graduates in 2016. In 2021, the Director-General of MESCC (Ministry of Higher Education, Science and Culture) noted that there were now 63,944 students currently studying in the 19 accredited HEIs, which include both Universities, Institutes and Vocational Institutes, throughout the country (MESCC, 2021).

Young people are using tertiary studies as a way to occupy their time and gain qualifications that will help them find some paid work. In 2021, MESCC issued a graph that outlined the distribution of active students in the higher education sector.

Other key players that have emerged with the different Ministries of Education include the Instituto Nacional de Ciência e Tecnologia (INCT), *Fundo de Desenvolvimento de Capital Humano* (FDCH) and the National Commission for United Nations Educational, Scientific and Cultural Organization (UNESCO) in Timor-Leste.

INCT is the national body for the development of research and technology in Timor-Leste. It was established in 2011 as part of the National Strategy Development plan of 2011–2030 to ensure human capital development. It is an autonomous body that works closely with the Ministry of Higher Education, Science and Culture (MESCC) to encourage research within HEIs. The institute sees science, technology, and innovation as critical elements for the future growth of Timor-Leste. The institute handles disseminating research to all HEIs and acts as a storehouse for newly published research.

The *FDCH* – The Human Capital Development Fund was created in 2011. Its mission is to contribute to developing national human resources in various strategic areas of development. This fund was set up to provide educational support for young people who do not have the economic capacity to complete tertiary studies. In mid-2021, HEIs accepted 480 young people into several different courses to increase the number of professionals in the labor market (Tatoli, 2022). These students commenced their studies close to the end of an academic year, so to keep their scholarships, they were expected to do catch-up work to progress through their degrees. Whether they can do so remains to be seen.

The National Commission for the UNESCO has been part of the growth of education in Timor-Leste since 2003. Its work has included the higher education sector. Though based in Indonesia, UNESCO aims to assist in research and innovation in higher education in science and technology in Timor-Leste to promote the attainment of Sustainable Development Goal 4. In addition, UNESCO helps the Timorese government plan and implement "equal access to education for all, including persons with special needs, linguistic minorities and teenage mothers" (UNESCO, n.d., p. 8).

The following sections will discuss key issues in the country's HE sector: student demand and transitions; quality versus quantity; ASEAN membership inclusion and Sustainability Development Goal (SDG) 4.3.

STUDENT DEMAND AND TRANSITION IN HIGHER EDUCATION

The need for further higher education services has occurred because of the increased demand for education by the growing number of secondary school graduates each year. Since 2003, when approximately 5,000 students enrolled in the new universities and institutions, the number of tertiary students has increased as the demand for higher education grows. The number of students who are currently active has grown from less than 10,000 in 2003 to more than 65,000 in 2019 (MESCC, 2021, p. 17). There are now 23 accredited institutions and other institutions such as the Catholic University, are in the process of meeting requirements for accreditation (de Sá, 2023).

In addition, the lack of work opportunities drives young people into the tertiary sector as the only way to occupy their time and gain qualifications that will help them find some paid work. In 2021, the MESCC outlined the distribution of active students in the higher education sector (Fig. 1).

Since most tertiary institutions tend to be in the larger urban centers, young people travel from home to attend the courses of their choice. The concentration of young people is in Dili or Baucau (the second largest urban center), though new institutions are opening in other municipalities. For example, there is a polytechnical college in Betano, Maufahi, for Petroleum and Geological Studies, a Coffee

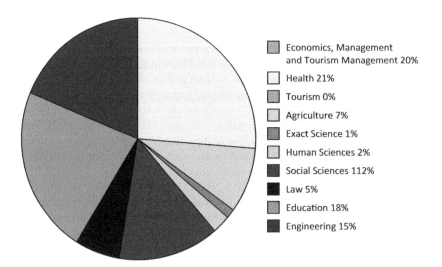

Fig. 1. Distribution of Students According to Study Choice (2021).
Source: MESSC (2021, p. 34).

and Agribusiness Institute in Ermera Municipality, and campuses from Dili institutions set up in the municipalities encourage people to undertake tertiary studies locally. While this practice has not been legally recognized, these institutions employ teachers from local secondary schools to provide tertiary-level education in education, nursing, finance, and business. This opportunity to study in their municipality offers an opportunity for ambitious people to continue their education to find better employment. Most recently, in 2021, the 8th Constitutional Government of Timor-Leste decided to build a new campus in Aileu, with benefits to offer the academic community teaching and learning conditions in an environment that is far from usual city living. It will provide both accommodation and separate faculty areas, thus providing a single, model campus with both formal and practical learning experiences (MESCC, 2021). In addition, for the first time in Timor-Leste, this university will offer wireless connections throughout, using optic fiber cabling that is coming from Australia. As a result, the university will be able to provide both face-to-face and distance teaching and learning (MESCC, 2021). As this is still in the planning stage and needs huge financial funding from the government, it will take time to implement such a bold project.

Although government funding enables comparatively low fees for students at UNTL, private and religious tertiary institutions must charge fees at a level that many students and their families find impossible to pay. The result is that many enrolled students drop out to find paid employment to pay for their tuition or frequently are forced to drop out, never to return to complete their studies. In addition, a new decree-law issued in February 2022 now gives students two years in which to complete their current degree after the usual time framework (Jornal da Republica, 2022). This time limitation will put pressure on poorer students to find financial support to complete their studies or force them out of tertiary studies altogether.

Another difficulty facing those who do graduate is that they do not have the skills required by the local labor market. This mismatch between the supply from HEIs and market demand and the competence between the needs of the labor market and the skills of graduates continues to impede the social contract and development of the country. Ximenes (2022) notes that the supply of labor from HE courses far outweighs the labor demand. As a result, new graduates have limited opportunities to obtain employment. As an example, in 2017, there were 3,605 university graduates from 7 universities though only 298 vacancies were advertised online from January to September in 2017 (SEJT, 2018). The demand for positions in the different labor areas also ends up being filled by internationals, rather than local Timorese.

QUALITY AND QUANTITY OF HIGHER EDUCATION

The first Education Act of 2008 was a milestone for the developing education sector that set out the process for the development and governance of the education sector, including tertiary education. This law was significant because it spelt out how the Ministry of Education was to be organized at national and district levels across each sector of education.

In July 2008, the Council of Ministers approved the document that looked at initial licensing and accreditation in the HEIs of Timor-Leste. It stressed the need for both rigour and quality of these institutions as had been requested by the Government.

In 2009, a team of four Timorese academics and a visiting professor involved in Indonesia's national accreditation process worked with existing tertiary institutions to learn how to complete the documentation required for accreditation. They offered training through several workshops that examined each component that needed to be completed before the accreditation inspection took place (National Agency for the Academic Accreditation and Evaluation, 2022). It was a complex process since, until this time, universities had not been accountable for their organization or daily procedures. Therefore, the need for preparation for Quality Assurance (QA) at both an internal and external level became essential in preparing for each institution's accreditation. Initially, institutions found it difficult to appoint a specific staff member to carry out this work, but institutional certification has become a regular part of the work of tertiary institutions. Once implemented, the number of licensed tertiary institutions fell to 9 from 13 (National Agency for the Academic Accreditation and Evaluation, 2022). In 2013, there were only 11 HEIs registered as accredited, but by 2020, there were a further 7 institutions registered (National Agency for the Academic Accreditation and Evaluation, 2022) and new applications for accreditation from other institutions continue to be received, so this number is assumed to increase, with ambitious plans for a "university city" to be situated in Aileu, about a 2-hour trip out of the capital city, to become a reality in the "near future" (MESCC, 2021). As institutions have met the accreditation requirements, and other Universities open, there is an expectation that this number will continue to increase. In all, 23 HEIs are now accredited either fully or partially (National Agency for the Academic Accreditation and Evaluation, 2022; de Sá, 2023).

In 2018, the Ministry of Education was split into two to cope with the increasing number of students, teachers, and institutions. For the higher education sector, the Ministry for Higher Education, Science and Culture (*Ministério Ensino Superior, Ciência e Cultura*) became the body for oversight of universities and tertiary institutions. Some of the most important goals of MESCC include that one-third of all teachers in the Higher Education Universities should have gained a doctorate by 2030. At the moment, MESCC has tabled that most of those lecturing in Universities and HEIs have only a Licentiate – equivalent to a Bachelor's degree. Furthermore, MESCC aims to commence an internal QA system through ANAAA and provide a formation program for teachers working in Higher Education and Polytechnics. These goals have added another layer to the existing *Agência Nacional para Avaliação Acreditação Académia* (ANAAA), as the national body for accreditation.

While the availability of courses in HEIs in Timor-Leste continues to expand, at an internal level, there is a tendency for institutions to establish new courses based on sufficient availability of their resources. These resources include the

Developing Higher Education in Timor-Leste 145

qualifications and ability of the lecturing staff available for teaching rather than the relevancy of the scientific areas and their respective graduates to the needs of labor market demand. Many of the courses are not yet accredited, with only 105 of 200 study programs having undergone program accreditation. None of these programs has achieved an A grade (excellent), with most (76.2%) still in the C (satisfactory) classification, and only 18.1% achieving a B (good) level (de Sá, 2023; Viegas, 2020).

Students choose their course of study without career guidance, but what path they can follow depends on their results from the National Secondary Exams. Students provide three options in their applications for tertiary studies that they are interested in, and the universities and institutions decide who they will accept. To offset this lack of informed choice, Hill (cited in United Nations Development Project [UNDP], 2018) suggests further reforms to improve the National University of Timor-Leste (UNTL). These suggestions include better selection processes, additional practical experiences, the need for vocational direction, and additional focus on why students want to study in particular disciplines. These suggestions could apply equally to all institutions. On a practical level, lack of access to print assessment tasks and finding relevant internet resources impede students' learning. The reality is that the number of computers available for students to use does not meet daily demand, and often, students are expected to pay for computer time, hindering many from being able to complete their work because of a lack of finances. In 2021, 64,589 pre- and post-Licentiate students are studying 1 of the 99 courses offered in the country. Many choose to study in Indonesia because of the lower cost of study and the breadth of courses available (MESCC, 2021).

In terms of student graduations, MESCC has a Department of Statistics that records and verifies every student's results before permitting the Universities and HEIs to graduate their students. This is a long and intensive process that is then repeated by the department for graduates to have their degrees legalized. The acknowledgement of the legalization process is finally published in the *Jornal da Republica*, the publication arm of the Government (Jornal da Republica, 2022).

Ximenes (2022) also cites the difficulties of attracting and hiring qualified human resources. Academic staff in HEIs often are called to teach in areas in which they have had no formal formation. Timor-Leste has a "one step up" level for teaching, but figures (Table 1) show that less than 50% of academic staff have a Licentiate degree, and 50.24% have a master's degree (ANAAA, 2019).

Table 1. Faculty Members by Academic Qualifications and Gender (2019).

Details	Gender		Total
	Male	Female	
PhD/Doctorate	90(89.1%)	11(10.9%)	101(5.6%)
Masters	681(75.7%)	224(24.7%)	905(50.24%)
Undergraduate	527 (66.3%)	268(33.7%)	795(44.12%)
Total faculty members	1,298(71.8%)	503(28.2%)	1,801

Source: ANAAA (2019).

Another issue relating to quality is a real difficulty in the languages that are used in education in Timor-Leste (Ximenes, 2022). As a multilingual country, school students are taught in the two official languages of Tetum and Portuguese, in varying degrees as they progress through school. Portuguese is expected to be taught and used in secondary schooling. However, the reality is that students complete their education with poor Portuguese capability. In the tertiary sector, language is even more diverse, with the language of instruction being the language most common in the various fields of study. One example is that for those studying Economics, the course is taught in Indonesian, since this is the language most common to the financial sector in Timor-Leste. However, those who work in government need strong Portuguese, while teachers in the lower grades of schooling need both Tetum and Portuguese. Some lecturers in HEIs continue to use Indonesian as their Portuguese is not strong enough to teach in that language (Taylor-Leech, 2015).

MEMBERSHIP INCLUSION IN ASEAN

The issues confronting higher education in Timor-Leste are not only about numbers. Applying for membership in ASEAN and meeting several conditions of Mutual Recognition Arrangements (MRA) and Mutual Recognition (MRS) have changed the institutional organization processes. In 1922, education was included as a prime exchange with other ASEAN countries, but *ANAAA* is preparing for this eventuality. As a result, the higher education sector has shifted requirements for its institutions, often leading to confusion about organization and performance indicators that had not been part of earlier requirements for accreditation. For academics, trying to produce the same indicators for higher education in a country that is only 20 years into its independence adds a further layer of difficulty in the organization processes. Academics themselves stress that there is a level of autonomy that best suits their specific specialties, while the administration tries to make it "one size fits all" (Garwe, 2021). DiMaggio & Powell (as cited in Garwe, 2021), argue that while harmonization between countries allows for broader opportunities for both academics and students, "the importance of academic freedom in higher education is often overlooked" (p. 9). To demand the same program structure for all tertiary offerings can degrade the unique needs of specific disciplines.

Timor-Leste is committed to becoming part of the ASEAN group of nations, in which education plays an important role. With an international expert from one of the ASEAN countries being part of the annual accreditation process, the panels of assessors raise the standards required with each annual assessment and inspection. However, there is an ongoing need for better training for institutions to prepare for the yearly review. This additional training is crucial to those institutions out of the capital that cannot visit ANAAA with offices in Dili easily. When it comes to the accreditation process, with the limited financial resources and qualified staff who can perform their work objectively and effectively, ANAAA staff struggle to find external assessors from other HEIs, since experience has

Developing Higher Education in Timor-Leste

shown that they lack understanding of the roles and functions of the HEIs, so their work is often flawed and lacking in genuine assistance to their colleagues. ANAAA has provided training and a continuous internship program for its staff through a partnership with Malaysia, Indonesia, and the Philippines to remedy this. These experiences help build a more professional accreditation team capable of providing skills to the institutions with whom they work (Viegas, 2020).

On November 24, 2021, the Meeting of the Council of Ministers met to approve the Decree-Law that set out the

> legal regime of the national standard curriculum for higher education and regulates the binary system, the legal regime of degrees and diplomas of higher education, the conditions for their attribution, the corresponding credit system, the academic calendar, the system of assessment of course units and the completion of a study programme. (RDTL, 2021)

This Decree-Law aims not only to improve the whole higher education sector at the institutional level but plans to allow for international mobility for jobs and further study. It also recognizes degrees obtained overseas by East Timorese students. This decree-law is to improve the opportunity for membership in ASEAN, by allowing for international study and teaching by HEIs. It presumes that those who apply for teaching and study will find HEIs with similar courses that will accept applicants from Timor-Leste. In addition, the MESCC has already commenced disseminating this new Decree-Law by holding a seminar on March 29, 2022, to ensure that all training offered in the country is in line with the requirements of the global market (De Deus, 2022).

SDG 4.3

Timor-Leste is committed to achieving the SDG and has mapped out its own "roadmap" to achieve these goals. Quality Education (SDG 4) is key to achieving other sustainable development goals, so this goal has become the over-reaching umbrella for achieving all goals. To attain these goals, a realistic and increased budget for education needs to be implemented in the annual budget decision-making. While there has been increased spending on education in general for the past 10 years, in reality, the proportion of the total national budget allocated to education has decreased (UNESCO, n.d., p. 8). With the potential to create both employment opportunities and to help students become work ready (Inder, 2021), investment in education, both private and public, has real worth. In fact, the Economic Recovery Plan (2020) for Timor-Leste, suggested a doubling of the education budget in the near future (Inder, 2021). However, it is difficult to find concrete evidence that shows that the government is working with ANAAA and MESCC to provide funding that will allow for the achievement of the goals.

The Covid-19 pandemic has affected all learning environments worldwide, not least in the tertiary sector. Many publications have described, analyzed, and researched student and staff reactions, and suggested options to cope with the options that least affect the teaching and learning process in universities and tertiary institutions (Camilleri, 2021; Chitpin & Karoui, 2021; Noori, 2021; Robinson-Neal, 2021; Scarborough, 2021; Tee, 2021). In Timor-Leste, the

MESSC has responded in several ways to lessen the impact of lockdowns, lack of vaccinations, and internet access difficulties for online learning. After the initial total shutdown in 2020 of all tertiary institutions, MESSC encouraged online learning for students to continue their studies. It quickly became evident that some serious issues arose from this option: poor internet access, lack of money to purchase internet access, and lecturers' lack of capacity to provide online learning all made the process untenable for most students.

To overcome some of these problems, in mid-2021, MESSC offered all students funding to purchase internet access so they could continue with their studies. While the idea was excellent, the disbursement management was challenging to implement. Each institution struggled to find student telephone numbers that had remained constant for the payment of funds. The National Parliament also passed a decree providing funds to MESCC to pay for student fees for both semesters of 2021 due to the downturn in the economy during the worst of the COVID-19 epidemic (RDTL, 2021). However, in early 2022, the last payments were finalized, with each institution having to provide a detailed account of students' receipt of this funding.

Although the government of Timor-Leste developed its NESP in 2011 (Ministry of Education, 2011), stating specific targets and goals for the following 19 years, the actual budget has always been less than anticipated. The reality is that about 8–9% only is allocated to education, and this continues to be lower than most other countries in the world. In 2020, the difference between the projected budget decided in 2011 and the actual budget had dropped to a 67% shortfall, leaving student funding from UD$450 per student down to less than US$300 in 2019 (Kraik, 2020).

It has been mentioned that HEIs in Timor-Leste are primarily in the private sector and that only the National University receives funding. Private institutions rely on student fees as the main source of income. Because of this HEIs find it extremely difficult to maintain sustainability and rely on outside donors. The government is limited to offering diverse ways to help the private sector by offering overseas study opportunities for lecturing staff of HEIs to upgrade qualifications and to take out credit to carry out building projects (RDTL, 2021). The government has also encouraged HEIs to take on extra students who are paid for by the government as a way of increasing the number of students in tertiary study, but also by injecting funds into the private sector (RDTL, 2021).

CONCLUSION

The higher education sector continues and will continue to grow in the future because of the burgeoning number of youths graduating from secondary schools. The young of Timor-Leste want to continue their education to increase their academic learning because employment opportunities for school leavers are so limited. Therefore, the higher education sector must look to the needs of the labor market, the width and depth of academic offerings, and the development of quality teaching and learning in all disciplines being offered in HEIs. For the most

Developing Higher Education in Timor-Leste 149

part, HEIs struggle with finding funds for research, community engagement and cooperation as well as finance for expanding resources, infrastructure and information systems and obtaining stakeholder feedback (Viegas, 2020).

According to the Constitution (RDTL, 2002), education is the right of all citizens. This right to education was emphasized when the Prime Minister of Timor-Leste spoke at the World Teachers' Day celebration in Dili (Araujo, 2016). It is stressed that although education is the transmission of knowledge for the future of a society, it is also essential as the road for young people to contribute to the development of Timor-Leste and is the most pertinent to the role of higher education in Timor-Leste. To achieve quality in the sector as well as to achieve the SDGs, the implementation of the aims and objectives of the Política Nasional de Ensino Superior (MESCC, 2021) provides a blueprint as the way forward but without including how this potential implementation will be funded or brought into fruition.

REFERENCES

Araujo, R. (2016). *Education as a cornerstone for building democratic values*. Retrieved October 24, 2021, from http://timor-leste.gov.tl/wp-content/uploads/2016/10/Education-as-a-Cornerstone-for-Building-Democratic-Values_12.10.2016.pdf

Chitpin, S., & Karoui, O. (2021). Covid 19 and educational leadership: Resolving educational issues. *Academia Letters*, Article 229. https://doi.org/10.20935/AL229

De Deus, I. L. (2022, March 29). MESCC promotes seminar on the new national standard curriculum for higher education. In *TATOLI*. TATOLI. Retrieved April 30, 2022, from http://www.tatoli>home>EDUCATION

De Sá, J. (2023). *73% of Higher Education in Timor-Leste has accreditation at level C.*

Garwe, E. C. (2021). Harmonization of higher education tensions: Does one size fit all? *Academia Letters*, Article 785. https://doi.org/10.20935/AL785

Inder, B. (2021). *Timor-Leste's Youth Population: The employment challenges of a 'Youth Bulge'. Centre for Development Economics and Sustainability*. Monash University. Retrieved April 30, 2022, from www.monashintimor.orgpublications

Institutu Superior Cristal (ISC). (n.d.). Retrieved April 30, 2022, from https://web.iscjournal.com/

Jornal da Republica. (2022). Retrieved November 23, 2022, from https://www.mj.gov.tl/jornal/?q=node/7045

Kraik, T. I. (2020). *Economics of Education in Timor-Leste*. Retrieved April 16, 2021, from https://laohamutuk.blogspot.com/2020/03/economics-of-education-ekonomiku.html

La'o Hamutuk. (2003). Retrieved February 5, 2022, from https://www.laohamutuk.org/Bulletin/2003/Mar/bulletinv4n1b.html#table02

Ministério do Ensino Superior, Ciência e Cultura (MESCC). (2021). *Política Nasional de Ensino Superior*. MESCC.

Ministry of Education. (2011). *National Education Strategic Plan (2011-2030)*. Retrieved November 30, 2022, from http://www.moe.gov.tl/pdf/NESP2011-2030.pdf

National Agency for Academic Evaluation and Accreditation (ANAAA). (2022). Retrieved November 23, 2022, from https://anaaa.gov.tl/akreditasaun-institusional/

Noori, A. Q. (2021). *Online learning experiences amid the COVID-19 pandemic: Students' Perspectives*. Retrieved January 8, 2022, from https://doi.org/10.20935/AL4307

Robinson-Neal, A. (2021). Reflections on educational practice: COVID-19 influences. *Academia Letters*, Article 176. https://doi.org/10.20935/AL176

Scarborough, R. (2021). Faculty as nonpersons at pandemic U. *Academia Letters*, Article 247. https://doi.org/10.20935/AL247

Taylor-Leech, K. (2015). *Multilingual education for all?* Retrieved November 30, 2022, from https://apsa.us/wp-content/ellipsis/10leech.pdf

Tee, A. (2021). Maintaining quality and standards in higher education through time of rapid change. *Academia Letters*, Article 2069. https://doi.org/10.20935/AL2069

UNESCO. (n.d.). *Timor-Leste Country Strategy, 2018-2021*. Retrieved October 23, 2021, from https://unesdoc.unesco.org/ark:/48223/pf0000263496?19=null&queryId=7ba635e1-4ced-4186-9301-38066d369f63

United Nations Development Project (UNDP). (2018). *National human development report 2018: Planning the opportunities for a youthful population*. UNDP.

University of Dili (UNDIL). (2022). *Profile page*. Retrieved February 5, 2022, from https://undil.tl/perfile-undil.html

Viegas, E. (2020, December 7). *Movement of Professionals*. PowerPoint presentation to Higher Education Institutions Timor-Leste. AEC Interface.

World Population Review. (2024). Retrieved March 9, 2024, from https://www.worldometers.info/world-population/timor-leste-population/

Ximenes, P. B. (2022). Higher education in Timor-Leste. In L. P. Symaco & M. Hayden (Eds.), *International handbook on education in South East Asia* (pp. 222–251). Springer Nature.

CHAPTER 11

ACHIEVING VIETNAM'S SUSTAINABLE DEVELOPMENT GOALS IN THE HIGHER EDUCATION SECTOR

Le-Nguyen Duc Chinh[a] and Martin Hayden[b]

[a]Vietnam National University HCMC, Vietnam
[b]Southern Cross University, Australia

ABSTRACT

Vietnam is firmly committed to attaining the Sustainable Development Goals articulated in the United Nations 2030 Sustainable Development Agenda. Goal 4 concerns quality education, and target 4.3 refers to ensuring access by all men and women to quality and affordable technical, vocational and tertiary education, including university education. In 2017, the Prime Minister issued a directive that included five actions to be taken by Vietnam's Ministry of Education and Training to achieve target 4.3 in the context of the higher education sector. This chapter provides an opportunity to review some challenges the Ministry faces in implementing the five actions specified.

Keywords: Equity; gender equality; social inclusion; student loans; institutional autonomy; network reform; socialisation; qualifications framework; governance; access; accreditation

---

Higher Education in Southeast Asia
International Perspectives on Education and Society, Volume 49, 151–167
Copyright © 2025 by Le-Nguyen Duc Chinh and Martin Hayden
Published under exclusive licence by Emerald Publishing Limited
ISSN: 1479-3679/doi:10.1108/S1479-367920240000049011

INTRODUCTION

The 2030 *Sustainable Development Agenda* is highly relevant to Vietnam's needs and stage of development. Not surprisingly, therefore, Vietnam is firmly committed to its attainment. The Agenda identifies 17 *Sustainable Development Goals* (SDGs) to be addressed by all nations. Goal 4 concerns quality education, and target 4.3 refers to ensuring access by all men and women to quality and affordable technical, vocational, and tertiary education, including university education. In 2017, in *Decision No. 622/QD-TTg, dated May 10, 2017*, the Prime Minister directed the Ministry of Education and Training to take five actions relating to the attainment of target 4.3 in the context of the higher education sector. This chapter provides a context for and reviews some of the Ministry's challenges in implementing the five actions specified. Regarding the higher education sector, the Ministry of Education and Training was required to:

- implement strategies already approved regarding gender equality to ensure that all young people and adolescents, male and female, who have the required capacity, can access formal higher education services;
- raise the quality of tertiary education institutions by renovating their approach and management mechanism to link education to labour markets;
- implement policies to support social welfare beneficiaries, poor people, and people in vulnerable circumstances so that they can access higher education services according to their needs;
- accelerate reform of the network of higher education institutions, giving due importance to the quality of education and ensuring a system of higher education that is effective and in keeping up with regional and global trends; and
- give increased autonomy to higher education institutions based on their respective capacity, quality, and financial ability to reduce financial burdens on the State budget.

The chapter begins with a brief overview of the evolution and current circumstances of Vietnam's higher education sector. Then matters relating to each of the five actions are discussed.

EVOLUTION AND CURRENT CIRCUMSTANCES OF VIETNAM'S HIGHER EDUCATION SECTOR

Vietnam's commitment to higher education dates to more than 1,000 years ago when a Vietnamese emperor established a seat of higher learning in what is today the city of Hanoi. The institution founded was committed to the teachings of Confucius. Over the centuries since then, and until the early 20th century when French colonial authorities began establishing higher education institutions based on a Western model, Confucian academies dominated the national education system in Vietnam. These academies were highly selective and accessible only to males. The examination system was rigorous. Certificates of achievement equivalent to bachelor's and doctoral degrees were conferred. Graduates were rewarded with an appointment as a mandarin serving the royal court or as a military leader.

Vietnam was a French colony from 1848 to 1954. The French established a system of specialised higher education institutions to serve the elite in Vietnam and train locals in areas of specialisation needed to support the colonial administration. This system became increasingly fragile during the war of independence between 1945 and 1954. It was then abandoned by the communist government in the North when, in 1954, Vietnam was split into two countries. In 1975, when Vietnam was reunified under a hard-line communist government, the national higher education sector was comprehensively restructured along the lines of a Soviet model of higher education. Private higher education provision was abolished.

The modern higher education sector in Vietnam continues to be affected by many of the characteristics of the Soviet model. However, over the last two decades, it has undergone significant change, with market forces becoming increasingly influential in decision-making about governance, access, curriculum, and local and international engagement. Private higher education provision is now also encouraged within the higher education sector.

According to the most recent data, there were 242 higher education institutions in Vietnam's higher education sector, of which 67 were privately owned institutions, accounting for 22% of all enrolments in 2022 (Ministry of Education and Training [MOET], 2022). Of the 2,145,426 students enrolled in the higher education sector, 54.2% were female.

A distinctive feature of the sector is its rapid expansion since the early 2000s. The gross enrolment rate increased from 9% in 2000 to 29% in 2019 (World Bank, 2022a). However, the growth rate has recently slowed considerably, mainly among young males (GSO, 2023, p. 796). The likely reasons for this trend are that young people, especially young males, are becoming more inclined to study at vocational colleges or go abroad for work or study (Hậu, 2020; Thanh & Lê, 2022).

The establishment of many new universities and the appointment of many more academic staff members have accompanied the sector's expansion. A significant improvement in the qualification levels of academic staff members has also been observed. Whereas in 2009, only 10.16% of academic staff members held a doctoral qualification (*Report No. 760/BC-BGDĐT, dated October 29, 2009*), by 2021, the proportion had reached 32.4% (MOET, 2022). A generous provision of public funding has enabled this transformation, allowing many talented young Vietnamese to go abroad to complete their doctorates. These young scholars are having a significant impact on Vietnam's research productivity. Data from the Scimago Lab (Scimago, 2022) indicate a recent surge in the number of citable research documents coming from Vietnam. For example, whereas in 2016, Vietnam was the source of 5,877 citable documents, by 2021, the figure had climbed to 18,381 citable documents (Scimago, 2022).

However, improvements in research productivity tend to be concentrated across a few universities. In 2021, there were six universities (Vietnam National University in Ho Chi Minh City, Vietnam National University in Hanoi, Hanoi University of Science and Technology, Ton Duc Thang University, and Duy Tan

University) that accounted for more than one-half (53.2%) of all citable research documents from Vietnam (Elsevier, 2021). The University Ranking by Academic Performance (URAP) agency, a Turkish non-profit organisation, recently ranked 17 Vietnamese universities as worthy of praise for their publication and citation rates (Nguyen, 2022). The other side of this coin is that most universities in Vietnam were entirely teaching-focused and produced little or no research outputs.

ACHIEVING GENDER EQUALITY

The first of the Prime Minister's directions to achieve target 4.3 of SDG 4 concerned the need for the Ministry of Education and Training to implement strategies already approved for gender equality in higher education. Though not made explicit in *Decision No. 622/QD-TTg, dated May 10, 2017*, these strategies presumably included gender equality provisions embedded in a succession of legislative and regulatory instruments concerning the higher education sector in Vietnam.

Vietnam's commitment to gender equality in the national education system is legally well-established. The *Education Law* of 2005 (*Law No. 38/2005/QH11, dated June 14, 2005*) declared that male and female citizens should have equal educational opportunities. This Law was followed in 2006 by another more specific legal document, the *Gender Equality Law* (*Law No. 73/2006/QH11, dated Jun 29, 2006*). It required male and female students to be treated equally when selecting career training areas and receiving benefits from education and training policies. *Decree No. 70/2008/NĐ-CP, dated June 4, 2008*, directed all ministries and ministerial-level agencies to promulgate measures for promoting gender equality. *Decree No. 55/2009/NĐ-CP, dated June 10, 2009*, subsequently replaced by *Decree No. 125/2021/NĐ-CP, dated December 12, 2021*, indicated penalties concerning violations of gender equality regulations. *Decision No. 2351/QĐ-TTg, dated December 24*, 2010, which approved a national strategy for gender equality over the period from 2011 to 2020, identified seven specific objectives for ensuring equality between men and women in access to opportunities for participating in and benefitting from political, cultural, and social activities in Vietnam.

In the higher education sector, Vietnam's first higher education law, the *Higher Education Law* of 2012 (*Law No. 08/2012/QH13, dated June 18, 2012*), prescribed that all higher education students should be equitably treated without gender-based discrimination (Article 60). More recently, there has been an emphasis on attaining specific gender-based participation targets. For example, the gender equality strategic plan for 2021 to 2030 (*Resolution No. 28/NQ-CP, dated March 3, 2021*) indicated that, by 2025, at least 50% of master's degree and 30% of PhD graduates should be female.

For many decades, Vietnam has asserted the importance of gender equality in the national education system. However, in higher education, females have traditionally been less well-represented than males. During the past decade, this situation has reversed. As shown in Fig. 1, female enrolment numbers moved ahead of male enrolment numbers in 2011 and have continued to lead since then. In 2022, 54.2% of higher education students were female, compared with only 45.8% of males

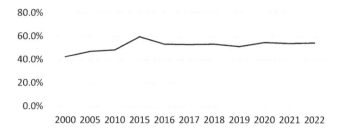

Fig. 1. Percentage of Female University Students. *Source*: Ministry of Education and Training [MOET] (2022).

(MOET, 2022). This pattern appears to result from females having higher retention rates than males at the upper-secondary level in the general education sector.

According to the Vietnam Household Living Standards Survey in 2020, the net enrolment rate for females in upper-secondary education was 79%, compared with a rate of only 73.5% for males (GSO, 2021, pp. 134–135). The reasons females now remain longer than males at the upper-secondary and higher education levels of the national education system need to be better understood. Exploration by the Ministry of Education and Training is warranted. The focus of policy concern now needs to be poorer male participation rates beyond the completion of lower-secondary education unless the problem is that females remain longer in the education system because they have fewer opportunities than males to find employment in the labour force.

However, within the higher education sector, some disparities suggest female disadvantage. One of these relates to participation in science, technology, engineering, and mathematics (STEM) programs, which tend to be dominated by males. The reverse situation occurs in the humanities and social sciences. Data from the World Bank (2022b) show, for example, that only 37% of STEM graduates in 2016 were female. This pattern is also evident within individual universities. For instance, at the Vietnam National University of Ho Chi Minh City (VNU-HCM) in 2019, 80% of students admitted to the College of Information Technology and 74% of students admitted to the College of Technology were male (Nguyen, 2019). In 2019, 74% of students admitted to the College of Social Sciences at VNU-HCMC were female, as were 69% of students at the College of Economics and Law. The pattern tends to be repeated at most, if not all, leading universities in Vietnam.

This gender disparity may reflect traditional gender-based attitudes in Vietnam regarding the appropriateness of females choosing to study natural sciences and engineering (Institute for Social Development Studies [ISDS], 2015, p. 38). However, other countries have successfully improved female participation rates in STEM programs. Vietnam could learn from their experience. For example, Malaysia introduced a policy with detailed targets and timelines to reduce the gender gap in STEM fields. It also launched a program to place female secondary school students who were good at STEM subjects into the STEM stream and provide them with an appropriate curriculum to become more confident to study at the tertiary level (Malaysia Ministry of Education, 2016, p. 18). Similarly, Singapore initiated specific programs to fill the gender gap in STEM fields. For example, the Promotion of Women in Engineering, Research, and Science (POWER) program provides a support system that helps female students study STEM subjects at the tertiary level and advance their careers after graduation (Nanyang Technological University [NTU], 2022).

Another area of apparent gender disparity concerns participation in postgraduate education. According to a recent report from the Ministry of Labour, Invalids and Social Affairs on gender equality in 2019 (*Report No. 362/BC-CP, dated August 10, 2020*), more males (63.8% and 72%) than females (44.2% and 28%) enrolled in master's and PhD programs respectively in 2019. Traditional gender-based attitudes may also play a role here. According to one investigation, while there is encouragement in Vietnam for all young people to continue their studies to achieve the highest possible qualification, this encouragement may be more robust for males than for females (ISDS, 2015, p. 39).

LINKING WITH THE LABOUR MARKET

The second of the Prime Minister's directions concerned the need for higher education institutions to reform their orientation and management to enable better linkages with the labour market. The effectiveness of Vietnam's higher education quality assurance framework and accreditation is critical. Business leaders have traditionally complained about recent university graduates' lack of employment readiness. Recently, however, as more universities are achieving certification under the higher education quality assurance framework, employers' views appear to be much more positive (Nga Nguyễn, 2022).

The higher education quality assurance framework is a recent development in Vietnam. The framework's process may be dated back to 2003 when the Ministry of Education and Training created a General Department of Educational Testing and Accreditation (Phạm & Nguyễn, 2019). In 2005, the *Education Law* declared the purpose of institutional accreditation to be helping higher education institutions identify progress in implementing their educational objectives, programs, and contents (Article 17). The Law also indicated that the results of institutional reviews must be publicly announced after an institution is accredited. Over the following 10 years, the ministry focused on developing institutional and program accreditation criteria. It also established independent quality accreditation centres. Then, in 2016, it issued quality standards and criteria for assessing academic programs (*Circular 04 No. 04/2016/TT- BGDĐT, dated March 14, 2016*); and, in 2017, it issued quality standards and criteria for institutional accreditation (*Circular No. 12/2017/TT-BGDĐT, dated May 19, 2017*). National quality accreditation centres were subsequently established to implement institutional accreditation. Institutions were also permitted to obtain certification for their quality by reputable international accreditation agencies.

The sector has made solid progress since 2017 with institutional accreditations. In August 2023, 194 of the 242 universities were fully accredited for the first time, and five were accredited for a second time (MOET, 2023; Tường, 2022). International accreditation agencies accredited nine universities. Progress with program accreditation has been slower. In 2022, only 10% (609) of the 6,000 academic programs being delivered by universities had been accredited (Quý, 2022).

Various quality standards and criteria for institutional accreditation identified in *Circular No. 12/2017/TT-BGDĐT, dated May 19, 2017*, addressed the linkages between universities and the labour market. For example, higher education institutions were directed to involve employers in establishing an institutional system for designing, developing, monitoring, and approving academic programs (Article 17). They were also required to record, monitor, and compare the employer satisfaction levels with a view to implementing self-improvement activities (Article 25). Recent research is identifying the beneficial impact of these provisions. The accreditation process at one of the constituent universities in the VNU-HCMC network of universities is reported to have had a markedly positive effect on the quality of the academic programs offered (Phạm & Nguyễn, 2020). These programs were closely linked with the labour market and had been modified to meet employer preferences (Phạm & Nguyễn, 2020, p. 52).

ADDRESSING SOCIAL INCLUSION

The third Prime Ministerial direction concerned the implementation of policies supporting access to higher education by social welfare beneficiaries, poor people, and people in vulnerable circumstances, according to their needs. A commitment to equal opportunity is fundamental to government policy regarding Vietnam's national education system. Vietnam's *Constitution* requires, for example, the provision of assistance to disadvantaged groups to enable their access to education (Article 61). Consistent with this commitment, the *Higher Education Law* of 2012 expressed the Government's commitment to providing preferential policies for students from poor homes or belonging to ethnic minority groups (Article 12). In 2015, *Decree No. 86/2015/NĐ-CP, dated October 2, 2015*, indicated that higher education students could waive or reduce their tuition fees if they were disabled, orphaned, or from a low-income family or an ethnic-minority group. In 2017, *Circular No. 36/2017/TT-BGDĐT, dated December 28, 2017*, required all higher education institutions to show their scholarship policies on their websites. In 2018, the revised *Higher Education Law* (*Law No. 34/2018/QH14, dated November 19, 2018*) required public higher education institutions to redirect a portion of their total tuition fee income to provide financial support for poor students (Article 65).

The extent of social inclusion in the national education system has improved remarkably over the past 30 years. The gross enrolment rate in primary and lower-secondary education is now above 95% (Le & Hoang, 2022, p. 2), meaning that, except for ethnic minority communities living in remote countryside locations, all social groups are now well represented in primary and lower-secondary education. The gross enrolment rate in upper-secondary education has also increased significantly since the early 2000s and was estimated at 65% in 2020 (Le & Hoang,

2022, p. 2). Improvements in social inclusion in the education system reflect Vietnam's strong economic growth, improved living standards, and significantly reduced levels of national poverty since the early 1990s. The level of gross domestic product (GDP) per capita (current US dollars) increased from 95.2 USD in 1990 to 3,694 USD in 2021 (World Bank, 2022c), and the national poverty headcount ratio fell from 58.1% in 1992 to 6.7% in 2018 (World Bank, 2022d).

However, in the higher education sector, which enrols less than one-third of the relevant age group, social inclusion policies have been relatively slow to have an impact. Higher education participation rates are not equal across all regions in Vietnam. It is also evident that young people from better-off homes are more likely to participate in higher education.

Differences between regions in higher education participation rates are significant. As shown in Fig. 2, there is a sizable gap in the number of higher students per 10,000 of the population between the two groups of regions. Between 2015 and 2020, the Red River Delta region (centred on Hanoi) and the Southeast region (centred on Ho Chi Minh City) had two to three times more higher education students per 10,000 population than four other more rural, and, in two cases, more remote, regions. Therefore, certain areas of Vietnam are better represented than others among the higher education student population.

There are also significant differences between the richest and the poorest households regarding access to higher education. Drawing on data for 2014 and 2021 (UNESCO, 2022), the poorest quintile of households accounted for 3.48% of attendance at higher education institutions in 2014 and 4.35% in 2021. In contrast, attendance rates at higher education for the richest quintile were 65.42% in 2014 and 64.59% in 2021. The gap was very significant. More recent data (GSO,

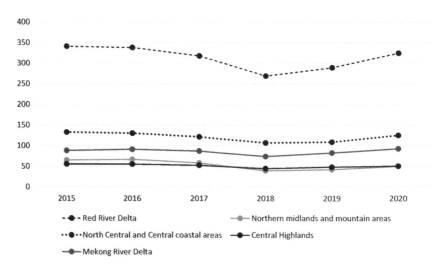

Fig. 2. The Number of Higher Education Students Per 10,000 Population by Regions. *Source*: GSO, 2023 (pp. 931–932).

2021, pp. 119–121) confirm a significant higher education participation gap between the richest and the poorest households. In 2020, the proportion of those over 15 years of age holding a bachelor's qualification or higher was 28.5% for the richest quintile of households in Vietnam but only 1.6% for the poorest. The proportion of those over 15 who never went to school or held no qualifications in the poorest quintile was 33.3%, which was five times higher than for those over 15 years of age in the wealthiest quintile.

Access to higher education in Vietnam also appears to lag compared with access rates across the ASEAN region. While all nations, and especially Vietnam, have experienced growth in these rates, Vietnam's gross enrolment rate continues to fall behind the rates for other countries in the region, including Singapore, Malaysia, Indonesia, and the Philippines (World Bank, 2022e).

Therefore, the challenges for the Ministry of Education and Training in developing policies that will improve access to higher education are formidable. A significant constraint on access in Vietnam is that there are currently few options for poor students to obtain the funds required to pay higher education student tuition fees and meet study costs. Government loans are the primary option. Other funding sources to support higher education attendance are loans from public and private commercial banks and scholarships from universities, civic organisations, or kind-hearted individuals. Loans can be challenging to obtain because students or their parents must demonstrate a capacity to make regular monthly repayments for the loan period. Scholarships tend to be of minimal value and, in most cases, must be obtained competitively.

The public student loan scheme was introduced in 2007 when the Prime Minister issued *Decision No. 157/2007/QĐ-TTg, dated September 27, 2007*, which sought to provide a loan scheme for students from low-income families or who were orphaned or experiencing financial difficulties. The maximum loan amount was set at VND 800,000 (around USD 40) monthly, with an interest rate of 0.5%. In 2022, the maximum loan amount was increased to VND 4,000,000 (around USD 160) per month, and the interest rate was increased to 0.65% per month (*Decision No. 853/QĐ-TTg, dated June 3, 2011, and Decision No. 05/2022/ QĐ-TTg, dated March 23*, 2022). According to the Vietnam Bank for Social Policy (Hương, Linh, & Nương 2021), the amount loaned to students was VND 2,807 billion (around USD 140 million) in 2007. The loan amount peaked at VND 35,802 billion (around USD 1.8 billion) in 2012. Since then, the size of student loan debt has been declining (Nguyen et al., 2021).

However, the loan amounts available are generally insufficient to cover the tuition fees and stipends for high-quality programs at public universities. They would certainly not cover tuition fees for most programs delivered by private universities. There are also various constraints affecting their availability. In 2018, only 2.6% of all enrolled higher education students accessed government loans (Doan et al., 2020, p. 8). The approval process for obtaining loans is widely considered too complicated (Doan et al., 2020, p. 32; Nguyen et al., 2021). For example, first-year students find it challenging to get approved for a loan before they confirm acceptance of a place at university and pay their tuition fees. There is also intense pressure to repay the loans.

According to guidelines from the Vietnam Bank for Social Policies, which manages the loan program, students must repay their loans within one year of graduating (*Decision No. 157/2007/QĐ-TTg, dated September 27, 2007*). They may obtain an extension on grounds such as having no work or experiencing financial difficulty, but the maximum extension period is strictly limited. For example, a full extension for a student who completed a four-year degree program would be two years only. Exceeding the extension period would incur payment of a penalty loan interest rate of 150%. There is also the problem of many students and their families not knowing about the availability of loans. Nguyen et al. (2021), who reviewed the implementation of the loan scheme over the past 10 years, discovered that around 19% of the survey participants had received no information about the loans.

Vietnam should improve the public student loan scheme to help more students from lower-income groups. First, the loan amount should be large enough to cover the tuition fees and provide a living stipend. Other countries adopt this principle. Thailand, for example, provides mortgage loans from 60,000 (about 1,800 USD) to 150,000 (about 4,500 USD) baht per year for tuition fees and other educational expenditures and 24,000 baht (720 USD) a year for a living stipend (Salam, 2018, p. 66). This level of provision is much more generous than is available in Vietnam. Second, the repayment period should be extended, and students should not start to repay their loans until their incomes are higher than the average cost of living in Vietnam. *Decision No. 157/2007/QĐ-TTg, dated September 27, 2007*, determined that loan funds must be repaid within one year of graduation, whether the graduate is employed or not. Extensions are provided, as reported earlier, but the penalty for exceeding the due date after an extension is severe. In general, the existing repayment duration is very short. According to Chapman (2013), low-income graduates in Vietnam must save 40% to 70% of their income to repay the loan. Thailand, in contrast, allows for a repayment duration of 15 years (Salam, 2018, p. 67).

Apart from reviewing the public student loan scheme, the Ministry of Education and Training might also review policies related to providing infrastructure for online program delivery. A recent equity concern that came to light when universities closed because of COVID-19 was that university students from low-income families, mainly those living in rural and remote parts of the country, had poor access to online program delivery. Thien (2021) and Hong (2020) reported on this concern in mountainous provinces, such as Son La, Dien Bien, Quang Nam and Dak Lak, where many ethnic minority groups live. While most universities tried to switch to online program delivery, students living in rural and remote regions faced many challenges with continuing their studies because of poor or non-existent online connectivity.

REFORMING THE UNIVERSITY NETWORK

The fourth Prime Ministerial direction concerned the need for a university network that meets Vietnam's demand for educational quality and an ability to become competitive regionally and globally. Issues relating to an appropriate

Achieving Vietnam's Sustainable Development Goals in the Higher Education Sector 161

university network for Vietnam have been a focus of attention for most of the past two decades.

A significant milestone in the reform of the university network was *Decision No. 47/2001/QĐ-TTg, dated April 4, 2001*, where the Prime Minister introduced a higher education network plan from 2001 to 2010. According to this document, the higher education system would have national universities, regional universities, key universities, academies, vocational and professional colleges, open universities, and community colleges. No criteria for classifying any of these types of institutions were ever specified.

The topic was addressed again in *Resolution 14/2005/NQ-CP, dated November 2, 2005*, concerning the comprehensive reform of higher education by 2020. It emphasised the need to develop key universities that should become national scientific and technological centres. It proposed that specialised research institutes, which functioned independently of the higher education sector at the time, should be merged with the key universities. It also envisaged the establishment of many private higher education institutions.

The Prime Minister introduced a more specific institutional classification framework in *Decision No. 121/2007/QD-TTg, dated July 27, 2007*. It proposed adopting a three-sector model by 2010 that would include universities ranked in the 'top 200' universities in the world, research-oriented universities, and universities and colleges with an applied-knowledge orientation. This plan was completely unrealistic, given that, at the time, hardly any universities in Vietnam were even 'research-oriented' (Hayden & Le-Nguyen, 2020, p. 23). A subsequent planning document, *Decision No. 37/2013/QD-TTg, dated June 26, 2013*, for the period up to 2020, proposed the same three-tiered institutional classification system, but the three tiers were now research-oriented universities and academies, application-oriented universities and academies, and vocationally oriented colleges.

How this structure was to be implemented was not addressed. However, the new *Higher Education Law* of 2012 introduced a notion of ranking higher education institutions according to their prestige and quality. This notion was developed in *Decree No. 73/2015/ND-CP, dated September 8, 2015*, which proposed a stratification and ranking mechanism for the sector. The mechanism proposed was essentially unworkable. The government's decision in 2016 to give responsibility for all vocational education to the Ministry of Labour, Invalids and Social Affairs diverted attention from the need for a classification scheme involving stratification and ranking.

The amended *Higher Education Law* of 2018 made no mention of the matter. Instead, individual universities were permitted to obtain ranking by a reputable national or international ranking agency if that was consistent with their institutional vision. In *Decision No. 69/QD-TTg, dated January 15, 2017*, more realistic aspirations for the network of universities were proposed. This document sensibly indicated that Vietnam should have at least four universities ranked among the top 1,000 universities globally by 2025. By 2024, two Vietnamese universities had achieved top-1000 status on the world university rankings produced by Times Higher Education, and four others were among the top 1,500 universities (Times Higher Education, n.d.).

Progress was finally made regarding the need for a higher education qualifications framework when, in 2016, the Prime Minister announced the establishment of a Vietnamese Qualifications Framework (*Decision No. 1982/QD-TTg, dated October 18, 2016*). The impact of this development on the higher education sector was negligible because of the decision in 2016 to transfer vocational education to the Ministry of Labour, Invalids and Social Affairs. Most of the complexities requiring resolution through reference to the Vietnamese Qualifications Framework were related to vocational education and training rather than higher education.

The place of 'non-public' institutions in the higher education sector has been politically awkward for Vietnam, given its communist ideology and traditional commitment to socialism. Private higher education providers were first permitted during the early 1990s. At the time, they were referred to as 'non-public' institutions. The number of these institutions expanded rapidly during the 1990s. In 2006, there were 30 non-public universities and 17 non-public colleges, accounting for 12.6% of all higher education enrolments (Hayden & Dao, 2010, p. 216). In 2006, *Decree 75/2006/ND-CP, dated August 2, 2006*, introduced a significant change of policy direction by declaring that all future non-public higher education institutions must be 'fully private', that is, owned by private shareholders. Underpinning this change of policy direction was a renewal of commitment to the idea of 'socialisation', whereby private owners could be regarded as contributing to the public good by investing their funds in the provision of public services.

There was a surge in the number of private higher education institutions after 2006. Still, uncertainty remained about how much profit their owners could safely make before attracting attention from the Government. Many claimed to be 'not-for-profit', principally to avoid the payment of company tax rates. Confusion about their taxation status was resolved to an extent in 2013 when, in *Decree 141/2013/ND-CP, dated October 24, 2013*, 'not-for-profit' private higher education institutions were declared to be institutions generating a shareholder dividend below the rate of interest available from government bonds. Five years later, in the amended *Higher Education Law* of 2018, the government introduced a stricter definition of 'not-for-profit' that, in effect, made all private higher education institutions in Vietnam 'for-profit', given that they all needed to make a profit to survive.

The capacity of the Ministry of Education and Training to address network issues in Vietnam's higher education sector remains severely restricted by the high level of fragmentation in the sector's governance and management. As many as 18 ministries and more than 60 public instrumentalities (including provincial governments) exercise line-management supervision of public universities in Vietnam. The Ministry of Education and Training has line-management responsibility for many of the leading universities in the sector but not for the two national universities (VNU-HCMC and VNU-Hanoi), both of which report directly to the Cabinet. While the Ministry of Education and Training is responsible for providing a regulatory framework for the higher education sector, its capacity to enforce regulations is limited because other ministries and provincial authorities may not always be inclined to support the rules approved by the

Ministry of Education and Training. Other ministries and provincial authorities would most likely fiercely resist any attempt by the Ministry of Education and Training to take control of their universities or close any of them down. In 2005, *Resolution 14/2005/NQ-CP, dated November 2, 2005*, identified the need to eliminate line-ministry control of public higher education institutions as one of the objectives to be achieved by 2020. The extent of attention given to that objective to date has been negligible.

ACHIEVING INSTITUTIONAL AUTONOMY

The fifth Prime Ministerial direction concerns increasing the autonomy of higher education institutions based on their respective capacity, quality, and financial ability to reduce financial burdens on the State budget. Issues relating to institutional autonomy in the higher education sector have been a focus of policy attention since at least 2005 (Hayden & Lam, 2007).

In 2005, in the *Education Law*, institutional autonomy for public universities first began to be entertained. Article 60 declared that public higher education institutions could have decision-making freedom across a range of areas, including: developing educational programs, textbooks, and teaching schedules for approved training majors; deciding on enrolment quotas, organising the enrolment and training process, approving students' graduation, and offering degrees; developing their organisational structure, implementing recruitment, managing their human resources, implementing incentive compensation; creating, managing and using different resources; and collaborating with other national and international organisations form the commercial, educational, cultural, medical, and scientific research sectors.

In 2010, a University Charter *(Decision No. 58/2010/QD-TTg, dated September 22, 2010)* sought to guide higher education institutions on how to exercise institutional autonomy. It also indicated various activities that public higher education institutions could perform independently.

The *Higher Education Law* of 2012 went further, stating in Article 29 that universities should enjoy autonomy in teaching and research, management of technology, finances and international relations, and decision-making about organisational structures. However, this freedom was conditional on institutional quality appraisal processes. These processes were unavailable until the Ministry of Education and Training issued regulations on institutional accreditation (*Circular No. 12/2017/TT-BGDDT, dated May 9, 2017*) and academic program quality assessment standards (*Circular No. 04/2016/TT-BGDDT, dated March 14, 2016*).

In the meantime, however, the Ministry of Education and Training issued an updated University Charter (*Decision No. 70/2014/QĐ-TTg, dated December 10, 2014*), which granted some additional freedoms to all public universities. Even more important, in 2014, the government approved *Resolution No. 77/NQ-CP, dated October 24, 2014*, which introduced a pilot project to grant substantial institutional autonomy to approved public higher education institutions willing to become financially self-reliant, that is, no longer dependent on the state for their financial viability. Universities willing to engage in this initiative could develop their own programs, manage their own organisational structures and personnel, and set their own tuition fee levels. This policy was implemented initially with a small number of volunteer universities. In 2020, 23 public universities had volunteered to become financially self-reliant in exchange for their increased institutional autonomy (Tran & Do, 2022, p. 17).

In general, progress in granting more institutional autonomy to public universities in Vietnam has been slow. Though the Prime Minister's *Decision No. 622/ QD-TTg, dated May 10, 2017*, gave the Ministry of Education and Training a direction to provide increased autonomy to higher education institutions based on their respective capacity, quality, and financial ability, many obstacles would need to be overcome. First, as noted earlier, most public universities in Vietnam are not directly responsible to the Ministry of Education and Training. This means that granting increased institutional autonomy to these institutions must be negotiated with many other governmental stakeholders. Second, most public universities cannot survive financially if they cannot rely on public financial support, so they cannot trade increased financial self-reliance for more institutional autonomy. Third, all governing councils of all public universities in Vietnam must comply with the policies of the Communist Party of Vietnam. Therefore, their independent decision-making capacity is always subject to the party's right to veto any decision.

CONCLUSION

Vietnam was prompt in seeking to implement the 2030 *Sustainable Development Agenda* of the United Nations. In 2017, it approved a detailed set of actions to achieve all 17 SDGs in the Agenda. Goal 4 referred to quality education, and target 4.4 referred expressly to ensuring access by all men and women to quality and affordable technical, vocational, and tertiary education, including university education. The Prime Minister proposed five actions regarding higher education improvements, with responsibility for their attainment delegated to the Ministry of Education and Training. This chapter has provided a context for the proposed actions and a review of some challenges the ministry will encounter in addressing them.

Based on the analysis reported in this chapter, specific directions for the future are suggested. First, strategies must overcome the delays between approving policies for the higher education sector and their implementation. Existing policies regarding increasing female participation in STEM programs and PhD training are soundly based and highly appropriate to Vietnam's national aspirations. Still, processes for their speedy implementation are not well developed. There tends, therefore, to be too much delay in achieving policy priorities. This delay is also evident in the slow implementation of the sector's institutional accreditation policy. One source of delay is the lack of a national coordinating agency for the whole higher education sector.

As reported earlier in this chapter, as many as 18 ministries and more than 60 public instrumentalities (including provincial governments) exercise responsibility for public universities in Vietnam. In these circumstances, achieving a synchronised approach to policy implementation is complex. Second, the system for providing public loan funds for less-privileged university students requires extensive review. The level of the individual loans given to eligible applicants is inadequate, given the high cost of the student tuition fees now being charged by most leading public and nearly all private universities. The loan repayment schedule is also too stringent. Many students struggle within their first few years after graduation to earn the income needed to repay their loan debt.

Third, the trade-off forced by the government between institutional autonomy and financial self-reliance is causing those public universities that have accepted institutional autonomy to become preoccupied with securing funds formerly provided by the government. Increasing student tuition fees is the only realistic avenue for replacing the government revenue. However, the higher tuition fees make these universities less accessible to young people from poorer families. Indeed, the concern is that these universities are becoming enclaves for the rich in Vietnamese society.

REFERENCES

Chapman, B. (2013, March 10). Funding tertiary education in Southeast Asia and beyond. *East Asia Forum*. Retrieved November 19, 2022, from https://www.eastasiaforum.org/2013/03/10/funding-tertiary-education-in-southeast-asia-and-beyond/

Doan, D., Kang, J., & Zhu, Y. (2020). *Financing higher education in Vietnam: Student loan reform*. Working paper 51. Oxford Centre for Global Higher Education. Retrieved November 19, 2022, from https://www.researchcghe.org/publications/working-paper/financing-higher-education-in-vietnam-student-loan-reform/

Elsevier. (2021). *Scival*. Retrieved September 6, 2021, from https://www.elsevier.com/solutions/scival

General Statistics Office (GSO). (2021). *Result of the Vietnam household living standards survey 2020*. Statistical Publishing House.

General Statistics Office (GSO). (2023). *Statistical Yearbook of Vietnam 2022*. Statistical Publishing House. https://www.gso.gov.vn/en/data-and-statistics/2023/06/statistical-yearbook-of-2022/

Hậu, H. (2020, July 15). A significant decrease of the number of students choosing to study at universities. Is this an opportunity for vocational schools? *An Ninh Hải Phòng*. Retrieved December 19, 2022, from http://anhp.vn/hoc-sinh-vao-dai-hoc-giam-manh--co-hoi-cho-truong-nghe-d36949.html

Hayden, M., & Dao, K. V. (2010). Private higher education in Vietnam. In G. Harman, M. Hayden, & P. T. Nghi (Eds.), *Reforming higher education in Vietnam: Challenges and priorities* (pp. 215–225). Springer.

Hayden, M., & Lam, Q. T. (2007). Institutional autonomy for higher education in Vietnam. *Higher Education Research & Development*, *26*(1), 73–85. https://doi.org/10.1080/07294360601166828

Hayden, M., & Le-Nguyen, C. D. (2020). A review of the reform agenda for higher education in Vietnam. In L. H. Phan & B. N. Doan (Eds.), *Higher education in market-oriented socialist Vietnam: 'New' players, 'new 'discourses', 'new' practices* (pp. 21–39). Palgrave.

Hong, H. (2020, April 17). Many students in difficult areas cannot access online learning. *Dan Tri*. Retrieved November 19, 2022, from https://dantri.com.vn/giao-duc-huong-nghiep/rat-nhieu-hoc-sinh-vung-kho-khong-the-tiep-can-phuong-phap-hoc-truc-tuyen-20200417073529686.htm

Hương, N., Linh, T. N., & Nương, N. N. (2021). Effectiveness of Credit Policy towards Vietnamese Student. *Review of Finance*, *751*(2), 53–57.

Institute for Social Development Studies (ISDS). (2015). *Social determinants of gender inequality in Vietnam*. ISDS. Retrieved November 19, 2022, from https://vietnam.embassy.gov.au/files/hnoi/ISDS_Report_Binh%20dang%20gioi_EN_PDF-2.pdf

Le, A. V., & Hoang, P. H. (2022). Basic education in Vietnam. In L. P. Symaco & M. Hayden (Eds.), *International handbook on education in South East Asia*. Springer. https://link.springer.com/chapter/10.1007/978-981-16-8136-3_38-1

Malaysia Ministry of Education. (2016). *Sharing Malaysian experience in participation of girls in STEM Education*. UNESCO International Bureau of Education (IBE). Retrieved September 5, 2021, from http://www.ibe.unesco.org/sites/default/files/resources/ipr3-boon-ng-stemgirlmalaysia_eng.pdf

Ministry of Education and Training. (MOET). (2022). *Statistics on higher education sector 2021-2022*. Retrieved March 5, 2024, from https://moet.gov.vn/thong-ke/Pages/thong-ko-giao-duc-dai-hoc.aspx?ItemID=8831

Ministry of Education and Training. (MOET). (2023). *Higher Education 2001-2022: Prosperity due to persistence*. Retrieved March 5, 2024, from https://moet.gov.vn/tintuc/Pages/tin-tong-hop.aspx?ItemID=8732

Nanyang Technological University (NTU). (2022). *POWER*. Retrieved November 24, 2022, from https://www.ntu.edu.sg/women/powers/about-us

Nga Nguyễn. (2022, August 5, 2022). *The quality of education is measured through employment opportunities*. Báo Phụ Nữ TP.HCM. Retrieved from https://www.phunuonline.com.vn/thuoc-do-chat-luong-dao-tao-la-co-hoi-viec-lam-cua-sinh-vien-a1469853.html

Nguyen, D. (2019, December 8). The university changes the landscape because of ... more female students. *Thanh Nien*. Retrieved November 19, 2022, from https://thanhnien.vn/truong-dai-hoc-thay-doi-canh-quan-vi-nhieu-sinh-vien-nu-post907336.html

Nguyen, H. (2022, July 4). Top 17 universities in Vietnam entered university ranking by academic performance. *University Ranking by Academic Performance (URAP)*. Retrieved November 19, 2022, from https://vietnamtimes.org.vn/top-17-universities-in-vietnam-entered-university-ranking-by-academic-performance-43131.html

Nguyen, M. H., Nguyen, T. L., & Nguyen, T. N. N. (2021, May 16). Research on the effectiveness of credit policy for Vietnamese students. *Tai Chinh Journal Online*. Retrieved November 10, 2022, from https://tapchitaichinh.vn/ngan-hang/nghien-cuu-ve-hieu-luc-cua-chinh-sach-tin-dung-doi-voi-sinh-vien-viet-nam-333806.html

Phạm, T. H., & Nguyễn, D. H. N. (2020). Impact of quality assessment of training programs by AUN-QA standards: A case study of Vietnam. *Vietnamese Journal of Education, 492*(2), 51–55. Retrieved November 19, 2022, from https://tapchigiaoduc.moet.gov.vn/vi/magazine/492-ki-ii-thang-12/10-tac-dong-cua-hoat-dong-danh-gia-chat-luong-chuong-trinh-dao-tao-theo-bo-tieu-chuan-aun-qa-mot-nghien-cuu-truong-hop-o-viet-nam-7717.html

Phạm, T. H., & Nguyễn, C. H. (2019). History of quality assurance in Vietnamese higher education. In C. Nguyen & M. Shah (Eds.), *Quality assurance in Vietnamese higher education*. Palgrave Macmillan. https://doi.org/10.1007/978-3-030-26859-6_3

Quý, H. (2022, April 22). Vietnam had only around 10% of higher education programmes accredited. *Thanh Niên*. Retrieved November 21, 2022, from https://thanhnien.vn/ca-nuoc-moi-co-khoang-10-chuong-trinh-dai-hoc-duoc-kiem-dinh-post1451321.html

Salam, A. (2018). Thai student loan fund and its current status. *Journal of Asia Pacific Studies, 5*(1), 62–75.

Scimago. (2022). *Scimago journal & country rank*. Retrieved November 24, 2022, from https://www.scimagojr.com/countryrank.php?region=Asiatic%20Region&year=2021

Thanh, H., & Lê, H. (2022, August 21). Why did 35% high school students not choose to study at universities? *Vietnamnet*. Retrieved December 19, 2022, from https://vietnamnet.vn/vi-sao-gan-35-thi-sinh-bo-xet-tuyen-dai-hoc-2022-2051825.html

Thien, C. (2021, September 15). Highland students face many difficulties in online learning. *Cong an nhan dan*. Retrieved November 19, 2022, from https://cand.com.vn/giao-duc/sinh-vien-vung-cao-gap-nhieu-kho-khan-trong-viec-hoc-online-i628206/

Times Higher Education. (n.d.). World university rankings. *Times Higher Education*. Retrieved March 7, 2024, from https://www.timeshighereducation.com/world-university-rankings

Tran, T. L., & Do, T. T. Q. (2022). Higher education in Vietnam. In L. P. Symaco & M. Hayden (Eds.), *International handbook on education in South East Asia* (pp. 1–22). Springer. https://doi.org/10.1007/978-981-16-8136-3_40-1

Tường, V. (2022). *List of higher education institutions accredited*. Retrieved November 25, 2022, from https://laodong.vn/chinh-sach-giao-duc/danh-sach-cac-co-so-giao-duc-duoc-cong-nhan-dat-tieu-chuan-chat-luong-1026351.ldo

UNESCO. (2022). *Country dashboard*. Retrieved December 19, 2022, from http://sdg4-data.uis.unesco.org/

World Bank. (2022a). *School enrolment, tertiary (% gross) - Vietnam*. Retrieved December 19, 2022, from https://data.worldbank.org/indicator/SE.TER.ENRR

World Bank. (2022b). *Gender Data Portal*. Retrieved November 24, 2022, from https://genderdata.worldbank.org/indicators/se-ter-grad-fe-zs/?fieldOfStudy=Science%2C%20Technology%2C%20Engineering%20and%20Mathematics%20%28STEM%29&view=bar

World Bank. (2022c). *GDP per capita (current US$) – Vietnam*. Retrieved December 19, 2022, from https://data.worldbank.org/indicator/NY.GDP.PCAP.CD?locations=VN

World Bank. (2022d). *Poverty headcount ratio at national poverty lines (% of population) – Vietnam*. Retrieved December 19, 2022, from https://data.worldbank.org/indicator/SI.POV.NAHC?locations=VN

World Bank. (2022e). *School enrolment, tertiary (% gross) – Indonesia, Vietnam, Singapore, Malaysia, Thailand, Philippines*. Retrieved December 7, 2022, from https://data.worldbank.org/indicator/SE.TER.ENRR?end=2021&locations=ID-VN-SG-MY-TH-PH&start=2011&view = chart

INDEX

Academic freedom, 25–27
Access, 37–40, 94–95, 153
Accreditation, 156
Agência Nacional para Avaliação Acreditação Académia (ANAAA), 144
American rule, 92
Andragogy, 104
Articulation of aspirations of private HEIs, 7
Artificial intelligence (AI), 56
ASEAN International Mobility for Students (AIMS), 79
ASEAN University Network (AUN), 99, 130
ASEAN University Network Quality Assurance (AUN-QA) framework, 43, 124
Asia-Pacific Association for International Education (APAIE), 109
Asia-Pacific Economic Cooperation (APEC), 110
Asian Development Bank (ADB), 36
Association of Christian Schools, Colleges and Universities Accrediting Association Inc. (ACSCU-AAI), 96
Association of Local Colleges and Universities Commission on Accreditation (ALCUCOA), 96–97
Association of Southeast Asian Institutions of Higher Learning (ASAIHL), 131
Association of Southeast Asian Nations (ASEAN), 1, 3, 94, 124, 130
Assumption Business Administrative College (1975), 120
AUN30, 131

Autonomy, 2, 25, 37
in financial management, 25
in human resource management, 25
in policy implementation, 25

Badan Layanan Umum (BLU), 21
Board of Trustees (BOT), 24
Buddhism, 6, 121
Buddhism Education Institute, 36
Bumiputera community, 50, 54–55
Bureaucratic mindset, 123
Burma Socialist Programme Party (BSPP), 69

CALABARZON, 94
Cambodia's higher education sector, 7
goal-oriented university strategy, 7–9
SDG 4.3, 15–17
strategic, transformative university leadership, 9–11
strategic financial management, 13–15
strategic human resource management, 11–13
Centers of Development (COD), 97
Centers of Excellence (COE), 97
Centres for Business, 24
Centres for Innovation, 24
Centres of Intellectual Property Rights, 24
Chartered Colleges and Universities in the Philippines (AACCUP), 96
Children with disabilities (CWDs), 81
Chulalongkorn University Act B. E. 2551 (2008), 120
Chulalongkorn University, 100, 125
Civil disobedience movement (CDM), 71, 77

INDEX

Civil service management, 11
Civilian democratic governance, 72
College of Humanities and Sciences
(CHS), 113
Commission on Higher Education
(CHED), 92
Committee on University Education
Pathways Beyond 2015
(CUEP), 111
Comprehensive Education Sector
Review (CESR), 68
conNectUS, 112
Continuing Education and Training
(CET), 113
Cooperative and work-integrated
education (CWIE), 127
Corporation Law, The (1906), 94
Council of University Academic
Boards (CUAB), 74
Culture of borrowing, 125
Curriculum, 37, 105

De Montfort University, 7
Decree-Law, 147
Democratisation, 72
Department of Population (DOP), 81
Department of Statistics (DOSM), 59
Development Strategy for 2021–2030,
8–9
Digital transformation, 4, 108–110
Directorate General of Higher
Education (DGHE), 8, 28
Directorate of Research, Technology,
and Community Service
(DRTCS), 28
Disciplined democracy, 72
Distance education (DE), 70
Dual employment system, 13

East Asia Management University, 7
Education and Sports Sector
Development Plan
(ESSDP), 39
Education Law of 2005, 154
Education Law of 2007, 37

Education Sector Development Plan
(ESDP), 44
Educational Commission in
Education (EDCOM), 92
Employability, 96
Enhanced Education Act (Law) of
2013, 95
Enrolment, 36
Envision, enable, empower, and
energise (4Es leadership
framework), 8
Equity, 37–40, 160

Federation of Accrediting Agencies
of the Philippines
(FAAP), 96
Female labour force participation rate
(FLFPR), 59
Finance, 44
Financing, 44–45
Free higher education, 95
Free technical and vocational
education and training, 95
*Fundo de Desenvolvimento de Capital
Humano* (FDCH), 141

Gender equality, 154–156
Gender Equality Law, 154
Gender parity index (GPI), 40
Global Innovation Alliance
(GIA), 109
Global innovation index (GII), 29
Goal-oriented university strategy,
7–9
Governance, 45–46, 122–123, 153
Government Technology Agency
(GovTech), 108, 112
Gross attendance ratio (GAR), 39
Gross domestic product (GDP), 158
Gross enrolment ratio (GER),
40–41
Gross expenditure on research and
development (GERD), 29
Gross tertiary enrolment rate (GER),
21–22

Index 171

Higher Education (HE) *Act*, 92
Higher education (HE), 20, 68
  enrolments and growth in, 88
  need for quality in, 43–44
  in Southeast Asia, 1–4
  teacher/student ratios in, 89
  teaching and research staff in, 89
Higher education institutions (HEIs),
    2, 6, 20, 36, 92–93, 104,
    120, 140
  government, 21
  specialised, 36
  with provincial or community
    focus, 36
Higher Education Law of 2012, 154
Higher Education Modernisation Act
    (1997), 92
Human resource development
    (HRD), 126

Indonesian higher education, 20
  gross expenditure in R&D, 29
  history, 20–22
  institutional autonomy and
    academic freedom, 25–27
  leadership and innovation in
    Indonesian HE, 23–25
  SDG 4.3 in Indonesia, 22–23
  size, 21–22
  world-class research and
    innovation, 27–30
Indonesian National Research and
    Innovation Institute
    (BRIN), 30
Information and communications
    technology (ICT), 110
Innovation Management Institutes
    and Centres, 24
Institut Pertanian Bogor (IPB), 26
Institut Teknologi Sepuluh Nopember
    (ITS), 26
Institute for Social Development
    Studies (ISDS), 155
Institute Superior Cristal (ISC), 140
Institute Teknologi Bandung (ITB), 26

Institutes of Research and
    Community Services, 24
Institutional autonomy, 25–27,
    163–164
Institutional plans, 7
Instituto Nacional de Ciência e
    Tecnologia (INCT), 141
Interdisciplinary Collaborative Core
    (ICC), 113
Internal QA (IQA), 124
Internationalization, 98–99
Internet of Things (IoT), 56, 111
Internship-As-A-Service (IAAS), 112

Job-readiness of graduates,
    110–112
Junta's system, 79–82

K-12 reform, 95
Khmer Rouge regime, 6
King Mongkut's University of
    Technology Thonburi
    (KMUTT), 123
Knowledge-based economy, 105

Labour force participation, 59
Labour market, 156–157
  outcomes, 40–42
Lao People's Democratic Republic
    (Lao PDR), 35
  access and equity, 37–40
  governance and leadership,
    45–46
  labour market outcomes,
    40–42
  quality, 42–45
LASALLE College of the Arts, 106
Leadership, 9, 45–46
  in Indonesian HE, 23–25
Lembaga Akreditasi Negara
    (LAN), 52
Lifelong learning, 104
Limkokwing University of Creative
    Technology, 7
Local University Colleges (LUCs), 92

172 INDEX

Mahachulalongkornrajavidyalaya University (MCU), 120
Malaysia
 challenges facing higher education, 54–58
 higher education's impact on economy, 58–61
 history of higher education, 50–52
 low female labour force participation, 59–60
 shift to services, 60–61
 structure of Malaysian higher education, 52–54
Malaysian External Trade Development Corporation (MALTRADE), 61
Malaysian Qualifications Agency Act, 52
Massive Open Online Courses (MOOCs), 129–130
Membership inclusion in ASEAN, 146–147
Memorandum of Understanding (MOU), 127
Memorandums of Intent (MOI), 112
Memorandums of Understanding (MOU), 112
Middle-income trap, 61
Military coup, 82
Ministry of Economy and Finance, 14
Ministry of Education (MOE), 71, 113, 122
Ministry of Education, Culture, Research, and Technology (MoECRT), 24
Ministry of Education, Youth and Sport (MoEYS), 6, 8, 16
Ministry of Education and Sports (MOES), 36
Ministry of Higher Education, Science, Research, and Innovation (MHESI), 122
Ministry of Higher Education, Science and Culture (MESCC), 141
Ministry of Labour and Vocational Training (MoLVT), 6

Ministry of National Development Planning (MoNDP), 23
Ministry of Planning and Finance (MPF), 73
 compilation and extrapolation of data from, 88
Monitoring and evaluation (M&E) system, 8
Mutual Recognition (MRS), 146
Mutual Recognition Arrangements (MRA), 1, 99, 146
Myanmar, 68
 2011–2021 advances in, 75–77
 bureaucratic structure of HE, 74–75
 HE in conflict context, 77–79
 history of HE in, 68–72
 SDG 4.3 in Junta's system, 79–82
 size of HE in, 72–74
Myanmar Education Committee, 74

Nanyang Academy of Fine Arts (NAFA), 106
Nanyang Technological University (NTU), 105, 109
National Accreditation and Quality Assurance Committee (NAQAC), 75, 82
National Curriculum Committee (NCC), 75
National Education Act (1999), 120
National Education Committee (NEC), 75
National Education Policy Commission (NEPC), 71, 75
National Education Strategic Plan (NESP), 68
National HEIs, 36
National Institute of Education, 36
National Institute of Educational Testing Service (NIETS), 124
National Institute of Pedagogy, 36
National League for Democracy (NLD), 71
National Network of Quality Assurance Agencies (NNQAA), 97
National School of Fine Arts, 36

Index   173

National School of Music and
   Dance, 36
National Unity Government
   (NUG), 72
National University of Laos (NUOL),
   36, 42
National University of Singapore
   (NUS), 104
National University of Timor-Leste
   (UNTL), 140, 145
Ne Win's Revolutionary Council, 69
New Economic Policy (NEP), 3, 50
New Public Management (NPM), 25
Non-tax state income (NTSI), 26
NUS Centre for Future-ready
   Graduates (NUS CGF), 112

Office for National Education
   Standards and
   Quality Assessment
   (ONESQA), 124
Office of Higher Education
   Commission (OHEC), 122
Office of National Higher Education,
   Science, Research, and
   Innovation Policy Council
   (NXPO), 123
Operation Lalang, 51

Payap College (1974), 120
Payap University (1984), 120
Pedagogy, 104
Pensionado system, 92
People's Defence Force (PDF), 72
People's Socialist Community, 6
Perguruan Tinggi Kedinasan, 21
Persons with disabilities (PWDs), 2, 80
Philippine Accrediting Association
   of Schools, Colleges and
   Universities (PAASCU), 96
Philippine Association of Colleges
   and Universities
   Commission on
   Accreditation
   (PACUCOA), 96
*Philippine Qualifications Framework
   Act* (2017), 97

Philippine-California Advanced
   Research Institute (PCARI)
   project, 97
Philippines, 92
   related issues in HE, 93–99
Policy, 122–123
Private HEIs, 10, 21
Private higher education, 51
Private Higher Education Act of
   1996, 3
Private Higher Education Institutions
   Act, 51
Private School Law, The (1917), 94
Private Schools Registration Act, 69
Private tertiary education institutions
   (PHEIs), 51
Program for International Student
   Assessment (PISA), 54
Promotion of Women in Engineering,
   Research, and Science
   (POWER), 156
Provincial Education and Sports
   Services, 36–37
Public administrative institutions
   (PAIs), 6
Public HEIs, 3, 6–7, 9–11, 21, 44–45

Qualifications framework, 159
Quality, 42, 54–56, 95–98, 124–126
   in higher education, 2, 143–146
   issues of financing and, 44–45
   need for quality in higher
      education, 43–44
Quality assurance (QA), 37, 124, 144
   access to, 112–114
Quality Management System
   (QMS), 96
Quantity, 54–56
   of higher education, 143–146

Raffles International College, 7
Rectors' Committee (RC), 75
Regional Centre for Higher Education
   and Development
   (RIHED), 130
Regional HEIs, 36
Religious HEIs, 21

Republic of scholars, 21
Research and development (R&D), 3, 28, 29, 97, 132
Resistance, 68
Robotics, 56
Royal Institute of Law and Administration, 36
Royal Proclamation of the Private College Act of 1969, 120
Royal School of Medicine, 36

SATKER universities, 26
Scholarship Grant Program for Children and Dependents of Sugarcane Industry Workers, 95
Scholarship Program for Coconut Farmers and their Families (CoScho), 95
Science, technology, engineering and mathematics (STEM), 28, 56, 155
  shortage of STEM graduates, 56–57
Sijil Tinggi Persekolahan Malaysia (STPM), 55
SIM University, 106
Singapore, 104
  access to quality education, 112–114
  digital transformation, 108–110
  higher education in, 104–107
  job-readiness of graduates, 110–112
  Sustainable Development Goal 4.0 and Higher Education in, 107–108
Singapore Institute of Technology (SIT), 105
Singapore Management University (SMU), 105
Singapore University of Social Sciences (SUSS), 105
Singapore University of Technology and Design (SUTD), 105
SkillsFuture for Digital Workplace (SFDW), 110
SkillsFuture movement, 113
Smart Nation and Digital Government Group (SNDGG), 108

Smart Nation and Digital Government Office (SNDGO), 108
Social inclusion, 157–160
Socialisation, 162
Southeast Asia, higher education in, 1–4
Southeast Asia Ministers of Education Organization (SEAMEO), 130
Special education, 36–37, 92, 153, 161
State Law and Order Restoration Council (SLORC), 70
State Peace and Development Council (SPDC), 70
State University Colleges (SUCs), 92
Strategic, transformative university leadership, 9–11
Strategic financial management, 13–15
Strategic human resource management, 11–13
Student demand and transition in higher education, 142–143
Student loans, 2, 95
Students, 69
Superior Pedagogy Institute, 36
Support to Higher Education in the ASEAN Region (SHARE), 107–108
Surabaya, 26
Survey of National Social Economy (SNSE), 22
Sustainable Development Goal (SDG), 7, 22, 50, 93, 152
  SDG 4.3, 15–17, 22–23, 128–130, 147–148
  sustainable Development Goal 4.0, 107–108

"Teach Less Learn More" policy, 113
Teaching, 12
Teaching/learning, 37
Technical Vocational Education and Training (TVET), 111
Tertiary education subsidy (TES), 95
Thai Qualification Framework (TQF), 124

Index

Thailand, 120
    policy and governance, 122–123
    quality, 124–126
    SDG 4.3, 128–130
    Thai higher education in Southeast
        Asian Context, 130–132
    workforce preparation, 126–128
Thailand Cyber University (TCU),
    129–130
Timor-Leste, 140
    membership inclusion in ASEAN,
        146–147
    quality and quantity of higher
        education, 143–146
    SDG 4.3, 147–148
    student demand and transition in
        higher education, 142–143
Total Quality Management (TQM), 96
Transformative leadership, 9
Transnational Education (TNE), 98
Transnational Higher Education Act
    (2019), 93
Trends in International Mathematics
    and Science Study
    (TIMSS), 54

UNESCO Institute of Statistics
    (UIS), 37
Union Solidarity Development Party
    (USDP), 72
United Nations (UN), 22
United Nations Educational, Scientific
    and Cultural Organization
    (UNESCO), 141
Universal Access to Quality Tertiary
    Education Act of 2017
    (UAQTEA), 94–95
Universidade de Paz (UNPAZ), 140
Universitas Airlangga (UNAIR), 26
Universitas Diponegoro (UNDIP), 26
Universitas Gadjah Mada (UGM), 26
Universitas Hasanuddin
    (UNHAS), 26
Universitas Indonesia (UI), 26
Universitas Pendidikan Indonesia
    (UPI), 26

Universitas Sebelas Maret (UNS), 26
Universitas Sumatera Utara
    (USU), 26
Universiti Utara Malaysia (UUM), 52
Universities, 92
Universities Central Council
    (UCC), 74
University autonomy, lack of, 57–58
University Colleges Act, 51
University development strategy, 7
University Education Law, 74
University Mobility in Asia and the
    Pacific (UMAP), 79
University National Educational Test
    (U-NET), 124
University network, 160–163
University of Dili (UNDIL), 140
University of Santo Tomas (UST), 92
University of Singapore, 105
University of the Arts Singapore
    (UAS), 106
University of Timor (UNTIM), 140
University Ranking by Academic
    Performance (URAP)
    agency, 154

Vietnam National University
    of Ho Chi Minh City
    (VNU-HCM), 155
Vietnam's higher education sector
    evolution and current
        circumstances of, 152–154
    gender equality, 154–156
    institutional autonomy, 163–164
    linking with labour market,
        156–157
    social inclusion, 157–160
    university network, 160–163
Work-readiness, 111
Workforce preparation, 126–128
World Health Organization (WHO), 81
World-class research and innovation,
    27–30

Yangon University Distance
    Education (YUDE), 73

Printed and bound by CPI Group (UK) Ltd, Croydon, CR0 4YY
19/01/2025

14627897-0003